E Pluribus Unum

The Formation of the American Republic
1776–1790

First Great Seal of the United States,
used on all official documents from 1782 through 1841

Other Books
by Forrest McDonald

Alexander Hamilton: A Biography

The Presidency of Thomas Jefferson

The Phaeton Ride: The Crisis of American Success

The Presidency of George Washington

The Last Best Hope: A History of the United States
(with Thomas P. Govan and Leslie E. Decker)

The Boys Were Men: The American Navy in the
Age of Fighting Sail

Enough Wise Men: The Story of Our Constitution

Confederation and Constitution, 1781–1789

The Torch Is Passed: The United States in the
Twentieth Century

Empire and Nation

Insull

We the People: The Economic Origins of the Constitution

Let There Be Light: The Electric Utility
Industry in Wisconsin

E Pluribus Unum

The Formation of the American Republic
1776–1790

Forrest McDonald

LibertyPress

Indianapolis

Liberty*Press* is a publishing imprint of Liberty Fund, Inc., a foundation established to encourage study of the ideal of a society of free and responsible individuals.

The cuneiform inscription that serves as the design motif for our end-papers is the earliest known written appearance of the word "freedom" (*ama-gi*), or liberty. It is taken from a clay document written about 2300 B.C. in the Sumerian city-state of Lagash.

First edition published 1965 by the Houghton Mifflin Company, Boston. Second edition published 1979 by Liberty*Press,* Indianapolis.

Library of Congress Cataloging in Publication Data

McDonald, Forrest.
  E pluribus unum.

  Includes bibliographical references and index.
  1. United States—History—Revolution, 1775–1783. 2. United States —History, Confederation, 1783–1789. I. Title.
E210.M14 1979   973.3   79-4130
ISBN 0-913966-58-4

To Edwin J. Soares and
Miss Livia Appel for being,
and for having to do
with the like of me

Contents

Acknowledgments

For helping in one way and another—some unknowingly, some through kindness, others through hard work—to bring this book about, I am grateful to the following persons: Winifred Barton, George Billias, Ginie Callas, Paul S. Clarkson, Leslie E. Decker, Thomas P. Govan, James B. Hedges, Merrill Jensen, Ellen Shapiro McDonald, Henry Allen Moe, Jacqueline Taylor, Kenneth S. Templeton, John Worsley, Craig Wylie, and Pepe Rico y los otros Nerjaños.

Preface to the Second Edition

A book, like a child, has an identity of its own. It is therefore a strange experience to be offered, as I was, an opportunity to make changes in a book I wrote several years ago: it was almost as if one were invited to remake one's teenaged son. Tempting as such a prospect might be to many a parent, few could bring themselves to do it. The boy is himself, pimples and all, and to alter a single aspect of his character would be to destroy the integrity of the whole person. On that principle, I decided to decline the opportunity and—except for making some changes of form (principally by substituting footnotes for backnotes) and for correcting such factual errors as have come to my attention —to reissue the book as it originally appeared.

It might be useful to the reader, however, to know what changes I should be inclined to make, were I to make any. First, I should change somewhat the focus of the opening of the book. The alignment of republicans and nationalists was as I have depicted it, and so were the personal qualities and attitudes of the two groups of men; but further study has convinced me that the conceptual core of republican ideology was different from what I earlier supposed. Specifically, I have described the republicans as being rationalists and as believing in the inherent goodness or perfectibility of man. It now appears that to understand the more doctrinaire of them one must also take into account the quasi-paranoid ideas of the English Oppositionists—notably those of John Trenchard, Thomas Gordon, Viscount Bolingbroke, and James Bergh.

Second, I should probably handle differently my analysis, in chapter six, of the deal in the constitutional convention between John Rutledge of South Carolina and Roger Sherman of Connecticut. It is not that I believe my interpretation is wrong; indeed, it is the only way I know to reconcile the known facts about the hard-nosed trading that went on behind the scenes at the convention. But the direct evidence supporting my account is skimpy, and when the book first appeared a number of reviewers who otherwise reacted favorably balked on that point. Some, in fact, treated it as if it were central to my overall thesis, whereas it is actually tangential. That is to say, though it is important to understand that artful wheeling and dealing were necessary to effect the compromises which made the Constitution possible, it is not so important precisely how the deals were made. Accordingly, if I were doing the book over again I should probably couch this particular episode in more tentative or conjectural language, though doing so would disrupt the flow of the narrative.

Third, I should probably handle certain individuals somewhat differently. After further study of Alexander Hamilton, for instance, I have come to realize that his historical image as a wily and devious manipulator is unjustified; similarly, I have come to realize that James Madison was much more devious and considerably more able than I had thought. Most important, however, there was a dimension to the Founding Fathers which is neglected here: the ardent desire that some of them had for Fame, the secular equivalent of Christian immortality. The hope of winning the undying gratitude of posterity through noble creative statesmanship was clearly the "ruling passion" in Hamilton's life, and a similar urge impelled Madison, James Wilson, and other Americans of their generation.

That brings us to the final change I should be disposed to make. My respect and admiration for the Founders of the American constitutional system is large, yet most of the people who stalk these pages are described as driven by base motives, especially greed. That approach to the subject misled some into believing (or charging) that I had written a new economic interpretation to replace the Beardian economic interpretation I had previously challenged. If I were to redo the book (and if I knew how), I should attempt to make my central argument clearer. I do not maintain that the Constitution was the product of the interactions of grubby and greedy men. I do maintain that such interactions brought about the conditions in which a relative handful of men—whose idealism, fortunately, was tempered by a realistic understanding of their countrymen— could effect a constitutional revolution. If we would appreciate what the Founders did, we must understand their contemporaries as they did.

FORREST McDONALD

Coker, Alabama
November 1978

Preface to the First Edition

The first function of the founders of nations, after the founding itself, is to devise a set of true falsehoods about origins—a mythology—that will make it desirable for nationals to continue to live under common authority, and, indeed, make it impossible for them to entertain contrary thoughts. Ordinarily the founding, being the less subtle of the tasks, is also the easier, but with the American Founding Fathers the order of difficulty was reversed. On the one hand, widely different and deeply rooted local traditions separated the thirteen British colonies in North America, and space and the available means of communication separated them even further. Accordingly, logic dictated that if the colonies were to be independent of Britain they should be independent of one another also. They should be not one nation but several, and most Americans, including many devoutly patriotic leaders, so thought.

On the other hand, a condition inherent in British North America dictated that if the founding could be accomplished, the necessary myths would create themselves. For Americans reckoned values in the marketplace and by consensus, unlike the Europeans, who reckoned them through traditional institutions and by absolute standards.

Now, one of the peculiarities of the American way is that
when contests of ideas arise, the view held by the winning
side comes in time to be regarded as the unqualified truth,
the only possible view; indeed, all subsequent battles must
begin with the outcomes of earlier battles as unquestioned
premises. Before independence, for example, few Americans
espoused the doctrines about to be set forth in the Declaration of Independence, and hosts of divergent opinions were
perfectly tolerable; but once the Declaration was made, it
became not only immoral but virtually unthinkable to hold
any other position. Similarly, those who in the 1780s believed that the nation should be one instead of many had
rivals in abundance, but if they won, the winning itself
would create the necessary mythology, for it would retroactively transform the winners' view into the only view.

The nationalists won, and their victory established as
truth a pentad of fictions: (1) that the war for independence
had been a united war for national independence, not for
the independence of the several states; (2) that the question
facing the new nation was not whether it should have a
national government, but what form that government should
take; (3) that the first form, that of the Congress under
the Articles of Confederation, was unworkable and consequently public and private morality collapsed just after the
war ended in 1783; (4) that in the ensuing political chaos
and commercial stagnation Americans came to realize that
the Confederation was inadequate to promote the national
ends that all desired; and (5) that the wisest group of
men ever assembled in a single body, a group of demigods,
came to the rescue by writing a Constitution that would
assure the blessings of liberty to themselves and their posterity.

For a hundred years historians of this epoch dutifully

performed the function that was the universal function of historians: they preserved the myths and adapted them to the changing needs of a changing society. Down through the nineteenth century they did so: John Marshall, Jared Sparks, George Bancroft, Richard Hildreth, John Fiske, each in his turn, recited the myths anew, each embellishing them only enough to adjust them to changing times, as each viewed those changing times.

Then came a sudden aberration, one with many American roots but no American precedents: Around the turn of the present century, a small group of historians disowned their traditional function as preservers and adapters of myths, and audaciously proclaimed that they would thenceforth seek and report only the truth. So spoke the "scientific historians" of Johns Hopkins and elsewhere, and so spoke the "New Historians" led by James Harvey Robinson, Charles A. Beard, Frederick Jackson Turner, and Carl Becker. In a burst of creative scholarship, the followers of the New History unearthed an array of long-forgotten facts —most notably, facts demonstrating that the Fathers had been a cantankerous lot who fought one another, in unseemly fashion, for power and wealth—and devised a new interpretation of the national origins that would accommodate this information.

Such findings, like the truth-seeking heresy that inspired them, were scarcely welcomed. In a society in which the voice of the people is the voice of God, they were dangerous, subversive, downright blasphemous. Undaunted, the champions of the pursuit of truth in history fought the good fight for a whole generation, and in due course—because scholarly ideas, too, are evaluated at the marketplace—their interpretations came to prevail.

But then, in the early 1930s, Beard and Becker came to

believe (or realize) that their own works—even Beard's
An Economic Interpretation of the Constitution and Becker's *The Declaration of Independence*—had also preserved
and adapted the myths, adapting them differently only because of the rapidly changing circumstances of their own
times. Whereupon they solemnly recanted the whole blasphemous ideal of the pursuit of truth, and not only declared
that the historian should preserve and adapt myths to the
changing needs of changing times, but proclaimed that he
could in fact do no other. And where Beard and Becker
led, the rest of their profession soon followed.

So it went until a scant dozen years ago. Then the study
of history in America took still another turn: not because
anyone planned it that way or because the tenor of the times
so dictated, but because, as a result of a concatenation of
physical and economic circumstances, it suddenly became
possible and even easy to find out details about the American past, on a scale never before dreamed possible. The new
generation of historians, inspired almost to the point of in-
toxication by their rapid consumption of vast quantities of
new information, began to discover anew the blasphemous
ideal. The old generation watched the upstarts demolish
their every cherished interpretation—those having to do
with the national experience as well as those dealing with
national origins.

Ahead lay the gargantuan task of reconstructing all aspects of American history—that is, of building new narrative and interpretive frameworks that could accommodate
the newly learned data. These, like the older accounts,
would be products of the historian's imagination, mere
made-up stories; but if they were properly made up their
contours would reflect those of past reality—much as a

map, another product of man's imagination, reflects topo-
graphical reality—and not the immediate needs or aspirations of the present or any other generation.

The task would not be easy even if the new generation
were entirely free in undertaking it. But it is not. Most modern historians have shaken loose the fetters of the old generalizations about American history, but have not entirely
free themselves from the old dogmas. The old dogmas, the
philosophy of the New Historians in retreat, postulated that
all judgments are subjective and therefore (1) that all truth
is relative to the point of view of the observer, (2) accurate knowledge of the human past is not knowable, and
(3) not worth seeking.

Now any sophomore student of logic should be able to
perceive that it is indefensible to draw such inferences from
that premise, but historians, even the modern ones, have
somehow managed to believe that if the premise is sound
the rest necessarily follows. Some therefore have challenged
the premise, which is inherently a futile pursuit because the
premise is true by definition. Others have tried to ignore it,
but that is scarcely more satisfactory. Those who follow
neither of these courses have most often tried to accommodate it by devising an analytical style of writing in which,
instead of telling the reader what happened, they attempt
to recapitulate the thought processes by which they came to
believe that that was what happened.

I object to such writing on two grounds. One is simply
that it yields works so dull that no reasonable man will try
to wade through them.[1] The other is that it confuses the

---

[1] I cite as a prime example my own earlier work, *We the People: The Economic Origins of the Constitution* (Chicago, 1958).

three phases of the historian's cerebral processes—finding and taking in information, digesting and reducing it to meaningful generalizations, and writing it up. The first of these, ingesting, is systematic and logical: one utilizes one's training to find out where all the relevant materials are, and one by one takes them all in. The second, digesting, is partly logical but mainly intuitive and unconscious: the human brain can and daily does perform many thousand times as many calculations, reducing facts to generalizations, as can be performed on the brain's logical, conscious surface. The third, writing, is partly intuitive and partly a matter of hard and systematic work: one selects and arranges the data, not for their importance, but for their usefulness in communicating generalizations.

So believing, I have written a book which is unabashedly "subjective." It is myself: through the course of more than 20,000 hours of conscious work and several times that in unconscious work, I have taken in a hundred thousand or so scraps of information, and attempt here not to reproduce them but to tell you what they mean. Yet I believe that what I tell you is not only objectively true but also objectively verifiable. That is the purpose of the notes to this book. They are not—as it was once held that notes should be—designed to "prove," step by step, that each of the things I have said is true, so that the facts can "speak for themselves." Rather, they are designed so that anyone interested in doing so can undergo the mental gymnastics that I went through to arrive at my various generalizations (though without the false starts, dead ends, and other wasted motion that accompanied most of my efforts). I believe that if you read the materials they cite, in the order that they are cited, you will (in addition to noticing that like all people I make mistakes) reach essentially the same conclusions that I have reached, though you would doubtless state them somewhat differently.

It could be, of course, that what I say is true in every detail but does not constitute a story whose contours reflect past reality; I have not said everything and what I have said might not measure up to, or be confined to, its proper context. But I believe that the story told here is not only true but also valid as history. A valid historical context (1) dictates its own point of observation (which is to say, of generalization), (2) has terminal points in time and space, and (3) is reducible to a single question that is self-answering. Valid historical inquiry ends, rather than begins, with knowledge of the pertinent point of observation, termini, and question; when one knows them, one is ready to write. In the writing, one is concerned only with such things as are meaningful on the appropriate level of generalization— in this instance, the United States *as* United States during the years of its founding—and not, for their own sake, with the parts that made it up or a larger whole of which it was a part. If one follows this procedure, the story that results will necessarily conform to past reality.

Now, from the point of view of the United States as United States, the only question that had any meaning between 1763 and some point around the time of the Declaration of Independence was, Would the British colonies in North America find a viable means of staying within the British empire, or would they not? That being answered in the negative, the next meaningful question was, Would the States be able to win in war the independence they had declared? This is not to say that these were the questions that from day to day occupied every Jedediah Strong in New

England or Peter Van Blank in New York or Henry Lee
Carter in Virginia; perhaps they lived out their entire lives
without ever once thinking of them. But if one would be
concerned with the United States at these times, these questions and these only have any meaning.

And so, in the period under inquiry in this book, there
was also only one meaningful question: Would this be
politically one nation, or would it not?

If I have stated the obvious I do not apologize, for it is
the obvious that is often most difficult to see.

FORREST MCDONALD

Providence, Rhode Island
February 1965

E Pluribus Unum

The Formation of the American Republic
1776–1790

Chapter One

From One, Many

Where patriots stood, in the spring of seventy-six, depended upon whether they believed in Original Sin. Two vital questions had been settled: war could not be averted, for war had long been a fact; and the empire could not be held together, for in almost every colony patriots had seized control of the military, royal governors had fled, and revolutionary assemblies had established themselves as *de facto* governing bodies. But as to what to do next, disagreement was sharp and deep. The practical question was, shall independence be declared now, or shall a national government be created first? The underlying question was, is man rational and virtuous or is he evil; is he to be trusted or not?

The group that took the first position had two wings: one led by John and Samuel Adams, John Hancock, Elbridge Gerry and, off and on, other New Englanders; the other led by Richard Henry Lee and Arthur Lee, Patrick Henry, Thomas Jefferson, George Wythe and, off and on, other Southerners. These men thought of themselves as the part of Congress having the "forwardness and zeal" that the times required; they believed, as Paine put it, that one should "give the people the truth, and freedom to discuss it, and all will go well." From both aspects of their faith, it followed that the war with Britain could be speedily won by militiamen and volunteer citizen-armies, with but little direction from a Congress of delegates from the several aborning states. It also followed that the Continental Congress should be as expeditious about declaring independence as it was cautious about establishing a permanent union and a permanent government.[1]

The group that took the second position had three roots: one based in Pennsylvania and led by Benjamin Franklin, John Dickinson, Robert Morris, James Wilson and (until the showdown over independence came) Joseph Galloway; another based in New York and led by the Livingston family and its connections; the third based in the South Carolina low country and led by John Rutledge, Thomas Lynch, and Christopher Gadsden. These men thought of them-

---

[1] Edmund C. Burnett, *The Continental Congress* (New York, 1941), 16, 3–197, *passim;* Merrill Jensen, *The Articles of Confederation* (Madison, 1948), 54–103. My analysis of the mind of the republicans is based upon study of their writings: James C. Ballagh, ed., *The Letters of Richard Henry Lee* (2 vols., New York, 1911, 1914); William W. Henry, *Patrick Henry: Life, Correspondence, and Speeches* (3 vols., New York, 1891); Julian Boyd, ed., *The Papers of Thomas Jefferson* (16 vols. to date, Princeton, 1950–); Charles F. Adams, ed., *The Works of John Adams* (10 vols., Boston, 1850–56); James T. Austin, *The Life of Elbridge Gerry* (2 vols., Boston, 1828, 1829); Harry A. Cushing, ed., *The Writings of Samuel Adams* (4 vols., New York, 1904–08); Massachusetts Historical Society, *Warren-Adams Letters,* especially vol. 2, *1778–1814* (Boston, 1925); Edmund C. Burnett, ed., *Letters of Members of the Continental Congress* (8 vols., Washington, 1921–36); and many more. See also the interesting sketches in George W. Corner, ed., *The Autobiography of Benjamin Rush* (Princeton, 1948), 138–58, and Richard H. Lee, *Life of Arthur Lee* (2 vols., Boston, 1829).

selves as "the sensible part" of Congress; they believed, as Hamilton put it, that "the safest reliance of every government" is not the goodness of the people, but "men's interest." It followed that to attempt to wage a war without a national government was the height of folly. It also followed that there was no wisdom in merely declaring independence, "nor any other purpose to be enforced by it, but . . . giving our enemy notice of our intentions before we had taken any steps to execute them."[2]

During the prewar decade of resistance to British authority, the proto-nationalists had led the way, but they had lost leadership when the shooting started, and in 1776 the republicans swept to power. Under republican direction, Congress declared that British authority was nonexistent, and for practical purposes it created nothing that could properly be called either a union or a government. But the matter did not end there: in the ensuing eleven years, the pendulum would swing thrice again. As it swung, only these two groups—one believing fiercely in republicanism and

---

[2] Quotations from Hamilton, "A Letter from Phocion to the Considerate Citizens of New York," January 1784, in Harold C. Syrett and Jacob E. Cooke, eds., *The Papers of Alexander Hamilton* (7 vols. to date, New York, 1961–   ), 3:494, and Edward Rutledge to John Jay, June 8, 1776, in Burnett, ed., *Letters of Members of Congress*, 1:476. See also William G. Sumner, *The Financier and the Finances of the American Revolution* (2 vols., New York, 1892), vol. 1, *passim;* Charles Page Smith, *James Wilson, Founding Father, 1742–1798* (Chapel Hill, 1956), 62–89; Carl L. Becker, *History of the Political Parties in the Province of New York, 1760 to 1776* (Madison, 1909); Robert L. Brunhouse, *The Counter-Revolution in Pennsylvania, 1776–1790* (Harrisburg, 1942), 10–38; Richard Barry, *Mr. Rutledge of South Carolina* (New York, 1942), 103–93; Jensen, *Articles of Confederation*, 54–103. Jensen sees the same basic alignments but—like most of these writers—sees a different basis for them from that presented here.

but secondarily in the nation, the other believing fiercely in
the nation and but secondarily in republicanism—remained
essentially constant in their views. All others shifted as circumstance and opportunity and experience dictated, or as
the core groups were able to win their allegiance.

The hard-shelled republicans, Eastern and Southern,
shared a reverence for the classical republican virtues and
a tendency to carry them to vices. The rectitude of their
intentions was rarely questionable, but it sometimes veered
to petty self-righteousness; they believed in and practiced
simplicity, but ofttimes demanded impossible austerity of
others; they were dedicated, sometimes to the point of big-
otry, and militant, sometimes to the point of paranoia. In
public life, they heartily embraced the rationalist tradition,
which meant that their thinking was systematic and en-
cumbered by a minimum of superstition and sentimentality and that they believed in the natural rights of man and
the possibility of a clean, rational break with the past. It
also meant that when considering human affairs they tended
to reason in straight logical lines from generalities to par-
ticulars, even when observation told them that the path to
truth is variously curved. In private life, from aristocratic
cultivation in Virginia and from Calvinistic indoctrination
in Massachusetts stemmed a seriousness and sense of propriety that precluded enjoying humor or play or the plea-
sures of the flesh, save with a long hangover of guilt.
Elbridge Gerry's denunciation of the ribaldry of Annapolis, John Adams' horror at the immorality of London and
Paris, and Jefferson's revulsion at Marshall's swearing,
hunting, drinking, and whoring, were all of a piece. And
one can no more imagine Sam Adams or James Lovell or
George Wythe engaged in a passionate love affairs than

one can imagine Gouverneur Morris or Alexander Hamilton not so engaged.[3]

So far in common. Given these like attributes, others that might appear different resulted much the same. The South was agricultural, the East maritime; the South had staples, the East had none; Southerners viewed traders with suspicion and contempt, Easterners viewed plantation masters with suspicion and awe. But the end result, in terms of business and political morality, was scarcely distinguishable: the Southerners' habitual ways of doing things were as slipshod and cavalier as the Yankees' were shrewdly calculated, and thus neither was overburdened with veneration for the sanctity of agreements, nor even with hostility toward welching on a deal or toward cheating a bit.[4]

Finally, republicans from both places were, with rare exceptions, born and educated in British North America, and those who ever encountered Europeans or distant Americans did so only as adults, long after their attitudes and prejudices had crystallized. Consequently, their at-

---

[3] Gerry to Samuel Holten, April 21, 1784, in Burnett, ed., *Letters of Members of Congress,* 7:497–98; Samuel Adams to John Adams, July 2, 1785, in Cushing, ed., *Writings of Adams,* 4:315 ff.; Adams, ed., *Adams Papers,* especially vol. 9, and the same editor's *Familiar Letters of John Adams and His Wife;* Kenneth B. Umbreit, *Our Eleven Chief Justices* (New York, 1938), 150–52; and the sources cited in footnote 1, above. For a delightful letter on the immorality of Paris, see Abigail Adams to Mercy Warren, September 5, 1784, in *Warren-Adams Letters,* 2:242 ff. For an example of pushing militance to the point of paranoia, see R. H. Lee to Samuel Adams, November 18, 1784, in Richard H. Lee, *Memoir of the Life of Richard Henry Lee, and His Correspondence* (2 vols., Philadelphia, 1825), 2: 47–48.

[4] On the business morality of Virginians, see Isaac Harrell, *Loyalism in Virginia* (Philadelphia, 1926), *passim,* and chapter 3 herein; on that of the Yankees, see James B. Hedges, *The Browns of Providence Plantations* (Cambridge, 1952), 329–32, *passim,* and chapter 4 herein.

tachments—like those of most Americans—were local.
When Patrick Henry declaimed that "I am not a Virginian,
but an American," everyone knew he was merely indulging
in plausible oratory; but when Jefferson said "Virginia, sir,
is my country," everyone knew he meant it.[5]

The nationalists were more flexible and somewhat more
charitable in their views, of others as of themselves. All
men were ruled by avarice and ambition, and so must they
be; but some men were less so than others. Indeed, some
men were even worthy of trust: those who recognized that
their motives were a compound of good and evil. In war,
one served one's country out of patriotism, but also in pursuit of personal glory; in government, one filled public office out of esteem for a public trust, but all the while
pursued personal gain. Those who pretended otherwise
could never be trusted, for they were either knaves who
masked their evil behind virtuous utterances or fools who,
believing in their own purity, would also believe themselves
damned to total corruption upon committing their (inevitable) first corrupt act.[6]

In their personal lives, most nationalists had scarcely an
attribute that austere republicans approved. Take their
morality: no friend stood to lose their loyalty by turning
out to be weak or dishonest, yet any man, friend or foe,
stood to lose their respect simply by breaking a promise.

---

[5] The provincialism of the republicans and their lack of early exposure to
the outside world is clear from the sources cited in footnote 1. The contrast
with the backgrounds of the nationalists is striking.

[6] See, for example, Clarence L. Ver Steeg, *Robert Morris, Revolutionary
Financier* (Philadelphia, 1954), 37–40, 59–60; footnote 7, below, and
Hamilton Papers, vols. 1–2, *passim.* All references to the *Hamilton Papers,*
unless otherwise indicated, are to the Syrett and Cooke edition.

Or their manner: they spoke and carried themselves with a too easy, too natural grace that suggested pride, vanity, arrogance. They imposed harsh discipline on underlings, but were likely to be, or at least to appear, ill-disciplined themselves. They could work hard and long and endure great deprivation, but somehow things seemed to come easy to them, and they could appear indecorously happy—and often frivolous—on the soberest of occasions. Most were likely to be robust and lusty, and all, even the prissy and scholarly James Wilson, enjoyed a good drink and a not-so-good woman. Many of them were also incurable romantics, believing in nobility and honor and gallantry much more passionately than they believed in the rights of man.[7]

Indeed, though they were intelligent enough not to broadcast it, few of them believed in the rights of man at all, nor even in the rationalism that underlay them. They could think as systematically as any rationalist, but their systems were based in history, not in logic; accordingly, they believed that men have rights, but only such as have, over the

---

[7] My analysis of the mind of the nationalists is based upon their writings and upon various biographies, notably *ibid.;* the two biographies of Morris, previously cited; Smith, *James Wilson;* Barry, *Mr. Rutledge;* Anne Cary Morris, ed., *Diary and Letters of Gouverneur Morris* (2 vols., New York, 1888); Jared Sparks, *Life of Gouverneur Morris* (3 vols., Boston, 1832); Charles R. King, *Life and Correspondence of Rufus King* (6 vols., New York, 1894–1900); James Wilson Papers, Historical Society of Pennsylvania; Charles J. Stille, *The Life and Times of John Dickinson* (2 vols., Philadelphia, 1891); Otis G. Hammond, ed., *Letters and Papers of Major-General John Sullivan, Continental Army* (*Collections of the New Hampshire Historical Society,* vols. 13–15); Philip Schuyler Papers, New York Historical Society; the various nationalist-oriented newspapers of the period; and many others. For an excellent example of the disapproval of nationalists by republicans, see John Adams' denunciation of Franklin in a letter to James Warren, April 13, 1783, in *Warren-Adams Letters,* 2:208 ff.; see also Arthur Lee's letters to Warren, in the same volume.

years, been won and incorporated into tradition. As to the Age of Reason, Hamilton could offhandedly dismiss the whole idea: "A great source of error," he wrote, "is the judging of events by abstract calculations, which though geometrically true are false as they relate to the concerns of beings governed more by passion and prejudice than by an enlightened sense of their interests." And Dickinson could echo, "Experience must be our only guide. Reason may mislead us."[8]

Their nationalism itself was a product of experience. For one thing, in contrast to the republicans, almost all were either born or educated abroad.[9] For another, they were rooted primarily in the middle colonies and in South Carolina. There, because of the presence of both staples and commerce, intercolonial and international business were daily routine. Whereas New England farmers and Virginia planters might, from one year to the next, see no one from fifty miles distant, Philadelphians and New Yorkers in all walks of life came into regular contact with men and information and ideas from the entire Atlantic community. A broader national view among the latter was virtually inevitable.[10]

---

[8] Quotations from *Hamilton Papers,* 2:242, and Madison's Journal, August 13, 1787, in Max Farrand, ed., *The Records of the Federal Convention of 1787* (3 vols., New Haven, 1911), 2:278.

[9] For examples, Robert Morris was born in Liverpool, Hamilton in the West Indies, Wilson in Scotland, George Read and James McHenry in Ireland; Galloway, Dickinson, many of the members of the New York aristocracy, John, Hugh, and Edward Rutledge, and virtually every other important member of the South Carolina aristocracy were all educated in England.

[10] The observation regarding the frequency of contact is based upon the distribution of population, as indicated in the *Census of 1790,* and my tabulations of ship movements for the several American ports, from shipping news in the various newspapers. See also footnote 2, chapter 2, herein.

One more thing. The two groups, being recruited mainly from the same segments of the population—the lawyers, planters, and merchants who could afford the expensive business of public service—shared many attitudes on the proper relations between government and business, principally the belief that private rights to property were morally anterior to government. But on one cardinal point they differed sharply. The nationalists, placing their faith in persons and being skeptical of the people, were reluctant to allow a popular government to interfere with private business and not at all reluctant to conduct the business of government by interweaving its doings with those of private business and businessmen. The republicans, believing in the trustworthiness of the people and being skeptical of power located in any hands—that is, trusting man but not men—were far more willing to have the government interfere in private business and far less willing to have private business interfere in government.[11]

The initial turn of events on the military front seemed to prove the republicans unqualifiedly right. In mid-1775 General Gage, having witnessed the withering fire of New England militia in several engagements, wrote home that "These people . . . are now spirited up by a rage and enthusiasm as great as ever people were possessed of, and

---

[11] This difference in attitudes is best seen by comparison of the views of, say, Hamilton (*Hamilton Papers*) with Jefferson (*Jefferson Papers*), or Dickinson with Richard Henry Lee (see Forrest McDonald, ed., *Empire and Nation: Letters from a Farmer in Pennsylvania, John Dickinson, Letters from the Federal Farmer, Richard Henry Lee;* Englewood Cliffs, N.J., 1962, ix–xvi), or Robert Morris (Ver Steeg, *Robert Morris*) with George Mason (Kate Mason Rowland, *The Life and Correspondence of George Mason* [2 vols., New York, 1892]).

you must proceed in earnest or give the business up."[12] By
mid-1776 local militias and raw continental citizen-soldiers
had forced Gage himself to give the business up and evacuate Boston, and had, as well, repulsed a major siege of
Charleston, South Carolina. On June 7, when Richard
Henry Lee moved that Congress declare independence,
British troops commanded not a foot of soil in the thirteen
states.[13]

On the developing political front, events seemed to prove
the opposite. The first enemy of the Republic to appear
there (as it was soon to appear on the battlefield) was
state jealousy. Lee's motion included proposals that Congress seek foreign alliances and draw up a formal plan of
confederation, and the latter task was entrusted to a committee headed by John Dickinson. A month later, Dickinson reported with a draft of Articles of Confederation and
Perpetual Union. This draft provided for a single-branch
central government, consisting only of a Congress organized much like the existing one, but implicitly allowing
for such administrative agencies as Congress might establish. The powers of Congress were sketched in broad strokes
and were limited only by the reservation to the states of
control over exclusively internal matters. In general, the
plan seemed acceptable to most delegates, but certain aspects of it, those explicitly or implicitly defining the priv-

---

[12] The quotation is from Howard H. Peckham, *The War for Independence:
A Military History* (Chicago, 1958), 20. On the war, I have used Peckham's work, Douglas S. Freeman's *George Washington, A Biography,*
vols. 3 and 4 (7 vols., New York, 1948–57), John R. Alden's *The American
Revolution* (New York, 1954), and, occasionally, other and more special-
ized works.

[13] On June 7 the British did occupy Long Island outside Charleston harbor
in South Carolina, from which they were launching an unsuccessful siege.

ileges and obligations of the member states, occasioned debate that tore the scheme apart.[14]

Most of the argument turned around three questions. The first concerned voting in Congress. The Dickinson plan provided that the states should have one vote each, as in the existing Congress; delegates from the larger states contended for some form of proportional representation. The second concerned taxation. Dickinson's draft provided for raising money by assigning quotas to the state governments, rather than by giving Congress power to levy and collect taxes directly and generally on its own. Few objected to this, but a dispute arose over whether to assign quotas on the basis of population or land. Dickinson's plan was to assign them on the basis of population, which pleased the delegates from New England, where land values were high and people were fewer, and alienated those from the South, where land was cheap and people more numerous. The third issue was crucial. Dickinson's draft gave Congress power to limit "the bounds of those colonies, which by charter or proclamation, or under any pretense, are said to extend to the South Sea," and to dispose of all western lands thus separated from the states "for the general benefit of all." This engendered a fight between the "landed" and the "landless" states that would, now and in years to come, repeatedly jeopardize the very existence of the Union.[15]

---

[14] Jensen, *Articles of Confederation,* 126–39; Worthington C. Ford and others, eds., *Journals of the Continental Congress 1774–1789* (34 vols., Washington, 1904–37), 5:546 ff. (July 12, 1776).

[15] Joseph Hewes to Samuel Johnston, July 28, John Adams to Abigail Adams, July 29, Samuel Chase to Richard Henry Lee, July 30, 1776, in Burnett, ed., *Letters of Members of Congress,* 2:32; Burnett, *Continental Congress,* 219–29; Jensen, *Articles of Confederation,* 140–60.

The debates had been under way for a month when they were abruptly halted by a second weakness that would regularly plague national politics: no quorum was present in Congress. For most of the next seven or eight months a quorum was rarely in attendance, and whenever there was a quorum the press of more urgent matters precluded considering the formation of a permanent government.[16]

In the interim, still another weakness appeared: patriotism and the proximity of the enemy proved to bear an almost one-to-one relationship. Men loved their country—or were interested that its "government" do anything—whenever British troops were in sight, and with rare exceptions only then. The rage and enthusiasm around Boston left when Gage did; New York, with its principal city under occupation from September 1776 until November 1783, was intensely nationalistic throughout the war; and the Carolinas, until they were invaded by the British in the winter of 1779–80, were dedicated advocates of the protection of the sovereignty of the several states.[17]

Accordingly, when debate on the Articles of Confederation was resumed in April 1777, it was a North Carolinian, Thomas Burke, who led an assault against the proposed form of government, and it was congressmen from other states where the British were not who supported him. The outcome of their crusade was that when the Articles were finally approved in October 1777, they were but a shadow of Dickinson's original draft. The Union was expressly re-

---

[16] Burnett, *Continental Congress,* 229 ff.

[17] Troop movements can be traced in Peckham, *War for Independence,* 21–163; attitudes are reflected in the *Journals of Congress,* 1776–77, Burnett's *Letters of Members of Congress,* vols. 1–2, and in the published revolutionary records of the several states.

duced to a "league of friendship." Dickinson's article
granting broad powers to Congress was replaced by Burke's
article reserving sovereignty and independence to the several states. And the three controversial features were all
resolved in favor of state authority. The first remained the
same, the states retaining equal votes. As to the second,
the basis of levying requisitions on states was changed
from population to land. As to the third, Congress' power
over western lands was dropped altogether.[18]

In this insipid form the Articles were submitted to the
states for approval. To become effective, the document
(and future amendments to it) had to be ratified by every
state. In the contests over ratification, the smallest and
weakest states, despite having equal votes with the larger,
were the least enthused about the shadow-government being
established. (The more perceptive nationalists noted and
remembered this; later the same states would staunchly
support efforts to strengthen Congress, and still later, when
given opportunity to vote on a strong national government,
even without equal representation, they would support it
almost unanimously.) Virginia was first to ratify unconditionally; New York soon followed, and after seven months
all but four states had ratified, with or without proposing
amendments. The four holdouts were Georgia, Delaware,
New Jersey, and Maryland. Soon the first three came
through, and Maryland stood alone.[19]

---

[18] Burke to Richard Caswell, April 29, May 11, November 4, 1777, in Bur-
nett, ed., *Letters of Members of Congress,* 2:345–46, 360, 542; *Journals of
Congress,* 7:240 ff., 287, 300, 328, 351, 8:490, 492, 497, 501, 525, 628
(April–August 1777); Burnett, *Continental Congress,* 237–40, 248–58;
Jensen, *Articles of Confederation,* 249–70.

[19] Burnett, *Continental Congress,* 472–501; Jensen, *Articles of Confederation,* 185–97.

The reasons for opposition—as well as for support—
were many, but at bottom lay a single reason and the fourth
great enemy of the Republic. Behind the façade of slogans
about the rights of Englishmen and the rights of man, different colonies had supported the revolution in pursuit of
different goals, all local and few high-minded. If they failed
to obtain these, they would view Union and even Independence as barren gains.

The goal whose pursuit blocked ratification of the Articles was the ownership of the western lands. The question
had meaning in many places, for several states were "landless," having no claims or only nebulous claims to western
areas, and most of these landless states had as much population as their arable land, under existing technology, could
support. In New England the towns that were the most
crowded had been the most ardent in support of religious
radicalism in the 1750s, and in the 1770s they were most
ardent in support of political radicalism. But the problem
also had a more forceful and more focused applicability.
In Pennsylvania and Maryland the land supply had been
limited by features of their charters, under which the proprietors, the Penns and Calverts, reserved large tracts for
themselves. During the decade before Independence both
colonies had sought a two-part solution: abrogation of the
proprietary charters and releasing all lands west of the Al-
leghenies to buyers from all colonies. Among the Pennsylvanians this was a matter of seeking profitable outlet for
surplus capital acquired in mercantile ventures. In Maryland it was a matter of economic necessity. Maryland's
slave-labor plantation system was grossly inefficient, con-
suming great quantities of land, and its land disposal
system—whereby planters left the eldest son the home

plantation and gave the others money, slaves, and large acreage in the interior for establishing new plantations— required even more. By 1770 most of the land was taken up, and it was apparent that Maryland would soon either have to obtain some more land from somewhere or suffer the collapse of its entire socioeconomic system.[20]

In the tactical battle over disposition of the western lands, private and public interest were interwoven and narrow self-interest was indistinguishable from broad philosophical purpose. The ablest spokesmen for Pennsylvania and Maryland were several private companies, the most important being the Illinois-Wabash and the Indiana, that had acquired claims to huge tracts in various ways, particularly by buying "titles" from Indians. Many of the prominent stockholders of these companies were also prominent nationalist leaders—including Robert Morris, Benjamin Franklin, William Duer, James Wilson, and Charles Carroll of Carrollton. Because Congress would, until the Articles were ratified, operate extra-legally and thus have all such powers as it could get away with exercising, these nationalists were not eager for ratification anyway; and if they stalled, leaving Congress to cope with foreign powers

---

[20] See A. L. Olson, "Agricultural Economy and the Population in Eighteenth-Century Connecticut," in *Tercentenary Publications in the History of Connecticut* (New Haven, 1936); Roy H. Agaki, *The Town Proprietors of the New England Colonies* (Philadelphia, 1924); Charles Grant, *Democracy in the Connecticut Frontier Town of Kent* (New York, 1961); Avery O. Craven, *Soil Exhaustion as a Factor in the Agricultural History of Virginia and Maryland* (Urbana, Ill., 1926); Charles A. Barker, *Background of the Revolution in Maryland* (New Haven, 1940); Lewis C. Gray, *History of Agriculture in the Southern United States to 1860* (2 vols., Washington, 1933), 1:409–33, 541 ff.; Charles L. Lincoln, *The Revolutionary Movement in Pennsylvania, 1760–1776* (Philadelphia, 1901); and chapters 3 and 4 herein.

without being a legal power itself, perhaps they could force
the landed states to cede their claims. Unsurprisingly, the
state most bitterly opposed to Pennsylvania and Maryland
was Virginia, which had the largest and best-founded claim
to western lands and whose politics were largely dominated
by archrepublicans.[21]

Meanwhile, the war went on. Washington's army never
lost a major engagement, but it never won one either, for
it was Washington's design to play the Fabian and never
do battle unless victory were certain. It was working:
though Washington's men were usually ill-fed, ill-equipped,
and unpaid, and though Britain had thrown the world's
most powerful navy and a vast army against them, yet in
the fall of 1778 the two armies commanded almost exactly
the territory they had in the fall of 1776. In between, at
Germantown, Monmouth, and Newport, the Americans
heartbreakingly fumbled away what might have been decisive victories, but at Lake Champlain, Bennington, and
Bemis Heights they snatched victory from almost certain
defeat.[22]

Along the way, Washington's army became tough, seasoned, disciplined. When it was offered the faintest pretext
for good morale, its rage and enthusiasm were as high as
ever, but its respect for fellow agencies in the cause was
minimal. It learned to despise the militias, with whom
unreliability and cowardice proved more common than the
bravery they had first shown. Loyalty to the Congress was

---

[21] Jensen, *Articles of Confederation,* 198 ff. and *passim,* is by far the best
work ever done on this subject.

[22] Peckham, *War for Independence,* 58–101. For vivid reading on this
subject, see the *Hamilton Papers,* 1:198–604.

constantly strained but it never snapped; every soldier and officer may have cursed Congress fifty times for every word of praise, and most may have thought their hardship stemmed as much from congressional indifference, ineptness, and corruption as from unavoidable difficulties; but discontent rarely threatened to erupt into mutiny.[23]

Had they known in detail—instead of only suspecting—what was going on in high political places, the army's loyalty would have been even more strained. Intrigue and factional strife in Congress were common, and men of all factions embezzled public funds, profiteered in procuring army supplies, and speculated on the basis of secret information. A host of minor scandals broke. One major scandal—the dispute between Silas Deane (and by implication Benjamin Franklin and Robert Morris) and the Lee family, each of whom accused the other, with considerable justice, of grossly misusing public funds—created so many enmities and so hardened old enmities that Congress was almost paralyzed.[24]

And this was not the worst. The republicans in Congress, torn between fear of the army and dependence upon it, favored the despised militias whenever possible; the more so

---

[23] *Ibid.* For examples of the worthlessness of the militia, see Peckham, *War for Independence,* 145–54.

[24] For a good summary of these doings, see E. James Ferguson, *The Power of the Purse: A History of American Public Finance, 1776–1790* (Chapel Hill, 1961), 70–105; for details of the Deane affair, see Charles Isham, ed., *The Deane Papers* (*Collections of the New York Historical Society,* vols. 19–23, 1887–91); *Correspondence Between Silas Deane, His Brothers, and Their Business and Political Associates, 1771–1795* (*Collections of the Connecticut Historical Society,* vol. 23, 1930); Arthur Lee to James Warren, April 8, July 1782, in *Warren-Adams Letters,* 2:171–74; for an interesting example of corruption, see the Publius Letters, in *Hamilton Papers,* 1:562–63, 567–70, 580–82.

because many republican politicians, particularly those rising to power in the nationalist-dominated Middle States, were learning to use the militias with marked success in state and local elections. And late in 1777 they even endeavored by a circuitous route to oust Washington himself, in favor of the spurious hero of Saratoga, General Horatio Gates, whose political views were thought to be more republican and were certainly more favorable to the Lee family. (Through these machinations a single figure emerged as the symbol of opposition to the Lee-Adams junto: the Philadelphia merchant prince and erstwhile congressman, Robert Morris. To all sides, pro and con, Morris' every attribute qualified him for the role—his vast and complex network of mercantile ventures, his unqualified nationalism, his unwavering support of Washington, and his involvement with Deane, Franklin, and the Pennsylvania and Maryland land speculators. One can almost hear Arthur Lee referring to him as "They," with a paranoid's capital T.)[25]

Despite all this, given its practical difficulties, its internal strife, and its reliance on popular virtue instead of governmental power to enforce its measures, Congress performed almost incredibly well for more than three years. Having no taxing power itself—and it was politically impossible, at least temporarily, for the states to levy taxes—

---

[25] E. Wilder Spaulding, *His Excellency George Clinton: Critic of the Constitution* (New York, 1938), 52 ff., 92–93; Brunhouse, *Counter-Revolution,* 65, 105–7, 125–26, 262, *passim;* Freeman, *Washington,* vol. 4, chapter 23; Ver Steeg, *Robert Morris, passim;* Merrill Jensen, *The New Nation* (New York, 1950), 55–61, 366–67; see also Arthur Lee to James Warren, June 5, July 27, 1781, April 8, December 12, 1782, and Warren to John Adams, January 28, 1785, in *Warren-Adams Letters,* 2:166, 169, 171, 184, 248.

Congress resorted to issuing unsecured paper money or "bills of credit" that bore no interest. For a year and a half the bills were adequate; $25 million were issued and they bought more than $23 million worth of supplies and services. When the bills began to depreciate markedly, Congress turned to selling bonds or "loan office certificates"; by the end of 1778 certificates of a nominal value of about $20 million had yielded about $5 million worth of cash, and another $2 million (actual value) in money and supplies came in from loans from France, Spain, and Holland. But loans proved inadequate and Congress returned to issuing bills of credit; $76 million face value issued in 1777 and 1778 yielded the equivalent of roughly $16 million in gold or silver. Meanwhile, Congress mollified army discontent over the lack of pay by voting raises to all enlisted men and a bonus of half pay for life to all officers who would stick it out to the end.[26]

But the whole achievement rested on popular support, and now the well of popular support began to run dry. Public enthusiasm had sagged in the fall of 1777, but it surged upward after the victory at Saratoga and after the French alliance, and by the spring of 1778 most people thought final victory would soon be forthcoming. But then the Americans bungled a major opportunity at Monmouth, and for more than a year Washington failed to mount a single offensive and every effort to effect a cooperation with the French miscarried. One result was a huge popular psychological letdown; by mid-1779 the Spirit of Seventy-six was gone forever, at least in the states north of the Mason-

---

[26] Ferguson, *Power of the Purse,* 25–40, is an excellent account of these matters. On the half-pay bonus, see Burnett, *Continental Congress,* 311–16.

Dixon line. The ensuing military events were ill-calculated to rekindle it. In the winter of 1779–80 the British evacuated all their Northern military strongholds except New York City and launched a successful Southern campaign from Georgia up through the Carolinas. Soon thereafter, the French landed in Newport with a large fleet and 8,000 men. With the American armies gone and the seas relatively free, the basis of economic life in the North suddenly shifted from privateering and supplying American troops to "normal" peacetime commerce and supplying the French; and when the United States ceased to be everybody's most important customer, popular economic interest in supporting its paper vanished. As this interplay between psychological and economic factors unfolded, continental finance veered toward total collapse.[27]

From the fall of 1779 until the beginning of 1781, Congress' efforts to forestall the inevitable were a nightmare of frenzied finance. Congress resorted to check-kiting—issuing bills of exchange on its foreign ministers, hoping that by the time the bills were presented the diplomats could borrow funds to pay them, or could cover them by issuing new bills drawn on someone else. It sped up the paper-money machine, grinding out another $125 million, but the bills depreciated so fast that their cash buying power was less than $6 million. Then, in a wild effort to halt the depreciation, it devalued all the outstanding bills at forty to one, thereby reducing $200 million to $5 million, but that failed too, and soon the $5 million depreciated out of existence. It resorted to mass expropriation, with more

[27] Peckham, *War for Independence,* 89–101, 128–39; Ver Steeg, *Robert Morris,* 43–57.

success: the Quartermaster and Commissary departments, and sometimes the generals in the field, were empowered to take what they needed from whomever had it; they did so, leaving behind them a trail of embittered citizens, little consoled by pieces of paper saying that the United States in Congress assembled would reimburse them. Finally, Congress virtually abandoned responsibility, and turned and pleaded with the states to come to the rescue.[28]

The states' surprising response temporarily staved off collapse—and spelled trouble for the Union in the future. Throughout 1780 the states provided most of what the army had in the way of supplies and pay. For the former, they responded to Congress' requisitions payable in "specific supplies" rather than in cash. As for pay, Congress voted the soldiers still more postdated bounties and bonuses, but otherwise the states took on the full burden of paying the troops, the payments being largely in promissory notes. Almost all states complied when Congress asked them to assume responsibility for back pay due their soldiers in the continental army, and also to compensate them for losses sustained by having been paid earlier in depreciated currency. Nine states also took over payment of their soldiers for all or part of the next two years. In doing this the states took on public debts totaling almost as much as those of Congress, and by the end of 1780 most of them were also financially exhausted.[29]

The states' vigorous efforts derived in large measure from the same spring that had set off the financial debacle: the shift of the war to the South. The arrival of British

---

[28] Ferguson, *Power of the Purse,* 44–60.

[29] *Ibid.,* 50–69; *Journals of Congress,* 18:958–59 (October 21, 1780).

troops stimulated such a fit of nationalism among the erstwhile Southern states-righters that they not only began to
cooperate, but even removed the barriers to acceptance of
the Articles of Confederation. First, in the fall of 1780 Virginia suddenly reversed its long-adamant stand and ceded
all its lands north of the Ohio River to Congress. It imposed only one condition, that private claims to lands in
the ceded territory be explicitly rejected. This action dissolved Maryland's public reason for refusing to ratify the
Articles, though it left intact the private reason. While
Marylanders considered whether to ratify anyway and
hope that Virginia's condition could be obviated in Congress, the war gave them a nudge that settled the matter.
In January 1781 Maryland applied to the French minister
for aid in defending Chesapeake Bay against the British
navy, and the minister suggested that unless Maryland
should ratify, it would be impossible for the French to act.
The Maryland legislature promptly responded by authoriz-
ing its congressmen to subscribe to the Articles of Confederation.[30]

But it was too late; the Congress, or rather, the republicans' version of it, was doomed. An event on New Year's
Day, 1781, dramatically marked its passing. On that day
a thousand soldiers of the Pennsylvania line, disgusted
with their lot, rose up in mutiny and marched toward Philadelphia to seek redress from Congress. Instead, President
Joseph Reed of the Pennsylvania Executive Council met
them at Princeton and, after discussions, agreed to meet
their every demand. Satisfied, the mutineers drifted lei-

---

[30] Burnett, *Continental Congress,* 495–501; Jensen, *Articles of Confederation,* 228–38.

surely back to camp, where nothing was done to punish them. The die-hard republicans in Congress, thoroughly disgraced, at last faced up to the hard fact that they must establish public credit or the Revolution would be lost. This meant that Congress had to obtain power to collect taxes, or to find a miracle man to take over its financing. To the diehards each was a bitter pill, for they had long opposed vesting Congress with the power to tax, and the only eligible miracle man in sight was Robert Morris. But within a month and a half they had swallowed both.[31]

Now it was the nationalists who owned the "forwardness and zeal" that the times required. Hard-core nationalist leaders Robert R. Livingston, James Duane, and John Sullivan, strongly supported by temporarily nationalistic Southerners, speedily hammered out a radical new financial program. On February 3, 1781, Congress determined to ask the states to amend the not-yet-adopted Articles by granting Congress a permanent independent source of revenue, in the form of an impost—a five percent tax on all imports. Two weeks later Congress voted to reorganize and centralize its several administrative departments, placing each under a superintendent, and to ask Robert Morris to take over the crucial office of superintendent of finance. The powers vested in the office, together with others that Morris demanded and received before taking over in May, made him virtually the financial dictator of the United States. He expressly declined to supply the armies, and set

---

[31] *Pennsylvania Gazette,* January 24, 1781; William B. Reed, *Life and Correspondence of Joseph Reed* (2 vols., Philadelphia, 1847), 2:319–37; Burnett, *Continental Congress,* 481–82; Hammond, ed., *Sullivan Papers,* 3:253–65 (Sullivan to Washington, Reed, the French Minister, and President of Congress, January 7–13, 1781).

out only to reorganize the national finances on a business-like basis. That done, he said, public credit would be restored and Congress could then supply the troops as it saw fit.[32]

That was not the way it turned out. No sooner had Morris taken office when the extreme hardships of the army, the earnest pleas of Washington, and above all, the impending climax of the war in Virginia forced him into devoting full time to the business of supply. From May until the battle of Yorktown in October, Morris worked frantically at the task. He borrowed on his private credit as well as on public credit, using the first to establish the second, anticipated foreign loans by kiting bills of exchange, and adopted a system of supply through private contractors. The combination of these efforts with those of the states and of the army itself saw the troops through until the battle of Yorktown could be won.[33]

Brooding in the stillness after Yorktown, Morris was possessed of an idea, and a grand one. "This is the period of weakness," he reasoned, "between the convulsive labors of enthusiasm and the sound and regular operations of order and government." Audaciously, he determined to effect the transition himself, and thereby to do what Congress and the people had not yet seen fit to do, establish a permanent national union and a government to preside over it. The

---

[32] *Journals of Congress,* 19:102–3, 110, 112–13, 290–99, 432–33, 20: 545–48, 597–98 (February, March, May 1781); Joseph Jones to Washington, February 27, 1781, in *Letters of Joseph Jones of Virginia* (Washington, 1889); Sullivan to Washington, January 29, March 6, Washington to Sullivan, February 4, 1781, in Hammond, ed., *Sullivan Papers,* 3:276, 279, 292; Ver Steeg, *Robert Morris,* 58–64, 73

[33] *Ibid.,* 72–77; Sumner, *Financier and Finances,* 1:261–309.

tools for such a gigantic undertaking were at hand, though few had the imagination to see them as tools. The people of the United States shared a huge obligation and a huge piece of property, the public debt (which Morris calculated at around $25 million, or somewhere near as much as all the commercial property in the country) and the western lands (which were incalculable, but seemed likely to be twice as extensive as all the occupied lands in the country). The unimaginative, which is to say most people, saw the first as a curse and the second as a blessing, and proposed to use the one to cancel the other. Morris proposed instead to keep the lands out of the equation for now, and to come up with other means for servicing the debts. That done, the many, many thousands who held public securities would have a stake in supporting the national administration. Then, as an unrelated enterprise, Congress could begin to sell the lands, and soon many, many more thousands would have a stake in supporting the national administration. Soon, too, the national administration would have grown large and powerful.[34]

Servicing the debt, as Morris visualized it, was a two-part operation, for there were two kinds of creditors. First, there were the small farmers and shopkeepers who had become creditors more or less against their wills, by having provisions and supplies taken from them by the armies. These people needed cash payment as quickly as possible and needed to be protected against speculators while they waited. Under Morris' plan, their certificates would be quickly audited, scaled down to allow for inflation, and

---

[34] Ver Steeg, *Robert Morris,* 78–96, 105, 126–29; Ferguson, *Power of the Purse,* 117–24. At this time, of course, the public domain was still in process of creation.

exchanged for new, nonnegotiable certificates that would soon be paid off at par. Second, there were the large farmers and merchants who had furnished money or supplies voluntarily, either by subscribing to loans or by contracting for and delivering goods. Their certificates would be audited and scaled down and placed on a regular interest-bearing basis, but no provision would be made for redemption. Thus "funded," these securities would become a form of semipermanent investment and, after their market prices became stable, they would circulate as a form of money.[35]

To pull it off, what Morris needed were the authority and the money. Having neither, he simply assumed the one and set out to create the other. The annual cost of his plan would run around $2 million. If the states would ratify the impost amendment, the proceeds from import duties would provide a fourth to a half of the needed sum. For the rest, Morris proposed that Congress ask the states for power to levy a land tax of one cent per acre per year.[36]

In the meantime, all Morris had to work with were occasional loans from foreign governments and, what were even less dependable, payments by the states of their congressional requisitions; and thus to launch the program he had to resort to magic. First he got authority from Congress to establish a bank: the Bank of North America, capitalized at $400,000, to be raised through private subscriptions. Unsurprisingly, private subscribers did not appear, so Morris took out of the United States Treasury $250,000 of the proceeds of a loan from Europe, and bought bank stock with it. He and various of his friends raised the remainder

[35] Ver Steeg, *Robert Morris,* 92–94, 124–26.
[36] *Ibid.,* 93, 97 ff., 126 ff.

on their personal credit. Then the bank started operations, with Morris himself as a director and his business partner Thomas Willing as president. Much of the money that the bank lent to private individuals never left the bank, for borrowers usually deposited the money they borrowed and withdrew it at different times, or paid it to other depositors. Accordingly, the bank could safely issue notes for and lend eight to ten times as much as its capital. That made more than three million dollars out of four hundred thousand. The venture proved, investors clamored to buy stock, and Morris obliged them by selling the stock held by the Treasury.[37] The Treasury now had its money back and had a reliable source of short-term loans of several times its original investment.[38]

But Morris only appeared to be a magician. For all the imaginative sweep of his scheme and the brilliance with which he executed its details, it could work only if the economy was working and if permanent revenues were soon forthcoming. After Yorktown, the economy all but stopped working for a while. The land war was for practical purposes over, and the preliminary negotiations for peace were concluded within thirteen months. In the meantime, however, throughout 1782 the British carried on an effective war at sea, with the result that shipping from American ports was stopped almost completely. A severe nationwide

---

[37] Morris' critics, then and among historians later, severely condemned him for these operations; the reasons, apart from personal pique, lie in lack of understanding of the means of and need for the creation of credit.

[38] *Ibid.,* 84–89; Sumner, *Financier and Finances,* 21–35, 70; Lawrence Lewis, Jr., *A History of the Bank of North America* (Philadelphia, 1882), chapter 1; Burton A. Konkle, *Thomas Willing and the First American Financial System* (Philadelphia, 1937).

depression ensued, and Morris' chances of success dimin-
ished as the depression deepened.[39] Skilled as he was in
stretching a paucity of resources over a multitude of commitments, he was, by the fall of 1782, at wit's end.[40]

There was one hope: if the impost amendment could be
ratified soon, the income from spring imports in 1783 could
save the day. Morris did not leave the issue to chance.
He promoted the creation of "lobbies" of public security
holders in each of the Middle States, and stimulated these
(whose ranks included many of his enemies) to "pressure"
him and Congress and the states in behalf of favorable
action. So prodded, the states responded to the proposal
with unprecedented speed, and by the end of the 1782
legislative sessions, all states but two, Georgia and Rhode
Island, had ratified. Georgia, still under British occupation
and its restored royal government, did not count. If Rhode
Island would come through, Congress could take the position that the amendment had been ratified by every state.[41]

Rhode Island was understandably reluctant to support
the impost. As a state without any staples and with a pre-

[39] Toward the end of 1782 the economy was given brief but important relief
by the temporary opening of Havana to American wheat, an event that later
had significant political repercussions. See the *Philadelphia Pennsylvania
Packet,* March 29, 1785, and the *Philadelphia Evening Herald,* September
8, 1785, and the discussion of the Jay-Gardoqui negotiations, pp. 144–45,
herein.

[40] Peckham, *War for Independence,* 190; Joseph Reed to James Searle,
undated, in Reed, *Reed,* 2:295; Daniel of St. Thomas Jenifer to John
Hall, May 28, 1781, James Duane to Philip Schuyler, July 18, 1782, remarks of Witherspoon in Thompson's notes, August 6, 1782, all in Burnett,
Letters of Members of Congress, 6:101, 386, 426.

[41] Ver Steeg, *Robert Morris,* 123–24; *New York Packet,* October 24, 1782,
Pennsylvania Packet, July 6, September 5, 24, 1782; Philadelphia *Independent Gazetteer,* September 14, 1782; Virginia Delegates to Benjamin
Harrison, December 10, 1782, in Burnett, ed., *Letters of Members of Congress,* 6:558–59; Burnett, *Continental Congress,* 530–32.

dominately commercial economy, it sorely needed freedom of trade. Most of the goods it imported were soon re-exported, and unless the state could control import duties, and thereby reimburse its merchants through a system of refunds or drawbacks, it would be at an overwhelming commercial disadvantage in relation to other states. Furthermore, Rhode Island had its own sizable public debt, and the only conceivable source of revenue to support it was a moderate system of duties on goods imported for consumption inside the state.[42]

But there were less legitimate considerations as well. A dozen or so members of Providence's wealthy, shrewd, and opportunistic mercantile class—including John and Nicholas Brown, Thomas Jenkins, the firm of Clark and Nightingale, Zachariah and Phillip Allen, Joseph and William Russel, and Jabez Bowen—had speculated deeply in the public debt. Between them, they owned about $250,000, face value, of Continental Loan Office certificates. After all states but Rhode Island had ratified the impost amendment, it was easy enough for these men to convince mercantile correspondents in other cities that Rhode Island would soon also ratify. Indeed, the two Rhode Island delegates to Congress, Ezekial Cornell and David Howell, publicly assured Morris that Rhode Island would ratify it in the November session of the legislature.[43]

---

[42] Ver Steeg, *Robert Morris,* 126–29; *Providence Gazette,* throughout 1782; Frank G. Bates, "Rhode Island and the Impost of 1781," in American Historical Association *Annual Report,* 1894; David Howell to William Greene, Governor of Rhode Island, July 30, 1782, in Burnett, ed., *Letters of Members of Congress,* 6:399 ff.; see also the analysis of Rhode Island in chapter 4, herein.

[43] Ver Steeg, *Robert Morris,* 126; *Providence Gazette,* January 1782 to February 1783; List of Notes Issued for Consolidating the Securities Issued from the General Treasurer's Office, September 1782 to June 1784, in the

Their design was sinister. As soon as word got around that Rhode Island was about to ratify, continental securities everywhere began to rise in price, and state securities began to decline, for it was expected that if the states surrendered control of the impost, they would have great difficulty in paying their own debts. When the Rhode Island Assembly met in November, continentals had reached a peak and state securities had hit bottom. At just this moment, the Providence speculators dumped continentals and bought securities of New York, Massachusetts, and other states. Then the Rhode Island Assembly met and again refused to ratify. Continental securities dropped precipitously and state securities rose accordingly. As a result, the speculators doubled their investments.[44]

Unaware of these shenanigans, but expecting that the state could by some means be induced to ratify, Congress dispatched a delegation to try to persuade the legislature. They might have had reasonable expectation of success, for the speculators had now begun to unload their newly acquired state securities at relatively high prices and to buy newly depreciated continentals. But just then an old issue arose again to kill the impost forever: the struggle between the landed and the landless states.[45]

Congress had not yet accepted Virginia's conditional cession of the northwest territory, and Maryland—probably

Rhode Island Archives; Brown Papers, John Carter Brown Library and Rhode Island Historical Society, 1781–82, *passim.*

[44] Proceedings of the General Assembly, November 1782, in Rhode Island Archives; David Howell to Welcome Arnold, November 17, 1782, in Burnett, ed., *Letters of Members of Congress,* 6:542–43 (see also footnote at 542); and the sources cited in footnote 41, above.

[45] Burnett, *Continental Congress,* 533; *Journals of Congress,* 23:769 ff. (December 6, 1782).

supported by many of the Middle States nationalists, including Morris himself—had sought to force the state to drop its conditions. The matter was at an impasse until a group of Virginia political leaders decided to seize the opportunity offered by the financial crisis and force Congress into accepting its grant. Morris' idea of keeping the public lands in abeyance was a luxury that could be indulged only if Congress had other sources of revenue. If the impost collapsed, Morris' overall scheme would probably follow. The Virginians, having no love for Morris anyway and being eminently suspicious of his nationalistic designs, could head him off and perhaps ensure that Congress would accept the conditions of its land grant, simply by making sure that the impost amendment failed. Accordingly, in November the Virginia legislature rescinded its act of ratification. The congressional delegates on their way to Rhode Island learned of this action when they got to New York. In despair, they gave up and returned to Philadelphia. The impost amendment was dead.[46]

All hopes of creating a national government through more or less constitutional means died with it. Furthermore, the impending peace—at that moment preliminary articles were being signed, though Americans would not learn of it until March—would soon remove the greatest single stimulus for national action. But as it happened, something else was occasioning opportunity for a more drastic effort: the question of paying the army, which was now heavily concentrated in quarters at Newburgh, New York.

---

[46] Merrill Jensen, "The Creation of the National Domain, 1781–1784," in *Mississippi Valley Historical Review*, 26:323–42 (1939); Burnett, *Continental Congress*, 533; Gray, *History of Agriculture*, 2:621 ff.

The army had received virtually no pay in hard money in years. Morris had, on taking office, made clear what the priority of money for the use of the army would be: food first, clothing second, military stores and equipment third, attending the sick fourth, and only what was left over for pay; and there had never been any left over. So long as the fighting continued, enlisted men complained only moderately and sporadically about not being paid, and the officers temporarily almost forgot their promised bonus of half pay for life. But when peace loomed, and soldiers faced the prospect of returning home and losing their relative immunity from private obligations, that was another matter. Many officers, particularly, had suffered their personal affairs to fall into great disarray, and as Washington said, unless they received the bonus or substantial payments of back wages, many had nothing to look forward to except being thrown into jail for inability to pay accumulated debts.[47]

The demise of the impost amendment made their prospects appear dim, and in the following month—December 1782—grumbling grew rife and informal meetings of officers became common. For a time, the officers considered threatening to resign in a body, but late in the month they decided instead to draft a strong memorial to Congress. On the 29th a deputation consisting of General Alexander McDougall and Colonels Matthias Ogden and John Brooks arrived in Philadelphia, and on January 6 they presented their plea. In content and general tone the document was a respectful plea for justice, but it also dropped the ominous

---

[47] Ver Steeg, *Robert Morris,* 165; Washington to Hamilton, March 12, 1783, in *Hamilton Papers,* 3:286–87.

hint that "any further experiments on [the officers'] patience may have fatal effects."[48]

While Congress quaked, Morris and a handful of his inner circle saw opportunity. To seize it would require boldness, skill, and luck, and failure could be disastrous. But the men in the inner circle were, if nothing else, bold: Gouverneur Morris, Robert's sometimes extravagantly imaginative and daring assistant; Richard Peters, the active head of the Board of War; two congressmen, Morris' old friend James Wilson and his precocious new friend, Washington's former aide, Alexander Hamilton; and a handful of others. For a week or two, singly and in groups, they conferred with the McDougall committee, and thrashed out a nebulous plan for coordinating the power of the army with the influence of the newly organized public creditors. Together, they might be able to force adoption of Morris' permanent financial program—the funding of all continental debts, those to the army included, the assumption of all state war debts, and the establishment of adequate permanent revenues to support them.[49]

The conspirators did not intend to actually use the force of a rebellious army—not because they were particularly against it in principle, but on the practical ground that it

---

[48] Burnett, *Continental Congress,* 553 ff.; Madison's Minutes, January 6, 1783, in *Journals of Congress,* 25:846. One faction of officers thought that the states were a more likely source of payment; see Benjamin Lincoln to Knox, December 3, and Knox to Lincoln, December 20, 1782, in Henry Knox Papers, Massachusetts Historical Society.

[49] Hamilton to Clinton, January 12, 1783, in *Hamilton Papers,* 3:240; G. Morris to Jay, January 1, 1783, in Sparks, *Gouverneur Morris,* 1:249; Alexander McDougall to Knox, January 9, 1783, in Knox Papers, Massachusetts Historical Society; Smith, *Wilson,* 179–83; Jensen, *New Nation,* 69.

was not likely to work. Instead their goal was a quasi coup d'etat, inside the framework of the Articles of Confederation. This involved forcing two sets of formal actions: adoption by Congress of the necessary amendments and their ratification by the states. The first looked comparatively easy, the second less so; but virtually all the state legislatures were now in session or would soon convene, and if the army could be kept continuously threatening without exploding into outright violence, perhaps the states, subjected to more individualized pressures from the organized public creditors, could be rushed into it.[50]

Forthwith, the inner group went to work attempting to persuade influential men in state governments and in Congress to support the financial plan. With some they were bluntly honest, with others adroitly deceptive, and with still others they revealed just enough of the truth to win or force their support. With all, they played off "the terror of a mutinying army," as Arthur Lee wrote to Sam Adams, "with considerable efficacy." To cap the performance, Robert Morris suddenly and unexpectedly threatened to resign. On January 24 he sent a melodramatic message to Congress, feigning despair that public credit would ever be established. Declaring that he could "never be the minister of injustice," he advised Congress that unless his system were enacted by the end of May, he would unceremoniously quit his office and let Congress shift for itself. McDougall and Ogden were then sent back to army headquarters at Newburgh with a resolution well calculated to leave every-

---

[50] These plans are implicit in Hamilton to Washington, March 17, 25, 1783, in *Hamilton Papers,* 3:293, 306; see also Ver Steeg, *Robert Morris,* 176.

thing hanging in air: it said that Morris would pay the army "as soon as the state of public finances will admit."[51]

The stage being set, on the next day James Wilson proposed that Congress shelve its other business and concentrate on establishing a financial program. Congress agreed, and for a brief period it appeared that things would go smoothly. Wilson and Hamilton led the way, with the help of three new congressmen who were not in on the inner plan: Thomas Fitzsimons of Pennsylvania, James Madison of Virginia, and Hugh Williamson of North Carolina. Within a few days they had succeeded in tying all the parts of the program together in such a way that Congress had to consider them all as a piece.[52]

But they had just begun to gather momentum when things started to go awry. First the handful of hard-core republicans still in Congress—Arthur Lee and Theodorick Bland of Virginia, Jonathan Arnold and John Collins of Rhode Island, and Stephen Higginson of Massachusetts—began to throw up stumbling blocks. Even these were convinced that some kind of financial measures had to be adopted, but they were determined to prevent the establishment of Morris' overall system. By raising a series of

---

[51] Madison's Minutes, January 24, 1783, in *Journals of Congress,* 25:862; Arthur Lee to Samuel Adams, January 29, 1783, in Burnett, ed., *Letters of Members of Congress,* 7:27–28; see also Lee to James Warren, February 19, 1783, in *Warren-Adams Letters,* 2:190; Ver Steeg, *Robert Morris,* 170–71; Burnett, *Continental Congress,* 556.

[52] Madison's Minutes, January 25, 28, 29, February throughout, 1783, in *Journals of Congress,* 25:864–66, 870–85; Hamilton to Washington, February 7, Madison to Randolph, February 13, 18, 25, Hugh Williamson to James Iredell, February 17, Arthur Lee to James Warren, February 19, 1783, all in Burnett, ed., *Letters of Members of Congress,* 7:33, 44, 46, 49, 51, 57; Burnett, *Continental Congress,* 556–61.

minor objections and digressions, they caused the debates to drag through a week, and then through another. Now some of the New England delegates began to object to the impost part of the plan on the ground that their states could not pay their own debts without that source of revenue. When assumption of state debts was proposed as a counter to this objection, some of the Southern delegates protested against the huge debt being thus created and particularly against the direct tax on land that supporting it would entail. And crisis or no, some delegates began to wander home and thus to plague Congress with the old problem of keeping a quorum together.[53]

Hamilton and Gouverneur Morris were prepared to manage these difficulties by bringing a good deal more pressure to bear from the army. For ten days after the other two army delegates had gone, they had kept Colonel Brooks (a long-standing friend of Hamilton's) in Philadelphia for indoctrination. Then they sent him back to Newburgh with instructions to prepare the junior officers for "manly, vigorous association with the other public creditors." They also entrusted him with a letter to Henry Knox, one of the two influential generals whose support they knew they could count on. In a persuasive letter outlining the whole plan, Morris closed by saying that "after you have carried the post the public creditors will garrison it for you." A week later, Morris wrote to the same effect to the other trusted general, Nathanael Greene. Hamilton, having allowed time for Knox to get Morris' message, wrote to Washington.

[53] Madison's Minutes, January–February 1783, in *Journals of Congress,* vol. 25; Ver Steeg, *Robert Morris,* 172–74.

Sketching a picture of severe crisis in congressional finance (which surprised Washington, who had thought—accurately—that new funds, sufficient to alleviate the immediate problems, were on their way from Europe), Hamilton pleaded with Washington to use his great prestige to harness the army's demands for justice, and particularly to ensure that the pressure would be utilized not merely for immediate relief, but for the establishment of a permanent national system of finance. At the same time, Hamilton also urged that Washington exercise caution, so as to keep "a *complaining and suffering army* within the bounds of moderation." And just in case Washington were suspicious of the whole affair, Hamilton added in a casual postscript that it might be wise to consult General Knox, whom Hamilton knew Washington trusted.[54]

After allowing a couple of weeks for the re-agitation of the army to make its impression, Robert Morris did two spectacular things designed to force a climax. First, in an effort to embarrass Congress through public opinion, he published his earlier letter of resignation, which Congress had carefully kept secret. Then he issued a stark demand: that Congress set a deadline, perhaps of a year, for the total payment of the public debt. If the states did not, within that time, pay their full portions of the debt, then Congress (presumably with the army at its back) should assume power

---

[54] *Ibid.,* 172; G. Morris to Knox, February 7, McDougall and Ogden to Knox, February 8, 1783, in Knox Papers, Massachusetts Historical Society; John Armstrong, Jr., to Horatio Gates, April 29, 1783, in Burnett, ed., *Letters,* 7:155n; G. Morris to Nathanael Greene, February 15, 1783, in Sparks, *Gouverneur Morris,* 2:250–51; Washington to Hamilton, March 4, Hamilton to Washington, February 13, 1783, in *Hamilton Papers,* 3:254, 277.

to move into any delinquent state and collect not merely an impost, but all taxes necessary to fulfill the state's quota.[55]

But the end of the grand scheme was just two days away, for the two groups the nationalists had been exploiting got out of hand, and the dynamite they had been playing with finally exploded.[56] At the beginning of March Colonel Walter Stewart, a holder of a huge amount of public securities and a former aide-de-camp of General Horatio Gates, spent a week in Philadelphia. He invested a goodly part of his time in conferring with the leading members of Philadelphia's public creditors committee, most of whom were intimate friends of his and no particular friends of Robert Morris'—Blair McClenachan, Benjamin Rush, Charles Pettit, John Ewing, and others. On March 8 Stewart returned to camp at Newburgh and went directly to the tent of his former chief, General Gates. The erstwhile hero of the congressional republicans was possessed of bitter hostility toward both Washington and Morris, and for some time he had flirted with the audacious idea of increasing the agitation in the army and using it to overthrow Washington.[57]

---

[55] Morris to the President of Congress, February 26, March 8, 1783, in Francis Wharton, ed., *The Revolutionary Diplomatic Correspondence of the United States* (6 vols., Washington, 1889), 6:266, 277; *Pennsylvania Packet,* March 4, 1783.

[56] The account of the Gates-Armstrong affair given here differs from conventional historical accounts in one major respect: in holding that the army, on Gates' instigation, got out of hand; it is usually held that Hamilton and the two Morrises instigated the uprising all the way.

[57] Washington to Hamilton, March 4, 12, 1783, in *Hamilton Papers,* 3:277, 286; list of security holders in *Pennsylvania Packet,* July 6, 1782. These security holders were not all especially friendly toward one another; Rush, for example, despised Ewing and Arthur Lee, but was friendly with Gates. See Rush to Gates, June 12, September 5, 1781, and Rush to John

From Gates' tent immediately began to emanate a word-of-mouth campaign, rumors that Congress was going to do nothing for the officers and that the officers were gathering to take drastic action. From the same tent came two addresses, unsigned but written by John Armstrong, Jr. The first called for a meeting to discuss the relations of the army to Congress. To call such a meeting without the approval of the commander in chief was against regulations and implied casting off Washington's leadership and taking drastic action. The second called in effect for the officers to declare that they would not disband until they had obtained "justice." The second address also hinted that Washington was secretly in favor of such action, but was prevented by his position from taking an open stand. Accordingly, the officers should not be squeamish about disregarding Washington's public stance and acting independently.[58]

By a bold and decisive stroke that belied his underlying horror and fear, Washington was able to quell the immediate threat of insurrection. He surprised the rebellious by attending the meeting in person (March 15), and by virtue of rank he presided over it. By the dozen, officers came in, tempers blazing, only to sit in embarrassed silence as Washington addressed the group. He assured the officers that as their leader he would support their decisions, but pointed out the practical problems and attendant disgrace that would accompany rash action. Congress, he said, would see that justice was done, rumors to the contrary notwithstanding. (It was neither rank nor argument that carried the

---

Armstrong, March 19, 1783, in Lyman H. Butterfield, ed., *Letters of Benjamin Rush* (2 vols., Princeton, 1951), 1:263, 264–65, 294 ff.

[58] The two addresses are published in *Journals of Congress,* 24:294–98.

day: so commanding was Washington's personality that few men could stand up to him, face to face, and disagree with him, and it would take a Talleyrand to do so with motives that were less than impeccable.)[59]

For the moment, the rebels capitulated; a committee, headed by Knox, was formed and drafted resolutions affirming loyalty to Congress and repudiating the mutinous Armstrong-Gates address. The meeting formally ratified the resolutions and dispersed. But Washington and his intimates knew full well that their temporary victory could be sustained only if Congress soon showed ability and inclination to satisfy the officers' demands—some cash payment and good security for the balance of what was due them as well as the promised lifetime bonus.[60]

And as soon as they learned of the episode, Morris and his intimates realized that all hope was gone of using the army to achieve their long-range ends. Henceforth the two problems, paying and demobilizing the army and funding the public debts, had to be considered separately, and only the first had emergency priority. And at almost the very moment Newburgh was exploding, the other last hope of the archnationalists was vanishing. They had hoped that even if the alliance between creditors and army failed, the fear of a resumption of hostilities might perpetuate the emergency atmosphere that could stimulate nationalistic measures. But on March 12 news of the conclusion of a

---

[59] Freeman, *Washington,* vol. 5; Washington to President of Congress, April 18, 1783, in Fitzpatrick, ed., *Writings of Washington,* vol. 26; Burnett, *Continental Congress,* 567–69.

[60] *Ibid;* see also Hamilton to Washington, March 17, 25, and Hamilton's report in Congress, March 21, 1783, in *Hamilton Papers,* 3:290, 301, 305, 307.

provincial peace treaty with Britain arrived in Philadelphia, and on the 24th came news of the conclusion of a general peace.[61]

What followed was a three-part anticlimax, in which the victorious new nation all but disintegrated. First as to public credit: Congress made no provision for funding any of the public debt—continental, state, or army. Instead, by resolutions finally adopted on April 18, it merely asked the states to grant a watered-down version of the taxing powers Morris had sought. It repeated, with minor modifications and a time limit of twenty-five years, its request for an impost; it requested that the eighth article of the Confederation be amended to change the basis of requisitions from land to population; and it requested that the states establish effective revenues for the same twenty-five years, to yield, by quotas, $1.5 million to Congress annually. Finally, it repeated its request that delinquent states bring their cessions of western lands into acceptable form.[62]

The second step was the denouement of the army crisis. Upon receiving the news of the abortive revolt, Congress adopted a measure it had dawdled with for some time: it commuted the promised bonus of half pay for life into a promise to pay the officers full salaries for the ensuing five years. Then it decided, on Washington's recommendation, to offer the army three months' back wages in cash before discharging it, and it requested Morris to come up with the $750,000 that this would require. Morris demurred. It was impossible to do so, he protested, except through his personal credit, for Congress had no credit, and the sum was

---

[61] Burnett, *Continental Congress,* 563, 566.
[62] *Journals of Congress,* 24:256–62 (April 18, 1783).

beyond the means of the only other possible source, the Bank of North America. After some hesitation, Morris agreed to stay on as financier after the deadline he had established, and to issue the necessary notes, though this would require overdrawing his available resources, public and private, by half a million dollars. By June 7 the first of the notes was in the hands of the paymaster general, and despite the tediousness of the operation (for this first round Morris had personally signed 6,000 notes totaling $200,000), the rest were soon forthcoming.[63]

All this was conducted in an atmosphere of extreme tension, periodically broken by minor violence and threats of mutiny by the enlisted men. But upon the completion of peace large numbers in the army grew anxious to go home and trust their fates to their states (thereby the army became, as the public creditors would soon become, a powerful agency of national disintegration rather than of consolidation). Late in May Congress, in an artful stroke designed to weaken the army as a threat, directed Washington to grant furloughs instead of discharging his men. Within a month the army all but melted away, never having received any pay. A week later Morris' notes arrived in camp, and the major danger had passed.[64]

But enough malcontents remained together to force a final humiliation upon Congress. On Thursday, June 19, Congress received word that a band of eighty men from the Pennsylvania line had broken from their officers and were

---

[63] Burnett, *Continental Congress,* 568; Ferguson, *Power of the Purse,* 168–70; Ver Steeg, *Robert Morris,* 178–86.

[64] *Journals of Congress,* 24:364–65 (May 26, 1783); Jensen, *New Nation,* 81–82.

marching to Philadelphia to obtain justice. Some of the men threatened to rob the bank. Congress demanded that the Executive Council of Pennsylvania call out the local militia to protect them; the council refused on the ground that in the face of a restless popular mood, the militia could not be counted on. The next day the mutineers arrived and took possession of the barracks, where about four hundred other troops were already quartered. On Saturday morning, four or five hundred troops, bayonets fixed and well plied with liquor that anonymous Philadelphians had generously furnished, surrounded the State House, where both Congress and the Pennsylvania Executive Council were sitting. For three tense hours the two bodies exchanges insults and accusations of blame, while the mutineers milled outside, swearing, threatening, and occasionally terrifying a congressman or councilman by poking a bayonet inside a window. Finally, the congressmen screwed up their courage, voted to adjourn, and filed out through the mob. No violence ensued, but Congress discreetly decided to abandon Philadelphia and reconvene in Princeton.[65]

The nation no longer had a capital, and soon it had virtually no Congress, either. During the next six months there was rarely a quorum to do business. Not even on the matter of ratifying the peace treaty did sufficient delegates think it worth their while to attend; only through chance was the treaty ratified within the time limits agreed upon by the negotiators.[66]

---

[65] President of Congress to Washington, June 21, 1783, in Burnett, ed., *Letters of Members of Congress*, 5:193; Hamilton to William Jackson, June 19, and reports dated June 20, 21, 24, 1783, in *Hamilton Papers*, 3:397, 399, 401, 403; Burnett, *Continental Congress*, 575–79.

[66] *Ibid.*, 581–94.

Thereafter, such delegates as did attend Congress in adequate numbers to do business seemed determined to undo the few remaining bonds of union. When Morris resigned in 1784 they tore down his centralized system of administration, and their only definite achievements—the auditing of public accounts and the establishment of the national domain—looked to the dissolution, rather than the preservation, of the great cements of union.

The legacies of 1783 were fourfold. First, the revenue amendments of April remained pending; upon their fate at the hands of the state legislatures hung the fate of the Confederation. The next two weighted the outcome in favor of disintegration. On the one hand, Congress was in thorough disrepute. On the other, the public creditors, particularly those in New York and Pennsylvania, remained organized as militant pressure groups, and they now turned to the states to seek payment for their claims. The last was the most important of all: the pendulum had swung again, and the Revolution ended as it had begun, with republicans having their way. This meant that the "completion of the Revolution" would not, for now, involve the creation of a national government, but the fulfillment of the local aspirations which had, at the outset, impelled the several colonies to embrace the revolutionary cause.

Chapter Two

Completion of the Revolution: The Middle States

To nationalists, the war had ended on the sourest of notes, but there was abundant reason to believe that in their home territory the fibers of union would remain tightly woven. For one thing, people in the Middle States would not soon forget the military lesson the war had taught, that theirs was the most vulnerable part of America. New York had been held by the enemy for more than seven years; Philadelphia had been occupied for only one winter, but had lived under almost continuous peril of attack; and New Jersey and the lower Hudson valley saw perhaps more of the armies of both sides than did the rest of the country combined.

Should memory tend to lapse, a newly created institution would serve to renew it. In the spring of 1783 Henry Knox, a fat and sentimental Yankee who had become one of Washington's ablest generals, had reluctantly faced surrendering the glory and comradeship of war for the sake of his dull civilian life as proprietor of a bookshop. Finding others similarly disposed, he organized them into the Society of the Cincinnati, a fraternal association of ex-officers of the

Continental line. What Knox founded out of almost maud-
lin motives quickly hardened into an informed, influential,
and durable pressure group, interested both emotionally and
financially in strengthening the Union—and virtually the
only national organization except for Congress itself. As
quickly, it was denounced in New England and the lower
South as a long step toward hereditary aristocracy. But little
of such talk was heard in the Middle States, and there it
remained both powerful and socially respectable.[1]

Equally important were a number of purely physical considerations. Not the least of these was that here (and only
here) the great majority of the people had easy and regular
access to one another and to the rest of the world. Of the
Middle States, only Pennsylvania had a continuous line of
settlement deep into the interior, and even in that state
three-fourths of the population was concentrated in a small
area near Philadelphia. In the four Middle States combined
lived about a quarter of the nation's people, and fully nine-
tenths of them were no farther than a dozen easily crossed
miles from tidewater or within a day's land travel from New
York or Philadelphia. In turn, these two cities and points
between were connected by a daily coach service called the

---

[1] John C. Daves, ed., *Proceedings of the General Society of the Cincinnati*
[1784] (Baltimore, 1925); Wallace E. Davies, "The Society of the Cincinnati in New England, 1783–1800," in *William and Mary Quarterly,* 3d
Series, 5:3–25 (1948); Edgar E. Hume, "Early Opposition to the Cincinnati," in *Americana,* 30:613–14 (1936), and the same author's *General
Washington's Correspondence Concerning the Society of the Cincinnati*
(Baltimore, 1941); Aedanus Burke, *Considerations on the Society or Order
of the Cincinnati* . . . (Philadelphia, 1783); Henry Knox Papers, Massachusetts Historical Society; North Callahan, *Henry Knox: General Washington's General* (Philadelphia, 1958).

"Flying Machine." And into them, from every part of the Atlantic world, sailed almost two thousand ships a year. By comparison, the other parts of the country were almost unbelievably isolated.[2]

Such stimuli for the broad view, like the military stimuli, were reinforced by organized human doings. These were various, ranging from friendships born of wartime politics to intermarriages among the commercial and landed aristocracy, but most were connected, directly or indirectly, to Robert Morris. The Great Man (friends and enemies alike

---

[2] On population distribution in the Middle States, see Stella H. Sutherland, *Population Distribution in Colonial America* (New York, 1936), and Evarts B. Greene and Virginia Harrington, *American Population Before the Federal Census of 1790* (New York, 1932); the Census of 1790, published as *Return of the Whole Number of Persons Within . . . the United States* (Washington, 1802). Data on ship movements are tabulated from customs office papers in the Historical Society of Pennsylvania and the Public Records Division of the Pennsylvania Historical Commission, and from announcements in the New York *Daily Advertiser* and other New York newspapers and the *Pennsylvania Packet* and other Philadelphia newspapers. The entire subject of the time necessary to move from place to place in pre-steam America is a much neglected one, and one on which, in this volume, considerable stress is placed as a factor conditioning attitudes. Certain contemporary accounts, such as J. D. Schoepf's *Travels in the Confederation, 1783–1784* (2 vols., Philadelphia, 1911) and Christopher Colles' *A Survey of the Roads of the United States, 1789* (Cambridge, 1961), are useful; as are some of the older general transportation histories, such as Balthasar H. Meyer's *History of Transportation in the United States Before 1860* (Washington, 1917) and Archer B. Hulbert's *Historic Highways of America* (16 vols., Cleveland, 1902–05), and his *The Paths of Inland Commerce* (New Haven, 1920). However, there is not to my knowledge any published compilation of such data for eighteenth-century America. For this volume, I have depended heavily on an unpublished study done at Brown University by Arthur A. Anderson, "A Study of Communications in America Before 1801," a careful analysis based primarily on pamphlet literature in the John Carter Brown Library and ship logs and other manuscripts in the Rhode Island Historical Society.

called him that) had welded together a set of economic coalitions "whose interests knew no state boundaries and were truly national in their scope." The broadest based and best coordinated were public creditors, both original investors and speculators; they had been formed into militant organizations in cities from Baltimore to Boston and were strongest in Philadelphia and New York. They were also the greediest, most ruthless, and most insistent in demanding political action in their behalf.[3]

Next came the mercantile alliances and partnerships that Morris had formed, in office and out. Apart from his own house (Willing, Morris, and Swanwick) and a hand in several other firms in Philadelphia, Morris maintained partnerships, correspondent relationships, or other ties with some of the most affluent merchants in most major cities from Portsmouth to Richmond. Among these were John Langdon, Daniel Parker, Jeremiah Wadsworth, John B. Church, William Constable, William Duer, Matthew Ridley, William Turnbull, Mark Pringle, Tench Tilghman, and Benjamin Harrison, Jr. These, in turn, were closely tied in various ways with one another and with still other important houses. To follow through only one line of connections, Wadsworth and Church were partners; Alexander Hamilton was

---

[3] The quotation is from Charles A. Beard, *An Economic Interpretation of the Constitution of the United States* (New York, 1913), 325; Beard used it to describe a group which he inaccurately supposed existed in 1787–88 (see Forrest McDonald, *We the People: The Economic Origins of the Constitution,* Chicago, 1958), but it is a perfectly accurate description of the Middle States nationalists in 1783. On Morris, see Ellis P. Oberholtzer, *Robert Morris, Patriot and Financier* (New York, 1903); William G. Sumner, *The Financier and the Finances of the American Revolution* (2 vols., New York, 1891); and Clarence L. Ver Steeg's excellent *Robert Morris, Revolutionary Financier* (Philadelphia, 1954). The comments on public security holders are amplified below.

Church's brother-in-law, attorney, and agent; Tilghman, a member of Maryland's richest clan, was one of Hamilton's close personal friends, having served with him as an aide to Washington; Gouverneur Morris, a member of one of New York's richest clans, was intimate with both Hamilton and Robert Morris, and the Schuyler family, into which Hamilton and Church married, was intermarried with all the most important families in the New York aristocracy, including the Livingstons, the Van Rensselaers, the Van Cortlandts, and the Beekmans. These interconnections had an import far greater than merely business; because transportation and communication were synonymous and because information was normally carried as a subordinate cargo with goods, whoso controlled commerce also controlled, in large measure, the flow of ideas and information.[4]

Finally, there was the Bank of North America. On its capital of $400,000, the bank could issue notes up to perhaps three or four million dollars. The leverage—political as well as economic—that such a sum could provide can scarcely be overrated. In a country in which the sheer abundance of natural wealth dictated that the use for money would outrun its supply, this would in normal times be ten to twenty percent as much as all the hard money in circula-

---

[4] Ver Steeg's *Robert Morris* outlines most of Morris' connections and their origins. See also the Jeremiah Wadsworth Papers in the Connecticut Historical Society; the John Langdon Papers in the Historical Society of Pennsylvania; the Matthew Ridley Papers in the Massachusetts Historical Society; the William Constable Papers in the New York Public Library; John Platt's unpublished biography of Jeremiah Wadsworth (doctoral thesis, Columbia University, 1955); and Robert A. East's *Business Enterprise in the American Revolutionary Era* (New York, 1938). For Hamilton's connections, see Harold C. Syrett and Jacob E. Cooke, eds., *The Papers of Alexander Hamilton* (7 vols. to date, New York, 1961–63), especially volume 3, 1782–86.

tion. In the postwar period special circumstances conspired to reduce the money supply and thereby to make the bank's influence even greater.[5]

The bank's potential for profitable public service was thus immense. Lending money at six percent and earning dividends of fifteen or twenty, it could help governments place their finances on an orderly basis; it could lower prices for imported goods by enabling merchants to buy in ship-load quantity; and though it could not finance long-term manufacturing and agricultural development, it could help manufacturers by enabling master craftsmen to pay wages punctually and in cash, and it could benefit farmers by enabling merchants to pay more for farm products. And because it could vastly contract or expand the available money supply, it could serve as a regulatory mechanism to stabilize a large portion of the entire economy. Obviously, in corrupt or incompetent hands its destructive potential was equally great.[6]

---

[5] On the bank in general, see Lawrence Lewis, Jr., *A History of the Bank of North America* (Philadelphia, 1882); Bray Hammond, *Banks and Politics in America, 1783–1865* (New York, 1957), chapter 1; F. Cyril James, "The Bank of North America and the Financial History of Philadelphia," in *Pennsylvania Magazine of History and Biography,* 64:56–87 (1940); the manuscript Minutes and Letter Book of the Bank of North America, the Minutes of the Directors and the Minutes of the Stockholders of the Bank of North America, all in the Historical Society of Pennsylvania; and the previously cited biographies of Morris. On the reduction in the supply of specie, see, for example, "A Citizen," in the *Pennsylvania Packet,* July 6, 1782; Daniel Clymer's remarks in the Pennsylvania Assembly, December 28, 1786, as quoted in the Philadelphia *Evening Herald,* January 17, 1787.

[6] The most thorough arguments about the merits and powers of the bank, as well as much useful information, are contained in the debates in the Pennsylvania Assembly over the question of its charter, as published in the *Evening Herald,* especially the issues of September 7, 8, December 28, 31, 1785, January 4, March 29, April 1, 5, May 6, 1786, and January 13, 17, and 20, 1787.

As an adhesive of the Union, its efficacy derived from two sources. First, it welded ever tighter interstate coalitions of mercantile interests, for its stockholders included moneyed men in virtually every city from Baltimore to Portsmouth, and its two largest stockholders were a New Yorker and a resident of Hartford, John B. Church and Jeremiah Wadsworth. Second, by its control of the money supply it could serve—and was dedicated to the idea of serving—as a deterrent to state fiscal systems that would weaken national ties or as a stimulus to measures that would have the opposite tendency.[7]

The most likely sources of danger to the nationalist cause were the state governments, but after some bad moments those too appeared to be well in hand at war's end. New Jersey and Delaware were no problem. Jersey was often rent with factional strife between its eastern and western parts, and at the moment the triumphant East Jerseyites were jubilantly persecuting the Tories and pacifists who abounded in West Jersey, but on matters concerning the Confederation the two factions were unswervingly nationalistic. Delaware was plagued by the secessionist (almost anarchistic) tendencies of its southernmost residents, but in the state as a whole nationalism was dominant;[8] and besides,

---

[7] As to stockholders, see the list of original subscribers to the issues of 1781 and 1784 in Lewis, *Bank of North America,* 133–47; Morris' speech of March 31, 1786, quoted in *Evening Herald,* May 3, 1786; and the correspondence between Alexander Hamilton, Jeremiah Wadsworth, and John Chaloner, cited below. Examples of the bank's political stance are also cited below; for a clear example of it, see Morris' speech in the Pennsylvania Assembly, December 22, 1785, as reported in the *Evening Herald,* December 28, 31, 1785, and January 4, 1786. See also Burton A. Konkle, *Thomas Willing and the First American Financial System* (Philadelphia, 1937).

[8] Richard P. McCormick, *Experiment in Independence* (New Brunswick, 1950); John A. Munroe, *Federalist Delaware* (Philadelphia, 1954).

the state's government was firmly in the hands of dedicated nationalists, many of them from Philadelphia.[9]

In New York the threat of rampant, state-oriented republicanism had flickered briefly but apparently had died. In 1777 George Clinton, a popular Whig leader and second-string aristocrat, had become the state's first governor through political maneuvering with the militia, much to the chagrin of Philip Schuyler, who also aspired to the office. But since then Clinton had served two three-year terms, provided orderly government, thwarted all extreme radicalism, and proved unwaveringly devoted to the nation. It was true that Clinton showed a distressing zeal in persecuting Loyalists, many of whom were related to important members of the Whig aristocracy. It was also true that he showed a distressing preference for the rising and aggressive new-rich merchants of New York—Melancton Smith, the Sands brothers, Alexander McDougall, Isaac Sears, and others—as opposed to the mercantile branches of the old landed families. But all things considered, New York could count itself as having the most stable and conservative government in the country.[10]

In Pennsylvania extreme radical republicans had seized

---

[9] Pennsylvanians and Delawareans often lived in one state and held public office in another, a practice stemming from the fact that until the Revolution the two colonies were partly joined, having separate legislatures but a common governor.

[10] E. Wilder Spaulding, *His Excellency George Clinton, Critic of the Constitution* (New York, 1938); Spaulding, *New York in the Critical Period, 1783–1789* (New York, 1932), 121–30; Harry B. Yoshpe, *The Disposition of Loyalist Estates in the Southern District of the State of New York* (New York, 1939), 32–37, 56–58; Alexander Hamilton to Robert Morris, August 13, 1782, and to Clinton, June 1, 1783, in *Hamilton Papers*, 3:132–43, 367.

leadership in 1776, proclaimed a constitution, and established what was little short of a totalitarian democracy. A tightly knit band of doctrinaire, uncompromising zealots, the radical republicans in Pennsylvania drew their power from and wielded it through the militia and the city mob, which they controlled by a brilliant system of organization. For some years the fortunes and even the lives of nationalists whose conduct or sentiments were suspect had been in danger of occasional but controlled mob action; more than one devout nationalist had to turn his home into a fort or flee the city. But the predominance of the radicals in Pennsylvania came with the ascendancy of republicans in Congress, and when their congressional counterparts were discredited in 1780, their power likewise faded. At the end of the war Philadelphia nationalists (who styled themselves Republicans and whom the radical republicans styled anti-Constitutionalists or Morrisites) were firmly established in the driver's seat: they held an almost two-to-one majority in the unicameral legislature and dominated the Executive Council. With the war over and the occasion for extremism therefore gone, the nationalists expected to stay there.[11]

So the nationalists in the Middle States thought they had good reason for cautious optimism. What they were leaving out of account was that human greed, now apparently har-

---

[11] The standard work on Pennsylvania during the period is Robert L. Brunhouse, *The Counter-Revolution in Pennsylvania, 1776–1790* (Harrisburg, 1942), which is useful but far from adequate. Also valuable are David Hawke, *In the Midst of a Revolution* (Philadelphia, 1961); Charles Page Smith, *James Wilson: Founding Father, 1742–1798* (Chapel Hill, 1956); and the Morris biographies and the sources on the bank cited earlier. The generalizations made here and in the following pages, however, are derived primarily from Pennsylvania newspapers and the manuscript and official government sources cited hereafter.

nessed to their cause, was a mighty engine that could pull both ways. Erelong, it would tear the Union asunder.

In New Jersey and Delaware organized and localized greed proved ineffectual, and therefore did little to diminish the nationalism of the inhabitants. To be sure, the public creditors there, like those elsewhere, wanted only to be paid and were not fussy about the political implications of who paid them; so they petitioned their legislatures to comply with Congress' April 18 revenue plan and, at the same time, to take direct state action in their behalf. Furthermore, the creditors in New Jersey had the attributes of a successful pressure group, being numerous and impatient, but the state was too poor to do much for them. It tried: in 1783 the legislature established a complicated scheme whereby it issued $83,000 in paper money (New Jersey's share of the proposed annual congressional requisition), paid it directly as interest to continental and state creditors instead of to Congress, recalled it through taxes, paid it out again as interest the next year, and so on. But the effort was as futile as it was ingenious, and served only to load the state with a greater fiscal burden than it could carry. In Delaware the holders of public debt, state or national, were few, and the state was easily able to service its major obligation, soldiers' depreciation certificates. It did so, and quickly ratified the revenue amendments, and sat and waited for the other states to do the same. In neither state did what happened make much difference.[12]

But elsewhere in the Middle States, a destructive chain of

[12] *Votes and Proceedings of the House of Assembly of the Delaware State* (published in Wilmington after each session), committee reports dated January 17, February 5, 1785, January 27, 1787; McCormick, *Experiment in Independence,* 173, 176–79.

events was engendered by an interplay between lobbying by public creditors and the treatment of Tories. In upstate New York violent persecution of Loyalists began several months before New York City was evacuated. The city, at that time, had in it many British and Loyalist merchants, a sizable measure of British goods, and a large quantity of gold. Had these merchants been able to expect fair treatment after the evacuation, which was ostensibly guaranteed by the peace treaty, they might have remained in the city and facilitated an orderly and quick return to peacetime commercial prosperity. But when the violence upstate was given official endorsement by discriminatory legislation—including a huge direct property tax on persons who had remained in the city during the occupation—these merchants decided to get out. Before going, they dumped their goods in New York City and the surrounding New Jersey and Connecticut countryside, draining off large quantities of gold in the process. When the evacuation finally took place, the city's economy was a shamble.[13]

But New York City got off to a roaring start, nonetheless, because of some highly artificial circumstances. One byproduct of the frenzied anti-Toryism (and with many no doubt a cause as well) was the passage of legislation confiscating the estates of Loyalists, the total market value

---

[13] Hamilton to Clinton, June 1, 1783, to James Duane, August 5, 1783, from Robert R. Livingston, August 30, 1783, from John Jay, September 28, 1783, to Gouverneur Morris, April 7, 1784, and Hamilton's pamphlet, "A Letter from Phocion to the Considerate Citizens of New York," January 1784, all in *Hamilton Papers,* 3:367–72, 430–31, 434–35, 459–60, 483–97, 528–29; *Journal of the Senate of the State of New York* (published in New York by sessions), March 30, 1784; *Laws of New York,* October 23, 1779, May 6, 1784; Alexander C. Flick, *Loyalism in New York During the American Revolution* (New York, 1901), *passim;* Yoshpe, *Loyalist Estates, passim;* Spaulding, *New York in the Critical Period,* 121 ff.

of which was roughly £750,000 New York current ($1,875,000). Less imaginative souls than Governor Clinton and his friends might simply have sold the estates, retired the state's debts, and been done with it. Not so with Clinton; no dullard was he. On the theory that one wins friends among the well-to-do by making them better-to-do, he and his allies arranged to dispose of the confiscated property according to a careful design.[14]

So as to ensure that the field of buyers would not be cluttered with small purchasers, the lands were sold in large blocks at public auction. So as to permit profits for speculators, it was provided that payments could be made on the installment plan and in certain kinds of public securities, at their face value. Since no provision had been made for paying either interest or principal on these securities, holders were willing to sell them for prices that returned handsome profits to buyers of confiscated estates. In effect, anyone who had the cash for doing so could buy securities on the open market at prices ranging from fifteen to twenty cents on the dollar and sell them to the state (not for money, but for confiscated estates) at one hundred cents. To raise the cash, speculators indulged in an orgiastic interchange of estates, securities, and goods. This interchange, in turn, created a market for everything, and thus started the city's economy going despite the absence of hard money.[15]

---

[14] The original confiscating act was passed October 22, 1779; the amendment that really set off the speculative orgy was passed May 12, 1784; the two laws are in *Laws of New York,* 1:173 ff., 736 ff.

[15] The manuscript records of the transactions in the Southern District and part of those for the Middle District are preserved in the New York Historical Society; some of those for the Middle District are in the New York Public Library. For an excellent description of speculation in the estates, see Yoshpe, *Loyalist Estates,* 59–60, 63–78, 114–15, and elsewhere.

It also whetted the greed of a number of influential citizens, the most prominent being members of the mighty Livingston clan. Robert R. Livingston, chancellor of the state, erstwhile superintendent of foreign affairs, possessor of vast landed estates and even vaster influence, had suffered reversals in his personal affairs during the late years of the war, and he was eager to more than recompense his losses. Opportunities were as rife as money was short. In normal times Livingston's personal credit would have staked him to speculative enterprises on a grand scale, but these were scarcely normal times, for there was no money to be lent at a gentlemanly six percent when gentlemen could earn upwards of thirty. Accordingly, Livingston brought together a hundred or so merchants, moneyed men, and would-be moneyed men who had in common (a) speculative fever, (b) some pretensions to respectability, and (c) the friendship and trust of the governor. Together, they refined and started work in behalf of a plan Livingston had conceived.[16]

The plan was to establish a bank, but not an ordinary

[16] Hamilton to John B. Church, March 10, 1784, in *Hamilton Papers,* 3:520–23; George Dangerfield, *Chancellor Robert R. Livingston of New York, 1746–1813* (New York, 1960), 200–203; Allan Nevins, *History of the Bank of New York* (New York, 1932); Henry W. Domett, *A History of the Bank of New York, 1784–1884* (New York, 1884), 4–10. That the bank was designed primarily for operators and speculators in securities and confiscated estates is not developed in any of the last three sources; but compare the lists of original directors (given in *Hamilton Papers,* 3:515n) and shareholders (given in Domett, *Bank of New York,* 131 ff.) with the lists of speculators in forfeited estates published in Yoshpe's *Loyalist Estates,* and with the speculators in public securities in New York and the New Yorkers who raided securities in North Carolina, as recorded in Records of the Loan of 1790, in the National Archives, volumes 22, 25, 32, 545, 548, 549, 551 (New York funded and assumed debts), and 1243 and 1244 (North Carolina assumed debts).

one. Any bank could create money, but only by multiplying what it started with, and Livingston's group was starting with far less than enough to found a bank large enough to provide for all. Livingston had a way around that problem. Using their influence with the governor and other high state officials—and extending it a mite by purchasing the support of up-country legislators, either for cash or for a modest share of the venture—the promoters would induce the state government to underwrite a larger operation than they could afford alone. In fine, under the plan they would raise $250,000 in gold and the state would furnish twice that amount in paper, secured by private real estate and the state's taxing power. For several weeks appropriate members of the group singled out appropriate officers of government and laid the foundations for a favorable reception of the scheme. Then, on February 17, 1784, a formal petition for the plan was presented to the New York Assembly.[17]

Already, that unwavering servant of the nation Alexander Hamilton, that unflinching champion of integrity in public affairs, had set to work to thwart Livingston's efforts. His motives, however, were not solely service to the nation or championship of public integrity. Hamilton, as a poor and ambitious young lawyer, was working furiously to bring his actual circumstances more nearly in line with the potential he had obtained by marrying Philip Schuyler's daughter. His most important client—almost his only solvent one—was his newly acquired brother-in-law, John B. Church. Church and his partner Jeremiah Wadsworth had immense liquid resources and even larger schemes. They

---

[17] Hamilton to Church, March 10, 1784, in *Hamilton Papers,* 3:520–23; see also *ibid.,* 3:508n; *New York Packet,* February 12 and subsequent issues, 1784; *Votes and Proceedings of the Assembly,* February 24, 1784.

proposed, among other things, to negotiate an absolute monopoly over the exportation of tobacco to France; and partly to facilitate the execution of that hoped-for arrangement and partly because it offered intriguing possibilities in its own right, they hoped to gain control of all the banking power of America. They had already become the largest stockholders in the sole existing bank, Philadelphia's Bank of North America, and they had already made plans for establishing a bank in New York, which they proposed to dominate. Livingston's plan, if successful, would obviously frustrate their own. But Wadsworth and Church were, at the moment, in France, seeking to negotiate their tobacco contract with the Farmers-General, the French organization that had control of such matters. In their absence and in their behalf Hamilton had to shift as best he could, and his opposition was formidable.[18]

He went to the more important of Livingston's backers in the city and tried to persuade as many as possible that Livingston's scheme was unsound. His arguments were plausible: it was dangerous to bring the state in, it was doubly dangerous to bring the upstate politicians in; and besides, the state's participation would only add more paper to what was already a surplus, and serve only to make the cycle of speculation run four ways instead of three. Many were convinced, but the result was not what Hamilton had hoped for. He sought to forestall the creation of any kind of bank, but his arguments were merely good reasons for keeping the state out of it. Unknown to Hamilton, a num-

---

[18] Church to Hamilton, February 7, 1784, Hamilton to Church, March 10, 1784, Church to Hamilton, May 2, 1784, June 15, 1784, in *Hamilton Papers,* 3:507–8 and note, 520–23, 558–59, 565; Platt, unpublished biography of Jeremiah Wadsworth, 47–68.

ber of the city's largest speculators and public creditors
decided to form a private bank with an original capital of
$125,000.[19]

This new promotion killed off Livingston's plan and
Church's and Wadsworth's as well. Hamilton learned of it
after about a week. When he did, it was hopeless to try to
stop it. Instead, he subscribed, for his clients, to as many
shares of the bank as possible, took a hand in the organization, and managed to become a director. The organizer soon
asked for a charter of the legislature, which was already
considering the Livingston scheme. The Assembly, not
knowing which way to turn, ended up by not approving
either plan. But the directors of the Bank of New York
decided to operate without a charter, and in July 1784 they
opened their doors for business.[20]

The political effect of all this was that, for the time being,
public creditors in New York were neutralized as an influence for governmental action. The bank, despite Hamilton's
efforts, began not primarily as a legitimate commercial bank
but as an agency for facilitating speculation, and as such it
was able to please a considerable number of the large operators in public securities. Accordingly, they stopped lobbying. The small public creditors in the state, who numbered
perhaps as many as six or seven thousand, never started.
Because the state's prospects for revenue were so poor, it

---

[19] This interpretation departs somewhat from those of Domett and Nevins,
previously cited; it is inferred from the sources cited in footnotes 16–18
and especially Hamilton to Church, March 10, 1784, from which sources
the inferences drawn here seem to me to be unmistakable.

[20] Nevins, *Bank of New York,* chapter 1; *Hamilton Papers,* 3:514–22 and
notes; on this whole episode, see also George Dangerfield, *Chancellor Livingston,* 200–203.

seemed unlikely that anything could be done for them; and anyway, they were not the militant organization that the large operators had been. The net result was that public creditors, large and small, ceased to be a militant force for union, but they were not yet a force for disunion.[21]

In the meantime, Wadsworth's and Church's man in Philadelphia, John Chaloner, had his hands more than full. The background of events there, as in New York, was the treatment of Tories, but their course was different. In Philadelphia, which had seen violent anti-Toryism during the war, persecution suddenly and surprisingly almost terminated with the end of the war. As a result, wealthy Loyalists and British merchants flocked into the city, bringing with them more than enough gold to replace what was being drained to pay for a large influx of British goods. But there were serious economic dislocations nonetheless. After mid-1783 the Bank of North America largely confined itself to purely commercial enterprises, which facilitated wholesome wholesale trade but had an odd by-product. Goods did not enter the speculative cycle in Philadelphia, as they did in New York, and privately held gold poured into the purchase and manipulation of the prices of public lands and securities. Thus, whereas speculation in New York arti-

---

[21] On the speculators, see the sources cited in footnote 16; the correspondence between Hamilton and Wadsworth, in *Hamilton Papers*, vol. 3; the Constable Papers in the New York Public Library; Ferguson, *Power of the Purse*, 251–86. The estimate of the number of small security holders is my own, derived from the New York volumes in the Records of the Loan of 1790, National Archives. A writer in the New York *Daily Advertiser*, March 5, 1788, estimated that at that time there were more than 5,000 holders of public debt in the state.

ficially created liquid capital, in Philadelphia speculation absorbed capital.[22]

Thereby, in times of what might have been plenty, a considerable shortage of money for ordinary purposes of retail business, manufacturing, and farming ensued. To fill the vacuum, a group of well-heeled Tories and new-rich Whigs formed a strange coalition, and together they more or less cornered the small money-lending market. Interest rates soared. (Said Gouverneur Morris of two of the usurers, "Archibald McCall [supplies] small sums, to men in distress, at a moderate interest; such as five, or ten, percent per month, according to their necessities . . . But if McCall has more of the milk of human kindness, Friend [George] Emlen as far exceeds him in the meekness of Christian love. He has therefore a more pious charity, and seeks more distressed objects on which to exercise it. This superior endowment has been justly rewarded, in some instances, with twelve percent per month. See how good a thing it is to be merciful to the poor.")[23]

The bank tried to alleviate the situation by expanding. Its officers and directors were feeling particularly bullish,

---

[22] John Chaloner to Jeremiah Wadsworth, February 14, 1784, in the Wadsworth Papers, Connecticut Historical Society; Gouverneur Morris to Hamilton, January 27, 1784, and Chaloner to Hamilton, February 12, 1784, in *Hamilton Papers,* 3:498–503, 509–10. The newspapers aired arguments for and against the return of Loyalists, but the very nature of the arguments against indicates that they were returning in numbers; see, for example, *Pennsylvania Packet,* June 17, July 31, August 7, 1783; *Freeman's Journal,* July 2, 1783. The fact that John Dickinson, who had refused to sign the Declaration of Independence, was elected president of the Pennsylvania Executive Council late in 1782 and reelected in 1783 shows the temper of the times; see *Pennsylvania Packet,* November 7, 9, December 31, 1782, November 11, 1783.

[23] Morris to Hamilton, January 27, 1783, in *Hamilton Papers,* 3:498–503.

partly because of the general optimism that prevailed and partly because the bank had earned and paid a whopping sixteen percent in dividends during 1783, and bank stock was selling at far more than its par value. Indeed, one regular complaint was that there was not enough bank stock in circulation to accommodate all who wanted to invest in it. Thus in addition to greatly expanding loans, the bankers decided to expand their base of operations by offering a new sale of stock. In January 1784 the stockholders voted to double the outstanding stock by offering a thousand new shares for sale. But in a fit of euphoria, they did so in a highly unrealistic way, designed to give themselves a bonus. The original stock had a par value of $400 a share. It was proposed that the new stock be sold at $500 but valued at $450, and that the difference of $50 be credited to the original shareholders, raising their shares to the same $450 par.[24]

The bullishness was premature, for a sequence of calamities was about to befall the bank (devilment, their main source, was the seasonal malaise of midwinter Philadelphia, because of the long confinement and restriction of normal business occasioned by the freezing of the river). On January 12 the bank's stockholders approved the plan to issue new stock. Nine days later a bizarre assortment of Tory usurers, Whig speculators, and radical politicians convened and determined to establish a new bank, to be called the Bank of Pennsylvania. Its stock was, for practical purposes, to be virtually limitless, and subscriptions to it, at a mere

---

[24] Chaloner to Hamilton, November 26, 1783, January 21, February 4, 1784, in *Hamilton Papers,* 3:477, 497–98, 504; *Pennsylvania Packet,* February 7, 1784; James, "Bank of North America," in *Pennsylvania Magazine of History and Biography,* 64:65–66.

$400 a share, were to be opened immediately. Investors snapped up the issue: by the end of the month—at which time subscriptions to the increased stock of the Bank of North America were to begin—the sponsors announced that the subscription was full and called a meeting to elect directors.[25]

When they had organized, the promoters applied to the legislature for a charter. At the legislative hearings in middle and late February, James Wilson and Gouverneur Morris appeared to oppose the charter; Jonathan D. Sergeant (an eminent speculator and Constitutionalist politician) and Jared Ingersoll (the son-in-law of another eminent speculator and radical) appeared to argue for it. During the discussions there arose another issue, unrelated to the question of the banks but intimately related to the larger question of the money supply. One of the radical legislators charged that the Bank of North America was responsible for the prevailing high interest rates, and opined that he would like to see not only the charter of a new bank, but an issue by the state of a sizable amount of paper money on loan as well. James Wilson, ever more facile at making promises than at fulfilling them, impetuously responded that the bank was such a friend of low interest rates that it would gladly lend the state $200,000 in credit to underwrite a paper money issue, and another $300,000 in cash to help fill the state's quota of continental requisitions for 1782 and 1783. That would prove to be the most significant remark made in the debates.[26]

---

[25] Gouverneur Morris to Hamilton, January 27, 1784, in *Hamilton Papers,* 3:498–503; *Pennsylvania Packet,* January 22, 27, 31, February 3, 7, 10, 1784.

[26] Chaloner to Church and Wadsworth, March 25, 1784, in Wadsworth Papers, Connecticut Historical Society; Chaloner to Hamilton, March 25,

As the question of chartering the new bank hung fire, subscriptions to the new stock of the old bank came in, but at a snail's pace: by the end of February, only half the proposed new issue had been subscribed. On the twenty-sixth, the directors called a special (in fact, an emergency) stockholders' meeting for March 1, to consider "altering the terms of the new subscription, and other important points respecting the corporation." At the meeting, not all the "other important points" were revealed, but enough were laid bare to jolt the stockholders with the news that the bank was in serious trouble: it had considerably overextended its loan at a time when unexpectedly and unprecedentedly large orders for spring importations were beginning to drain away gold.[27]

Officially, the meeting resolved to reduce the par value of the new stock to $400 and to increase the offering to 4,000 shares, enough to accommodate everyone in the city who wanted bank stock. Unofficially, the stockholders agreed that it was imperative to go all out to ally themselves with the subscribers to the Bank of Pennsylvania, lest the old bank should completely collapse. As John Chaloner put it, unless the moneyed people stuck together "the great exports of specie will dissolve all the *banks* in a very little time." A

1784, in *Hamilton Papers,* 3:524–25; *Minutes of the General Assembly of Pennsylvania* (published in Philadelphia by sessions, 1781–90), December 5, 1783, January 31, March 31, April 1, 1784; *Freeman's Journal,* March 10, April 14, 1784; *Pennsylvania Packet,* March 27, May 20, 1784; Smith, *James Wilson,* 147–48; Notes of Wilson's Arguments, March 2, 1784, in Wilson Papers, Historical Society of Pennsylvania. William Bradford and Miers Fisher also appeared for the new bank; Brunhouse, *Counter-Revolution in Pennsylvania,* 150–51.

[27] Chaloner to Hamilton, March 25, 1784, in *Hamilton Papers,* 3:524–25; *Pennsylvania Packet,* February 26, 1784; Brunhouse, *Counter-Revolution in Pennsylvania,* 151–52; Philadelphia Merchants' Committee to Boston Merchants, January 3, 1784, in Society Collections, Historical Society of Pennsylvania.

meeting of all the merchants and traders of Philadelphia was called for the very next day, "on business of the greatest importance to the commerce of this city." At that meeting, the bank's spokesmen bared their problems. The speculators, usurers, and radicals who had promoted the new bank were unmoved; but many of their backers, those who had proposed to invest in the new bank primarily because they could not invest in the old on favorable terms, agreed to the proposed coalition. Ten days later, a meeting of the stockholders of the Bank of Pennsylvania was called, and there the subscribers voted to withdraw their petition for a charter and accept the terms offered by the old bank. The day seemed saved.[28]

But within a week two new catastrophes struck. The first was simple and devastating: news arrived from England that more than $300,000 of Robert Morris' checks were bouncing—that is, that amount of his bills of exchange on Holland, drawn in his capacity as superintendent of finance, were being protested for nonacceptance. The news did not surprise him; he had, in fact, already taken steps to cope with the problem. He had arranged for John Adams, as minister to Holland, to cover the overdraft by writing bills payable by Franklin, as minister to France; by the time the bills reached Franklin, Adams could cover them with the proceeds of a virtually certain new loan from Amsterdam. But it was widely known that the Bank of North America had to stand ready to provide the sum if something went wrong in Holland; and the timing of the news could scarcely have

---

[28] Chaloner to Hamilton, March 25, 1784, William Seton to Hamilton, March 27, 1784, in *Hamilton Papers,* 3:524–27; *Pennsylvania Packet,* March 2, 18, 1784; *Pennsylvania Journal,* March 13, 1784; *Freeman's Journal,* March 17, 1784.

been worse. Because of what it did to further undermine confidence in the bank, as well as because of the curtailment it necessitated, the bank was forced to stop lending entirely and to call many outstanding loans.[29]

A full-scale panic was brewing. Some large speculators and a few more conventional businessmen—those who depended on daily circulation—were wiped out. Despite this, the bank might easily have ridden out the storm and soon been able to restore order, but for one cardinal fact: that in times of economic crises in a democratic society, no one is so perilously exposed as the very wealthy, if the very wealthy have the necessary attributes of a scapegoat. The bank had them in abundance, and its enemies, with malicious glee, pointed them out: the bank was a powerful monopoly, created by government but not by the people; for mysterious reasons, an abundance of money had suddenly turned into a dangerous shortage; the bank controlled the money supply and therefore the bank must be responsible.[30]

Plausible evidence of the bank's culpability was soon forthcoming. The Assembly, pondering a proposal to ease the money shortage by issuing paper money to be lent against real estate mortgages, remembered James Wilson's

---

[29] Ver Steeg, *Robert Morris,* 193; Seton to Hamilton, March 27, 1784, Chaloner to Hamilton, May 26, 1784, in *Hamilton Papers,* 3:526–27, 561–62. According to Chaloner, discounting was resumed sometime in mid-May.

[30] General business conditions are revealed in the correspondence between Chaloner, Hamilton, Wadsworth, and Church, previously cited. Attacks on the bank were sporadic throughout the year and may be seen in the various Philadelphia newspapers; see, for example, "A Friend to Liberty," in the *Pennsylvania Packet,* October 9, 1784. See also Benjamin Franklin to George Whatley, May 18, 1787, in John Bigelow, ed., *Works of Benjamin Franklin* (10 vols., New York, 1887–89), 9:388.

rash promise. Accordingly, it appointed a committee to call on the bank's president, Thomas Willing, for a large loan to underwrite the paper money and perhaps, if the loan were large enough, do something for the continental creditors in the state. Flabbergasted, Willing refused. Thereby, for political purposes the bank had sinned again—not only had it caused widespread distress, it now, in direct violation of an earlier promise, refused to help the state relieve the distress. The bill was not passed; instead, it was published for public consideration and assigned for action when the legislature reconvened in the fall.[31]

In the interim, three overlapping sets of enemies of the bank gathered for the kill. The first set was Morris' arch-republican political foes in Pennsylvania, some of whom were eager to cripple the bank out of sheer personal hostility to Morris, others out of a genuine fear of the concentration of money power. The second set (whose personnel included many who were also in the first group) was composed of the large-scale operators in public securities. These men were beginning to view the bank as a menace because it was not a reliable source of support for their speculations and because of its influence in preventing the state from assuming the continental debts held in Pennsylvania. The third set (whose personnel included many who were also in the second group) was made up of the usurers. These men bitterly opposed the bank because its officers were not corruptible, at least not by them. Not only had the bank refused to finance expansion of their lucrative operations, it had actu-

---

[31] Chaloner to Hamilton, March 25, 1784, in *Hamilton Papers,* 3:524–25; Chaloner to Church and Wadsworth, March 25, 1784, in the Wadsworth Papers; *Minutes of the General Assembly,* March 31, April 1, 1784; *Pennsylvania Journal,* May 15, 19, 1784; *Pennsylvania Packet,* May 20, 1784.

ally entered the small loan market in January and forced the interest rate down from twelve and a half percent a month to two and a half percent.[32]

The plan of attack was drawn up primarily by Charles Pettit, a Philadelphia merchant, Constitutionalist political leader, speculator in public securities, and brilliant financial operator. He was abetted by several men of similar description, including John Steinmetz, John Bayard, John Ewing, Blair McClenachan, William Moore, and William Irvine; by such back-country stalwarts of the Constitutionalist Party as William Findley, Robert Whitehill, Joseph Heister, John Hanna, and John Bishop, who came in for a share of the loot; and by other Constitutionalist leaders, including Joseph Reed, John Smiley, and George Bryan, who came in for more idealistic reasons.[33]

Pettit's plan required complete political control of the state, and its political implications, state and national, were large. Among the foreseeable consequences were transforming the state into a speculator's paradise, destroying the Bank of North America, and dissolving the financial bands which connected Pennsylvania with the Union. To gain the necessary political control, in the summer and fall of 1784 the Constitutionalists waged an all-out campaign directed

---

[32] The observation regarding usurers and interest rates is derived from *Pennsylvania Packet,* February 3, 1784, and Gouverneur Morris to Hamilton, January 27, 1784, in *Hamilton Papers,* 3:498–503.

[33] Brunhouse, *Counter-Revolution in Pennsylvania,* 170–74. The rosters given here are worked out from Brunhouse; from lists of members of public creditors committees as cited in the *Pennsylvania Packet,* July 22, August 14, 1784; from votes in the Assembly, as recorded in the *Minutes,* November 1784 session; and from lists of operators taking advantage of the act, as indicated in the manuscript volumes entitled New Loan Certificates, in the Public Records Division of the Pennsylvania Historical and Museum Commission—see footnote 39, below.

at—and almost succeeding in—re-creating the vigilante atmosphere of the late 1770s.[34]

In the extreme back country, where small handfuls of voters regularly returned to office anybody who would make and fulfill a few promises (they would, in fact, vote for almost anyone willing to make the arduous four-week trip to Philadelphia and neglect his private affairs all winter long, for the sake of his pittance of a salary as a legislator), Smiley, Findley, and their friends won easily on the strength of promises to destroy the monster banking monopoly and make everybody rich by lending them paper money on easy terms.

In midstate, Constitutionalists used the militias with the same effectiveness and in the same way that they had used them during the war: marching them to the polls to cast previously prepared ballots and to intimidate anyone disposed to vote the wrong way.

In and around Philadelphia the primary attack was not aimed at the bank as such, for its enemies were already enemies and its friends were not likely to be swayed. Instead, Morris and his followers were blasted (with the aid of Tory campaign money) as pro-Tory, largely on the ground that they had sought to repeal the state's test oath, a wartime measure that had formed the basis for much radical strength by disfranchising Quakers and Mennonites. Setting the tone for these charges was a mob-action atmosphere that arose in the city, accidental but genuine: with the unprecedented

---

[34] The following account of the elections of 1784 has been drawn from the *Pennsylvania Packet,* October 6, 9, 13, 1784; *Freeman's Journal,* September 1–October 13, 1784; *Pennsylvania Journal,* September, October 1784; Philadelphia *Independent Gazetteer,* September 4, 18, 24, October 9, 1784. See also Brunhouse, *Counter-Revolution in Pennsylvania,* 163–65.

spring imports came unprecedented numbers of immigrants, largely Irish, and the wave continued through the year, running sometimes as high as 2,000 newcomers a week.[35]

In the October elections the Constitutionalists won by a landslide. They won all ten seats in Philadelphia City and County by comfortable margins and swept every other county except Chester, York, and Bedford, and even in those places they won some seats. All told, they controlled seventy-five to ninety percent of the Assembly.[36]

Between November 1784, when the new Assembly convened, and March 1785, when it adjourned, it ground out Pettit's program, down to the last detail, and then some. The positive aspect of the program, finally enacted in March 1785, was a complicated scheme; as one writer said of it, "to unravel the code of policy it contains, requires no small amount of sagacity and Machiavellian shrewdness." But its principal features were elemental: a calculated appeal to the speculators in Philadelphia and a scheme for enriching the out-state politicians who supported the program. By the terms of the act, Pennsylvania simultaneously made provision for the state debt and that portion of the national debt owned in the state, and issued £150,000 ($400,000) in paper money. Two-thirds of the new money was appropriated for the payment of back interest on the national debt. The remainder was issued on loan against real estate mortgages of thrice the amount of the loans. (There was little doubt that the state could continue to support interest pay-

[35] On the mob-action atmosphere and immigration, see *Pennsylvania Journal,* May 15, 22, and throughout July 1784.

[36] Brunhouse, *Counter-Revolution in Pennsylvania,* 328–42; party affiliations, when not given by Brunhouse, are arrived at by comparing all votes cast in the 1784–85 legislatures, as recorded in the *Minutes.*

ments on both state and state-held national debt: in 1785, thanks to duties levied on the huge amounts of foreign goods imported into Philadelphia, the state took in about $400,000.)[37]

The advantages to everyone—at least to everyone on the inside—were abundant. Speculators in public securities and legitimate public creditors as well reaped the fruits of a doubling, then a trebling, of the market prices of securities. There were also less obvious sources of profit. Too, as William Findley said, somewhat later, the act had quite favorable effects on purchasers of state-owned lands. Speaking (as was his wont) of the poor struggling back-country farmers, but referring (as was also his wont) to larger operators as well, he pointed out the virtues of the system to land buyers. A man, he said, could borrow £100 from the state on real estate he already owned, use the money to buy public securities on the open market at a third of their face value, turn these securities over to the state at par in exchange for public lands, repay his original loan, and emerge with considerable profit. It was magic, said Findley. The state as well as the speculator gained: the increased circulating medium made it easier for the state to pay the interest on its own and the nation's debts; and besides, by lending a

---

[37] *Minutes of the General Assembly,* December 4, 24, 1784, February 3, 1785 (see especially the communications between the Executive Council and the Assembly for those dates); James T. Mitchell and Henry Flanders, comps., *The Statutes at Large of Pennsylvania from 1682 to 1809* (17 vols., n.p., 1896–1915), 11:454–86, 560–72; Philadelphia *Evening Herald,* March 8, 1785. The Executive Council did question the ability of the state to carry the burden; see its message to the Assembly, recorded in the *Minutes of the General Assembly,* December 4, 1784. The Assembly's answer, however, seems an effective rebuttal. See also the Report of the Ways and Means Committee, *ibid.,* December 22, 24, 1784.

mere £100 in paper (on which it would receive £6 a year in interest) it brought about the cancellation of £300 of its public debt (on which it had been paying £18 annual interest). Beyond this, as Robert Morris pointed out in a moment in which he forgot his posture as a gentleman, there were even less apparent advantages: the back-country politicians could earn tidy sums by acting as agents, on commission, for their neighbors' speculations.[38]

As a result of the enactment of the Pettit plan the assortment of nonbank financial operators in Philadelphia, all holders of several thousand pounds of public securities, profited; and such Constitutionalists as Heister, Bishop, Findley, Hanna, and Whitehill, among many others, most of them back-country politicians who had not previously owned any securities, suddenly emerged with profits of several thousand dollars apiece from the enactment of the program.[39]

The negative side of the program—which Pettit and many of his Philadelphia friends were not enthusiastic about, but recognized as a necessary sop to their back-country allies— was the destruction of the Bank of North America. After a long, fierce, and fruitless debate, the Assembly voted in September 1785 to revoke the charter of the bank. (In doing so, it inadvertently raised two problems that would

---

[38] Findley's remarks were made in a debate in the Assembly, as reported in the *Evening Herald,* May 6, 1786; Morris' are *ibid.,* April 5, 1786. For an interesting analysis of the deeper and more philosophical implications of the plan, see the *Pennsylvania Packet,* March 31, April 1, 1785.

[39] New Loan Certificates, vol. A, accounts 1, 2, 3, 60, 225, 230, 262, 1775–1802, 1954–58, 2718–24, 4915, 4919–25, 5381; vol. B, accounts 10, 391, 6177–84, 10525–26, 10528; vol. C, accounts 37, 54, 120, 126; vol. D, 19235–41, all manuscript volumes in the Public Records Division, Pennsylvania Historical and Museum Commission.

forever plague the American people. The first and least important—because it was more fundamental and therefore
beyond the ken of the democracy—was the question of
sanctity of contracts: whether a people could, through its
government, commit itself and then revoke the commitment.
The second was much more superficial and thus far more
important: whether politicians, after denouncing one another, were obliged to take action against one another, or
whether they should, as became the norm, merely denounce
each other publicly and in private compromise their differences.)[40]

These doings, and the chain of events they set off, shook
the interstate nationalist coalition to its roots. As the attack
on the bank shaped up, virtually all the outside investors
had but a single thought, and that was to get their money
back. But this was not so simple. The market price of the
stock had plummeted from a high of over $500 in January
1784 to around $370 in the early fall of 1785, and if the
outside investors (who held about $500,000 of the stock)
dumped all their holdings at once, they would have realized
only a fraction of their original investments. Hamilton, con-
sulting with Wadsworth, proposed an orderly procedure: a
test case in the Pennsylvania courts to determine whether
the bank retained its corporate existence by virtue of its
charter from Congress. If the courts so ruled (it was certain,

---

[40] For a full discussion of the bank and related subjects, see *Freeman's
Journal,* January 19, February 2, 9, March 2, 1785; *Pennsylvania Packet,*
March 2, 12, 29, 31, April 1, 1785; *Pennsylvania Journal,* February 19, 23,
1785; *Evening Herald,* September 7, 8, 1785; and the sources cited in footnotes 41, 49, and 50, below.

from the proceedings of the state's Council of Censors, that they would not, but Hamilton did not know this), there was nothing to worry about. The price of the stock would rise and Church and Wadsworth could pull out without much loss. If the courts ruled otherwise, Wadsworth and Church could, in conjunction with others, sue and force the bank to return their money.[41]

Wadsworth had already done something that ensured that what followed would be attended by a maximum of acrimony and a minimum of order. Seeking to find out what was going on in Philadelphia, he wrote to the one man in the city with whom he had had satisfactory dealings and who was not in the inside bank group. That man was Charles Pettit. Wadsworth, not knowing that Pettit was the grand architect of Pennsylvania's financial legislation of the year, confided to Pettit a suspicion that the directors had already provided for their own escape by borrowing from the bank sums equal to their investments. Pettit showed the letter around to friends in the legislature, and when the word got back to the bank directors, they were furious at Wadsworth. Said

---

[41] *Pennsylvania Packet,* February 3, 1784; Hamilton to Wadsworth, October 29, 1785, in *Hamilton Papers,* 3:625–27; *Evening Herald,* May 3, 1786; Pieter Van Berckel to Thomas Willing, in Stockholders Minutes, Bank of North America, January 9, 1786, in Historical Society of Pennsylvania; Journal of the Council of Censors, vol. 2, August 27, 1784, in Public Records Division, Pennsylvania Historical and Museum Commission. The latter, a decision concerning the constitutionality of the University of Pennsylvania Act of 1779, is a clear and carefully reasoned statement of the principle that popular assemblies can revoke charters at will. James Wilson argued to the contrary in a pamphlet published in the summer of 1785, *Considerations on the Bank of North America,* but Wilson was regarded as a "kept" lawyer of the company, and the Council of Censors more nearly represented the attitude of the Pennsylvania courts.

he, coldly, "I am perfectly willing they should think and act as they please if I can rescue my property from their grasp."[42]

Others were similarly disposed, and Wadsworth was besieged by offers from people who wanted to join him in getting out—but, it developed, for different reasons. Pieter Johan Van Berckel, Dutch minister to the United States, the Marquis Barbe-Marbois, French chargé d'affaires, Sampson Fleming, and William Edgar apparently wanted simply to get their money back. But with Edgar there were grounds for suspicion that something more was involved. He was, on the one hand, the brother-in-law and sometime partner of William Constable, one of Robert Morris' most intimate friends and admirers; and he was, on the other, the full-time partner of Alexander Macomb, one of George Clinton's most intimate friends and admirers, and it was no secret that Clinton was not opposed to wreaking financial havoc in Philadelphia so as to transfer financial power to New York.[43]

Another pair of New Yorkers had a different scheme. Walter Livingston and William Duer, engaged in huge marginal speculations in every manner of public securities, were "anxious to have a bank to play of[f] their continental paper with," and they felt that Edgar would join them. They tried to get Hamilton and Wadsworth to pull out with them, persuade others to do likewise, and use the proceeds to establish a new bank in New York. (Meanwhile, the Living-

---

[42] Wadsworth to Hamilton, November 11, 1785, in *Hamilton Papers,* 3:633–34; Platt, unpublished biography of Jeremiah Wadsworth, 152, footnote 2.

[43] Wadsworth to Hamilton, November 11, 1785, in *Hamilton Papers,* 3:633–34, and see the footnotes at p. 634; Spaulding, *George Clinton,* 200, 236–37.

ston clan itself was engaged in an interfamily brawl. Chancellor Livingston, still hard-pressed, was attempting what seemed little more than a raid on the property of his cousin [and Walter's father], Robert Livingston, third proprietor of Livingston Manor. Soon, the disputes between Livingstons would harden and make them into permanent and fierce political enemies.)[44]

Still another proposal came from Arthur Lee of Virginia. Lee had invested in the new offering of the bank's stock in 1784, up to the allowable limit of voting power; doing so was a rewarding way of becoming able to spy on his dearest enemy, Robert Morris, as well as to get in a position to do mischief. Now he proposed to induce as many people as possible to pull out as rapidly as possible, apparently in the hope that doing so would destroy at once Morris, the bank, and Philadelphia's financial power. (Lee had another motive in addition to vengeance. Robert Morris had just won the tobacco-monopoly contract that Wadsworth and Church had sought to obtain with the French Farmers-General. To profit from it, as Lee saw it, Morris had to drive the price of tobacco in Maryland and Virginia down to far less than its current level, which in turn was possible only if Morris could manipulate the money supply through the bank.[45]

---

[44] Wadsworth to Hamilton, November 11, 1785, Hamilton to Robert Livingston, April 25, 1785, from Robert Livingston, June 13, 1785, in *Hamilton Papers,* 3:608–10 and notes, 614–16 and notes, 633–34 and notes; Alfred Young, "The Democrat-Republican Movement in New York State, 1788–1797" (doctoral thesis, Northwestern University, 1958); Dangerfield, *Livingston,* see index entries under Robert Livingston, Jr., and Walter Livingston. Later Walter and the Chancellor made their peace; *ibid.,* 281–82.

[45] Lewis, *Bank of North America,* 144–47; Wadsworth to Hamilton, November 11, 1785; Arthur Lee Papers, Harvard University; Lewis C. Gray,

(That contract would cause other mischief as well. Its signing did nothing to cement relations with Wadsworth and Church, and apparently Morris' Virginia partner, Benjamin Harrison, Jr., broke relations with him because of it. Two of Morris' Baltimore partners, Mark Pringle and Matthew Ridley, decided to profit from it by double-crossing the boss; they would take advantage of the reduced prices, but outbid Morris' buyers fractionally and market the tobacco in Europe on their own account. And over this problem and some of its ramifications, Thomas Willing became disgusted and talked openly of dissolving the basic partnership.)[46]

Morris and his narrowing circle of friends were neither idle nor ineffectual as these events unfolded. Even as the storm clouds gathered, in the winter of 1783–84, Morris had launched the biggest and boldest venture that had ever been undertaken by an American merchant: he opened the China trade. With partners (Morris put up half of the money himself) he sent the 360-ton *Empress of China* to Canton, and on the eve of the cancellation of the bank's charter, the vessel returned with a cargo worth a third as much as the bank stock owned by all outside holders combined. Through the summer and fall of 1785, he fenced off his disgruntled associates; Wilson, the original Philadelphia lawyer, kept

---

History of Agriculture in the Southern United States to 1860 (2 vols., Washington, 1933), 2:603–4. For an appraisal of the actual meaning of Morris' contract, see chapter 3, herein.

[46] Mark Pringle to Matthew Ridley, November 12, 1785, in Matthew Ridley Papers, Massachusetts Historical Society; Jared Sparks, *The Life of Gouverneur Morris* (3 vols., Boston, 1832), 1:272–73; Ver Steeg, *Robert Morris*, 33–34, 190; William Hemsley Papers Relating to the Tobacco Business, 1784–86, in the Manuscripts Division of the Library of Congress. Ver Steeg says that the break with Harrison had to do with a dispute with John Holker, and that the Harrison-Morris connection was soon reestablished.

the attorneys for the hostile friends so confused that they rarely knew what they were about; and Gouverneur Morris, with his accustomed audacity, started a countermovement to bring the Bank of New York into a merger with the Bank of North America. Then, when the axe fell in September with the repeal of the bank's charter, Morris announced that he would personally become a member of the legislature and lead a fight for reincorporation. He did so, and he and reliable friends captured all ten seats from Philadelphia City and County in the October elections.⁴⁷

But the Wadsworth-Hamilton group was not easily diverted, and as a result of its pressure the annual stockholders' meeting in January 1786 was the most bitter in the bank's history. It was revealed at the meeting that the bank had been guilty of grave malpractices: particularly, it had lent Wilson almost $100,000 on questionable security, and the implications were strong that these transactions were by no means atypical. Wadsworth doggedly demanded the court actions that Hamilton had suggested; Morris himself "softened down much"; Willing tried desperately to calm tempers and gloss over the differences. In the end, the Wadsworth group got what it wanted, or so it seemed. The insiders, ostensibly admitting defeat, agreed to Hamilton's orderly course of legal disintegration, but in fact they had

---

⁴⁷ *Pennsylvania Journal,* May 18, 1785; Ver Steeg, *Robert Morris,* 189; Samuel Shaw to John Jay, May 19, 1785, in Henry P. Johnston, ed., *Correspondence and Public Papers of John Jay* (4 vols., New York, 1890), 3:144–49; Tyler Dennett, *Americans in East Asia* (New York, 1941), 4–7; Smith, *James Wilson,* 149–55; *Pennsylvania Packet,* September 29, 30, 1785; *Evening Herald,* October 15, 1785; Brunhouse, *Counter-Revolution in Pennsylvania,* 176–79. Gouverneur Morris had toyed with the idea of a merger for more than a year; see Gouverneur Morris to Hamilton, June 30, 1784, in *Hamilton Papers,* 3:569.

no intention of doing anything of the kind. Hamilton and Wadsworth were completely outmaneuvered: resorting to the courts by way of a friendly suit instituted by the bank itself simply gave the insiders opportunity to stall for a year and more. The outside investors could only stew and shout treachery.[48]

The tightly knit interstate economic group was coming unraveled.

As the fibers of union were being torn thus apart in private, others were reweaving the same stuff, in public, to create vested interests in state sovereignty. In Pennsylvania, this involved no more than strengthening the system that had been enacted in 1785.

In the state Assembly, Morris launched a powerful but vain counterattack even as he was doing battle with his allies; his design was to retie the interests of public creditors to the bank and the nation, and to obtain a rechartering of the bank. With his back to the wall, Morris fought brilliantly. His debate was skillful, his parliamentary operations shrewd, his appeal persuasive. Merging the best arguments of his opponents, he agreed that the paper money was "a wise measure"; he agreed that the bank should be subjected to regulation by the state; he argued that the state should have both the private bank and a governmental equivalent of a bank, the one to finance commerce and the public debt, the

---

[48] Pieter Johan Van Berckel, William Edgar, Sampson Fleming, William Denning, and Hamilton to Wadsworth, January 3, 1786, Wadsworth to Hamilton, January 9, 1786, in *Hamilton Papers,* 3:643–46; Willing to Wilson, June 10, 1784, and Wilson to Willing, July 29, 1784, in Minutes and Letter Book of the Bank of North America, and Stockholders Minutes, January 9, 1786, in the Historical Society of Pennsylvania.

other to finance agriculture and manufacturing, so as to arm the state in its economic warfare with its "dangerous rivals," New York and Baltimore.[49]

But the odds were too great. Morris' party fell just short of a reliable majority in the Assembly, and he faced two antibank Constitutionalist leaders who were more than a match for him. William Findley and John Smiley, a pair of Scottish bumpkins from the back country, picked their noses and talked through them, but in a contest of political maneuvers they had few peers. In spite of all Morris' efforts, when the legislature of 1786 adjourned Pettit's funding system was still on the books, now tightened and rendered permanent, and the bank was still without a charter.[50]

In New York political leaders had been slow to wander from their war-won nationalism, and even when others strayed, Governor Clinton exerted his influence to keep the state committed to Congress. Doing so was not easy. Many New Yorkers were angry over Congress' refusal or inability, in 1783, to take any decisive action on behalf of New York's claims to the renegade state of Vermont. Many were infuriated about the peace treaty, feeling that it gave unnecessary benefits to Loyalists. More important, many were disgusted with Congress' inability to force Britain to abide by the

---

[49] The debates are thoroughly reported in the *Evening Herald,* December 28, 31, 1785, January 4, April 1, 5, 1786; see also Thomas Paine's *Dissertations on Government, the Affairs of the Bank, and Paper Money, Addressed to the People of Pennsylvania, on the Present State of Their Affairs* (Philadelphia, 1786), a pamphlet Morris hired Paine to write.

[50] *Ibid.;* and also the debate on the Assembly's committee report of December 22–24, 1785, in the *Evening Herald* for March 29, April 1, 5, May 6, 1786; Francis Hopkinson to Jay, March 11, 1786, in Johnston, ed., *Jay Papers,* 3:183–84; *Minutes of the Assembly,* December 22–24, 1785, February 27, April 1, 7, 1786; *Statutes at Large of Pennsylvania,* 12:158–64 (March 1, 1786, chapter 1202).

treaty and abandon its garrisons inside the United States, five of which were inside the limits of New York. Their maintenance was costly as well as insulting, for it deprived New Yorkers of a share in the lucrative western fur trade. Playing upon these interrelated and emotionally charged issues, a radical faction of the legislature, led by a pair of up-state immigrants from New England (whom old New Yorkers despised and feared fully as much as they would despise and fear each succeeding immigrant group), sought drastic separatist action. In March 1784 they got it: the legislature delivered an ultimatum to Congress regarding these several complaints, and said that if Congress did not come up with a satisfactory response within nine months, New York would "be compelled to consider herself as left to pursue her own councils, destitute of the protection of the United States." Congress' response was weak. It merely resolved to do what it could, which was nothing, and authorized the states to attempt on their own to recapture the occupied western posts. Clinton, mustering all his influence, succeeded in persuading the legislature to accept that as complying with the ultimatum (after all, where would New York get the money to finance a military expedition against the British garrison?). During the remainder of the 1784–85 legislative session he was able to thwart other separatist action.[51]

---

[51] Burnett, *Continental Congress,* 540–46; Spaulding, *George Clinton,* 142–48; *Votes and Proceedings of the Senate,* March 2, 1784; *Votes and Proceedings of the Assembly,* March 2, April 22, October 18, 1784, and Clinton's messages to the legislature, recorded therein, January 21, October 18, 1784; Hamilton to Robert Livingston, April 25, 1785, to William Duer, May 14, 1785, in *Hamilton Papers,* 3:608–11.

But Clinton's nationalism rested primarily on a single assumption, that New York was among the Confederation's weakest members, and that assumption was about to vanish. The crucial pivot on which it turned was the state's lack of internal revenues. Lacking revenues, its economy seemed hopelessly bogged by the public debt and its military defense was impossible; only through Congress could it hope to deal with either. Lacking revenues, its natural attributes canceled one another: its rich soil, great port, and superb system of inland waterways were for nought, for the Mohawk was controlled by Indians and the trough of the upper Hudson and Lake Champlain were invitations to invasion from the north. Then all of a sudden New York had revenues in abundance, and all these considerations disappeared; the natural advantages loomed large, and it became possible to have a vision of New York as the Empire State.[52]

In December 1785—at just about the time Wadsworth and Hamilton were sitting down to discuss their strategy for the upcoming stockholders' meeting—Clinton sat down with State Treasurer Gerardus Bancker and perhaps a few intimate friends, to go over the books for the year. New York had experienced a year of unprecedented prosperity. The harvest was the greatest in history, the city did an import-export business far greater than it had ever done before the

---

[52] On New York's financial problems and their sudden disappearance, see the summary Report of the Committee on the Treasury, House of Assembly, January 16, 1788, published in the *New York Journal,* January 31, 1788; on consciousness of the impotence of the state resulting therefrom, see Clinton's message to the legislature, March 2, 1784, in the *Votes and Proceedings of the Assembly;* Clinton to Ezra L'Hommedieu, August 23, 1783, Hamilton to Clinton, October 3, 1783, in *Hamilton Papers,* 3:436, 464–69.

war, and most important, thanks largely to import duties the state's revenues had leaped from less than £38,000 ($95,000) in 1784 to almost £180,000 ($450,000) in 1785. A hundred and eighty thousand pounds! With that kind of money, the state could push the British out of the western posts by itself, it could chase every Indian back from the Mohawk, it could man the defensive posts at West Point and elsewhere on the Hudson, it could support a debt of seven, eight, perhaps ten million dollars; why, it could. . . .[53]

The George Clinton who delivered his annual message to the legislature a month later was scarcely recognizable as the timid, Congress-following governor of before. He had now become, and would remain for the next quarter-century, a bold leader of the state, forwarding its interests against all others. Under his leadership the legislature enacted, in the

---

[53] The financial data are from the Report of the Committee on the Treasury, cited in footnote 52; the remainder, including the statement that Bancker and Clinton actually sat down together, as opposed to Bancker's merely sending the information to Clinton, is inferential. The sources of the inferences are: regarding Bancker's making of year-end reports, Poughkeepsie *Country Journal,* February 3, 1789; on this and on prosperity in 1785, Clinton's 1786 message, as cited in footnote 54; and on the latter, commodity prices as quoted in the New York *Daily Advertiser* throughout 1785, and my tabulations of ship movements, 1784–90, from announcements in New York newspapers and the *London Daily Universal Register.* That the economy was booming in 1785 is also obvious from the growth pattern during the 1780s: postwar reconstruction did not begin until 1784, and 1786 was a year of temporary recession, but by 1790 New Yorkers owned almost 300 oceangoing vessels, measuring about 36,000 tons, and the tonnage clearing the port was more than 90,000 annually. All these figures are more than treble the prewar averages; Samuel D. McCoy, "The Port of New York, Lost Island of Sailing Ships," in *New York History,* 17:379–90 (1936). See also the tabulation published in the Newburyport *Essex Journal and New Hampshire Packet,* February 11, 1789.

spring of 1786, a long-range program whereby New York virtually seceded from the Union.[54]

By far the most important such measure was the financial program, patterned after the Pennsylvania plan but far more shrewdly put together. Paper money amounting to £200,-000 ($500,000) was issued, three-fourths of which was lent to individuals against real estate mortgages, thus satisfying the earlier advocates of a paper bank. By the same act, the entire state debt was serviced and two portions of the national debt were assumed: Continental Loan Office certificates and "Barber's Notes," certificates issued by the United States for supplies furnished the continental army. The reserved £50,000 of paper money was appropriated for immediate payment of one-fifth of the back interest due on these securities.[55]

The plan was well calculated to solidify the political power of George Clinton and his friends and, in the process, to reorient the state's energies toward New York's interests

---

[54] Clinton's message to the legislature, January 18, 1786, in *Votes and Proceedings of the Assembly,* 9th Session, 1st Meeting, 5 ff.; the legislative program can be traced in *Laws of the State of New York Passed at the Sessions of the Legislature* (3 vols., Albany, 1886–87), vol. 2.

[55] The act is Chapter 40 of the Acts of 1786, *ibid.,* 2:253 ff. Its passage through the Assembly can be traced in *Votes and Proceedings,* February 11–March 4, March 30, 1786, and through the Senate in its *Votes and Proceedings,* March 29, April 1, 1786. The first two dozen sections of the act are identical, except for punctuation and minor word changes, to the act of 1771 by which the colonial aristocracy emitted paper, and that act is virtually identical to one passed in 1738; *The Colonial Laws of New York from the Year 1664 to the Revolution* (5 vols., Albany, 1884), 2:1015 ff. and 5:149 ff. The crucial features of the act of 1786, those providing for funding and assumption, are in its article 54. Earlier writers on the subject—for example, Beard, Libby, Spaulding, and Cochran, in works previously cited —all treat the act as if it were a simple paper-money debtor-relief law.

instead of those of the United States. Some 5,000 holders of continental securities—about half the number of voters in a normal election—were provided for under the act. As the system was devised, these securities were neither paid off nor funded; they were simply lent to the state and the state assumed the task of paying annual interest on them. The system thus created, in effect, a list of 5,000 pensioners whose welfare was contingent on the state's welfare and not on the nation's. Seemingly the state was taking on a big burden, but actually it was getting off lightly. On the one hand, it relieved itself of obligation to pay any more congressional requisitions, for Congress now owed it more in annual interest on the securities it held than it owed Congress for requisitions. And on the other, the state government did nothing at all about the $3,600,000 of other kinds of continental securities held in the state, they being politically less potent because they were concentrated in the hands of only a couple of hundred persons. The scheme was, as one critic charged, "a studied design to divide the interests of the public creditors."[56]

But it was even more than that. It was also a means of doubly rewarding those who had loyally appreciated Clinton's past favors and of punishing those who had not. The rise in security prices which quickly followed the funding act caught the speculators in confiscated estates as bears in a bull market. That is, they were in effect short sellers, being committed to make future installment payments, in securi-

---

[56] For appraisals of the act and its effects, see the Report of the Committee on the Treasury, in *New York Journal,* January 31, 1788; Philip Schuyler's article in the Poughkeepsie *Country Journal,* March 10, 1789; *Daily Advertiser,* March 22, 31, 1787, February 2, 5, May 5, 1788; *New York Packet,* February 16, March 13, April 13, 1786.

ties, for the confiscated property they had bought from the state. Prices of securities trebled after the funding act, and so paying for their confiscated property cost them roughly three times as much as they had expected. Not surprisingly, many of them were broken and, indeed, because many were merchants who dumped goods on the market in a frantic effort to raise money to meet their maturing obligations to the state, New York City experienced a panic and commercial depression that lasted into the next year. Those who had proved most loyal and intimate friends of the governor, however, were protected by knowing that the funding would occur, what securities would be funded, and when the operations would take place. So informed, anyone could cover his position and even make a tidy sum by going long in the appropriate securities.[57]

The success of the program could only be told with time, but its popularity was apparent immediately. In the 1786 elections Clinton was personally so strong that his enemies

---

[57] Much of the foregoing is hinted at by "Gustavas" in the *New York Packet,* April 13, 1786, and by Assemblyman John Taylor, as quoted in the *Daily Advertiser,* March 22, 1787. I have nowhere seen it explicitly stated, however; it is my own analysis, derived from following the careers of various friends and enemies of the governor who were speculating in confiscated estates. Thus, for example, Isaac Gouverneur, John Lawrence, and Cornelius Ray, none friends of the governor and all speculators in confiscated estates, all went bankrupt in 1786. (Lawrence was an anti-Clintonian candidate for the Assembly in 1785; *New York Packet,* April 25, 1785; the politics of the others have been traced by more circuitous means. For their speculations, see Yoshpe, *Loyalist Estates,* 156; for their bankruptcy, see *Votes and Proceedings of the Assembly,* February 2, March 14, 1786.) On the other hand, the following are but a few of the Clintonians who speculated in confiscated estates, demonstrably prospered throughout 1786, and/ or emerged soon thereafter as "longs" in securities: Samuel Jones, John Smith, Melancton Smith, Jesse Woodhull, Anthony Ten Eyck, Ezra Thompson, James Clinton, Jacobus Swartwout, Peter Van Ness, and John Williams (for sources on these men, see McDonald, *We the People,* 304–8, notes).

could find no one to run against him, and he was reelected for his fourth consecutive three-year term. In the legislature the results were not so clear because the state did not have formally organized political parties, but the governor's unqualified supporters won at least two-thirds of the seats.[58]

In less than four years—by the winter of 1786–87—a once-solid wall of nationalism had come tumbling down. In its place stood four sovereign states, whose attitudes toward the Union now depended primarily on how they were faring in their involuntary experiments in independence.

New Jersey was worst off. The state's internal politics were rife with bitter fights between East and West Jersey. Its economy, potentially strong but continuously drained by commercial dependence on New York and Philadelphia, and crushed under the burden of an overambitious effort to service the public debt, simply could not operate. Many of its citizens had hoped that, with independence, they could relieve the pressure of overpopulation in the state and its lack of natural advantages by cooperating in grand schemes for buying from Congress huge tracts of western lands. Such dreams were dissipated by the ineffectuality of a Congress that New Jersey itself, in a seizure of myopia, had helped reduce to total impotence. Things were so bad that by 1787 no one could remember a year of peace when they had been worse. Despite the extremity of its particularist financial

---

[58] Some of the election returns are reported in the *New York Packet,* April 17, May 1, June 5, 1786; the efforts to find an opponent to Clinton in 1786 can be traced in Johnston, ed., *Jay Papers,* 3:151–87. The estimate of Clinton's strength in the legislature is based on my tabulations of all votes cast by every member—and comparison with the votes of every other member —in the 1787 legislature, as recorded in the *Votes and Proceedings of the Assembly.*

measures, New Jersey was more eager than ever to be under the roof of a strong national union.[59]

Pennsylvania had every reason for prospering but it was not. It was rich, powerful, populous, and bountifully blessed by nature, but it dissipated its energies in internal strife. From a curious admixture of greed and idealism, each of the two factions of Pennsylvanians fought for its own advantage at the expense of the other and, in the long run, to the detriment of both. In Pennsylvania political parties developed first, but there they were among the last to learn the genius of the American system: that the opposing parties do not oppose, but race in the same direction, albeit sometimes by different routes. A graph of the state's economy during the eighties, or of the history of the bank, or of the Constitution of 1776, or of the University of Pennsylvania, reveals the results: up-down, up-down, up-down, where there might have been only up. How Pennsylvania stood on questions of the Union followed the same cycle.[60]

Delaware, like New Jersey, was commercially dependent on its neighbors, but it had neither the oppressive debts burdening that state nor the internal dissension that debilitated Pennsylvania, and so it prospered. Even so, few in the state aspired to go it alone, and Delaware's nationalism was little diluted by the postwar experience.[61]

New York fared extremely well: never before had so

---

[59] McCormick, *Experiment in Independence,* 220–33, 252–78.

[60] Though Brunhouse's *Counter-Revolution in Pennsylvania* is in some respects superficial or factually in error, particularly on economic matters, its general running account of which party was on top and when is a useful and reliable guide, as are his two appendixes on the distribution of party strength by years, pp. 321–42.

[61] Munroe, *Federalist Delaware, passim.*

many had it so good. Its strong, energetic, and ably led economy made the transition from war to peace with enormous thrust; its strong, energetic, and ably led government made the transition from nationalism to state particularism with equal thrust. To be sure, in the political transition some were displeased and some were broken, but few believed that the change would be short-lived.

Chapter Three

Completion
of the Revolution:
The South

From the beginning, the South was a cliché. At the very
birth of the Republic men—wise and foolish, Southern
and non-Southern—already spoke glibly of the South, and
understood what they meant by the term, and were wrong.
Plantations, staples, tobacco, rice, aristocracy, slavery,
wealth, slavery, arrogance, slavery: these were the South,
these, almost everyone mistakenly agreed, made it a world
apart.

In point of fact, the safest generalization about the South
was one that nobody ever made: that each state in it differed
more from the others than did states elsewhere differ from
their neighbors. To be sure, every state in the South had the
"peculiar institution," Negro slavery; but then, so did every
other American state except Massachusetts, and so did virtually every other place where the British had planted
colonies. To be sure, in no American state outside the South
—with the partial exception of Delaware—was the economy
based on slavery; but then, neither was it in North Carolina,
most of Georgia, or Virginia west of the Blue Ridge.

It was somewhat more realistic to talk of two Souths,
upper and lower. Maryland and that part of Virginia east of

the Blue Ridge—the upper South—were economically almost twins. Each was dominated by planters who grew
tobacco as their principal staple and wheat as an important
secondary staple. In the process, through wasteful farming
methods, the planters consumed vast quantities of land.
(Men accused tobacco of destroying the soil, but it was not
tobacco, it was men: men devastated natural vegetation to
clear a patch of land, planted tobacco on the patch for six
or seven years, then abandoned it unprotected to the elements while they moved on to destroy new patches.) In the
process, too, because relatively healthful working conditions
permitted a natural increase, the number of slaves grew
greatly. Consequently, the upper South had a continuous
plethora of slaves and a continuous need for new land; until
the cotton gin arrived in the 1790s to solve their dilemma,
planters in large portions of the area chronically lacked
enough good land to keep their slaves profitably employed.
In keeping with the universal human habit of making a virtue of necessity, many planters in the upper South assumed
broad humanitarian stances and advocated one form or
another of abolition of slavery.[1]

---

[1] On soil exhaustion in the upper South, see Avery O. Craven, *Soil Exhaus-
tion as a Factor in the Agricultural History of Virginia and Maryland*
(Urbana, Ill., 1926); for observations on why it was abandonment of
land, not its culture, that "exhausted" it, see the analysis of Virginia, below.
On Maryland, see Charles A. Barker, *Background of the Revolution in
Maryland* (New Haven, 1940); Philip A. Crowl, *Maryland During and
After the Revolution* (Baltimore, 1943). On Virginia, see August Low,
"Virginia in the Critical Period, 1783–1789" (doctoral thesis, University of
Iowa, 1941), and his "Merchant and Planter Relations in Post-Revolution-
ary Virginia, 1783–1789," in *Virginia Magazine of History and Biography,*
61:308–18 (1953); Freeman H. Hart, *The Valley of Virginia in the Amer-
ican Revolution, 1763–1789* (Chapel Hill, 1942); Jackson T. Main, "The
Distribution of Property in Post-Revolutionary Virginia," in *Mississippi
Valley Historical Review,* 41:241–58 (1954–55), and his "The One Hundred," in *William and Mary Quarterly,* 3d series, 11:354–84 (1954). More

The lower South—South Carolina and the older, low-lands part of Georgia—was dominated by planters who grew rice as their principal staple and indigo as a major secondary staple. Because the quantity of swampland suitable for such crops was fixed, planters necessarily restored to intensive cultivation rather than the extensive cultivation employed in the upper South. In the process, because the swamps teemed with malaria, slaves perished at a rate that rivaled their rate of increase in the upper South. Consequently, the lower South often needed to import new slaves. Here, too, necessity dictated attitudes, but the attitudes were scarcely virtuous. The South Carolina planters' callous disregard for human life and suffering was probably unmatched anywhere west of the Dnieper. (The callousness applied, however, only to field hands; house servants and skilled laborers were regarded as human beings, their status depending upon whose human beings they were.)[2]

But the world of two Souths, however real in economic life, was only make-believe in other aspects of life. Indeed, it was in regard to social and political habits and attitudes (the South was aristocratic, read the cliché) that the stereo-

---

reliable than any of these, for economic and social history of the two states, is Lewis C. Gray's *History of Agriculture in the Southern United States to 1860* (2 vols., Washington, 1933).

[2] The standard works on these two states during the period are Charles G. Singer, *South Carolina in the Confederation* (Philadelphia, 1941), and Kenneth Coleman, *The American Revolution in Georgia, 1763–1789* (Athens, 1958). Again, Gary's *History of Agriculture* is more valuable, at least in regard to economics and slavery, than either special work. Also useful are Richard Barry, *Mr. Rutledge of South Carolina* (New York, 1942); George C. Rogers, *Evolution of a Federalist* (Columbia, 1962); D. Huger Bacot's "The South Carolina Up-Country at the End of the Eighteenth Century," in *American Historical Review*, 23:682–98 (1923), and his "The South Carolina Middle Country at the End of the Eighteenth Century," in *South Atlantic Quarterly*, 23:50–60 (1924).

type of a single unique South was most persistent and least accurate.

On one sociopolitical extreme stood the raw frontier state of Georgia. In Georgia, men hunted animals by setting fire to vast tracts of woodland; blithely heedless of the attendant destruction of domestic animals, houses, and even settlers, they scavenged the ashes for edible meat and salable skins. When men disagreed politically they attacked one another with knives or guns, or bit off the ears of enemies; when a man took a moderately unpopular political stand he dared not travel unguarded at night, and when he took an extremely unpopular stand his life expectancy became nominal. When the legislature made up its annual budget it was regularly faced with making allowances for the thievery of men with whom it had entrusted public monies the previous year; and often the legislature did not bother, for its members were too busy absconding with public property for their own account.[3]

On the other extreme stood the neighboring state of South Carolina, almost as decadently civilized as ancient Egypt. A single brushstroke reveals the picture. In 1784, during a celebration in Charleston, cannon were being fired from shore and from vessels in the harbor. One of the favorite house slaves of "Dictator John" Rutledge, the proudest of all the planters and head of the aristocracy, wished to see the

---

[3] For a description of fire-hunting, see the Savannah *Gazette of the State of Georgia,* November 18, 1784. For examples of violence and other rough-and-tumble political methods, see the *Gazette* for February 6 and April 3, 1784; and the Lachlan MacIntosh Papers, Georgia Historical Society. For examples of fraud, waste, and corruption, see the *Gazette* for March 13, 1783, January 8, 1784, December 1, 1785; and the Henry Osborne File, the Robert Middleton File, and the Journal of Proceedings of the House of General Assembly, January 8, 1784, February 7, 1786, all manuscripts in the Georgia Department of Archives and History.

celebration and firing of cannon. Rutledge sent her to the City Tavern, with instructions to request of William Thompson, the proprietor, permission to go on his roof for the purpose. The wench did so, but instead of identifying herself and asking the privilege—after all, she was "Mr. Rutledge's nigger" and Thompson was a lowly innkeeper—she emulated her master's pride and demanded it of Thompson. Thompson, dumbfounded, chased her away, perhaps with some violence and doubtless with some bad language. On hearing the slave's tearful, distorted account of the incident, Rutledge was furious. He summoned Thompson to appear at his house immediately. Rutledge demanded a public apology; Thompson, not yet understanding the situation, refused, whereupon Rutledge grossly insulted Thompson and Thompson responded with a challenge to a duel. Innkeepers, as everyone knows, do not challenge their betters to duels, and Rutledge scornfully had his Negro male servants throw Thompson bodily from the premises. He then had the state House of Representatives censure Thompson, charge him with contempt of the House (on the ground that Rutledge was a member), and order Thompson to behave himself lest he be forcibly removed from the state.[4]

And Virginia (which was what people most often meant when they said "the South") was scarcely aristocratic at all, at least by contemporary standards. The suffrage was widespread: a far greater percentage of its adult males regularly went to the polls than was the case in "democratic" Connecticut or Massachusetts. The rate of turnover of elected

---

[4] This episode is reported and commented on in the Charleston *Gazette of the State of South Carolina*, April 1, 29, 1784. Even the planters of Maryland and Virginia viewed the "profuse and luxurious . . . mode of living" of the South Carolinians with awe; see Richmond *Virginia Gazette,* October 22, 1785, Baltimore *Maryland Journal,* October 7, 1785.

officials was great, considerably more rapid than that in New Hampshire or even the "licentious republic," Rhode Island. The energy with which candidates sought office would not have been regarded as sluggish by Jacksonians half a century later, their techniques would not have been thought clumsy by ward heelers in big-city machines a century later, their appeals to the rights of man would not have been out of place among New Dealers a century and a half later. (It was not inconsistent that, once in office, Virginia politicians wielded power through tight little cliques, for so would successful American politicians do forever. Nor was it inconsistent that their society was based upon the enslavement of nearly half their numbers, for so had it been in the most successful republics the world had ever known, those of the ancients.)[5]

Finally, what each of the five Southern states desired and

---

[5] These are my own conclusions, derived from considerable study of primary sources in Virginia, and supplemented by an appreciative but somewhat skeptical reading of Charles S. Sydnor, *Gentlemen Freeholders: Political Practices in Washington's Virginia* (Chapel Hill, 1952); they depart considerably from conventional accounts. All conventional accounts, however, appear destined for the scrap-pile, in view of the almost unbelievably meticulous new study by Robert E. Brown and B. Katherine Brown, *Virginia, 1705–1786: Democracy or Aristocracy?* (East Lansing, 1964), especially chapters 7–11. Professor and Mrs. Brown kindly lent me a copy of their galley proofs of this work, which was scheduled for publication just after the present work went to press. As to the turnover of elected officials, my own tabulations show the following: between the sessions of May 1781 and October 1788 a total of 1,254 seats in the House of Delegates were filled. No less than 620 different persons held these seats—an average annual turnover of 44.8 percent, or a complete turnover every 2.23 years. The Virginia freemen elected an average of 158 representatives every year, an average of 71 of whom had never served in the legislature before. Tabulated from lists of delegates in Earl G. Swem and John W. Williams, *A Register of the General Assembly of Virginia, 1776–1918, and of the Constitutional Conventions* (Richmond, 1918).

needed in relation to the Union was different. Fundamentally similar as their economies were, in national politics Virginia and Maryland stood, in principle, for precisely opposite views, and in practice they were devout enemies. Georgia and North Carolina were largely indifferent to the fate of the Union; Virginia did not so much care what happened to the Union as it did that whatever happened, Virginia's should be the dominant voice. Maryland tended to be strongly nationalistic because it had much to gain thereby; South Carolina had little to gain from a stronger union but tended to be nationalistic nonetheless, because its aristocracy had a broad view that derived from the practice of educating all its young men abroad (usually in London), and because the necessities of commercial life threw its members into more regular contact with the outside world than was normal elsewhere.[6]

But whatever their aspirations and differences, the Southern states, like the states elsewhere, were left to go it alone for a while after 1783.

That suited Virginians just fine. Virginians, like other Americans, had long since worked out ways of integrating their relatively simple economy into the larger economy of the Atlantic community. Like other Americans too, they had filtered selected Anglo-Saxon ideas and institutions

---

[6] The disputes between Virginia and Maryland were referred to in chapter 1, above; for excellent information see also Merrill Jensen, "The Cession of the Old Northwest," in *Mississippi Valley Historical Review*, 23:27–48 (1936), and his "The Creation of the National Domain, 1781–1784," *ibid.*, 26:323–42 (1939). The other generalizations in this paragraph are drawn from the works cited in footnotes 1 and 2, above, and (inasmuch as I disagree with many of the conclusions drawn in those works) the sources cited under the individual states in the remainder of this chapter.

through the screen of their economic habits and evolved a distinct system of social, moral, and political views. But by the time of the Revolution their economic and philosophical "givens," unlike those of most Americans, had so hardened as to dictate to rather than to serve the people who held to them. So set were their economic ways that Virginians clung helplessly to them long after they had begun to work directly against their interests. So set were their philosophical principles that Virginians could do something for the crassest reasons, ingenuously describe the event in high-flown verbiage, and react with honest surprise and indignation if they were accused of acting from base motives. During the Revolutionary epoch, most of Virginia's doings were concerned with trying to disentangle from the economic givens and to carry out the logical implications of the philosophic.[7]

The basic unit of the economic system was the tobacco plantation. In Virginia east of the Blue Ridge, where about three-fourths of the state's inhabitants lived, the vast majority of the white adult males owned slaves. Sizes of plantations varied, but the typical plantation contained fifteen to thirty adult slaves and occupied six to twenty-five hundred

[7] My observations about the Virginia "givens" are drawn from a multitude of sources, ranging from Jefferson's *Notes on Virginia* to Gray's *History of Agriculture,* but in the main they come from two kinds of materials. The first is newspapers: I have read every line of every Virginia newspaper I could lay my hands on in repositories in Richmond, Washington, New York, Worcester, and Madison, for the years 1763–90. The second is biographies and personal papers. Among the biographies are Freeman's *Washington,* Brant's *Madison,* Conway's *Randolph,* W. W. Henry's *Henry,* Malone's *Jefferson,* Mays' *Pendleton,* Rowland's *Mason,* Brock's *Cary,* Lee's *Richard Henry Lee,* and Hilldrup's *Pendleton.* Among the published collections of personal papers used are those of Washington, Madison, Jefferson, R. H. Lee, Mason, Bland, and Randolph.

acres.[8] If a plantation fell significantly short of this ratio of land to slaves—fifty to eighty acres per field hand—its economic soundness was doubtful. Only a fraction of this acreage could be planted in tobacco, for slaves could cultivate, on the average, only about two and a half acres each; but the remainder was needed for gardens and grazing and, especially, for timber that would enable the slaves to be busy earning their keep during the winter. If a plantation's forests were pretty well stripped, its tobacco land spent, or its total area less than fifteen or twenty acres per field hand, it was not likely to be able to support itself within the framework of any tobacco prices that could reasonably be expected. These latter conditions were particularly common in the oldest and nominally richest parts of the state.[9]

To establish a typical plantation of, say, 2,000 acres and twenty-five field hands involved an investment of about $8,500, about $5,000 for slaves and the remainder for buildings and furniture, implements, livestock, a small boat, and other necessities. The land could be leased for about $500 a year, though it could vary almost as much as fifty percent more or less than that figure, depending mainly on proximity to navigable water. Given adequate land, operat-

---

[8] West of the Blue Ridge, where the plantation system had not yet developed, only about one family in four owned slaves; east of the Blue Ridge, the range of slaveholdings was from about ninety-five percent of the families in the northeastern portion (the Northern Neck) to about seventy-two percent in the southwest portion (the Southside). Just over one slaveholding family in four held fewer than ten slaves; about one in twenty-five held more than a hundred. See the sources cited in footnote 9.

[9] The economic analysis is drawn from Gray, *History of Agriculture,* 1:531, 541 ff. For distribution of landholding in Virginia, see Brown and Brown, *Virginia,* chapter 1; for distribution of slaveholdings, see *ibid.,* chapter 3, and Main's two articles, cited in footnote 1.

ing costs were low. Most plantations were largely self-sufficient, for slaves were trained in such skilled crafts as carpentering, weaving, coopering, and bricklaying, and plantation gardens and livestock produced most of the food. Other expenses, consisting mainly of foodstuffs purchased from the back country and rough cloths purchased from New England, amounted to about $25 per slave per year, over and above the off-season earnings from lumber and lumber products. Total annual costs of a plantation of 2,000 acres and twenty-five hands, including maintenance, depreciation, and interest (assuming that half the investment was on credit at six percent), would run around $2,100. Such a plantation would normally yield about 62,500 pounds of tobacco annually. Thus to break even the planter had to receive a net price of about twenty shillings Virginia currency, or $3.33, per hundredweight. To earn a net profit of six percent he had to receive about twenty-five shillings.[10]

Had Virginia planters received a reasonable fraction of the wholesale price that their tobacco fetched in foreign markets, they would have been wallowing in wealth. Instead, in the three decades before the war their net rarely if ever reached the twenty-shillings breakeven point, and yet in the same period wholesalers in London were paying several times that figure. The difference lay in the marketing system. In that same system lay the seeds of revolution.[11]

---

[10] Gray, *History of Agriculture,* 1:541 ff.; La Rochefoucauld Liancourt, *Travels Through the United States of North America . . . in the Years 1795, 1796, and 1797* (3 vols., London, 1800), 3:169. The estimated breakeven and profit prices are my own, calculated from the data given by Gray and La Rochefoucauld.

[11] Gray, *History of Agriculture,* 1:272–75; prewar prices from Williamsburg *Virginia Gazette* and occasional notices in London and Philadelphia

In the early days of tobacco culture, when plantations were concentrated on the lower tidewater, a loose system of direct or casual trading had prevailed. As tobacco production expanded it became increasingly necessary to have some form of regularized trade, for the uncertainty of arrival of ships, lack of information about the state of the market, and limited variety of imports all placed the planter at a serious disadvantage. By the beginning of the eighteenth century this need was filled by the development of the factorage and consignment system, under which British merchants dealt exclusively in the Virginia trade and established permanent houses in Virginia under the direction of agents called factors. Planters entered into a commercial relationship with factors by accepting credit (in goods or money) from them and by consigning their shipments through them to the parent merchants in Britain. The disadvantage of this system was that, once in debt to a British merchant, the planter had to continue to deal exclusively with him, and he could set prices at will. As Madison wrote, an instance "of a man's getting out of debt who was once in the hands of a tobacco merchant" was yet to be discovered.[12]

By the middle of the eighteenth century, the consignment system began to be supplemented by the direct purchase of tobacco in Virginia. One reason was the expansion of production above the falls of the rivers: the necessity of unloading and reloading at the fall line made the consignment system less practical on the piedmont. Too, Scottish mer-

---

newspapers; Allason Letter Books, 1757–93, in Virginia State Library; Francis N. Mason, ed., *John Norton & Sons, Merchants of London and Virginia* (Richmond, 1937).

[12] Gray, *History of Agriculture,* 1:409–33; Craven, *Soil Exhaustion,* 71–76; Mason, ed., *Norton & Sons,* 459.

chants began to enter the business at this time, and their best means of competing for the new customers was to furnish cash for crops. But the direct purchase system turned out to be no more advantageous than the consignment system, for it made prices dependent upon the money supply in Virginia rather than upon world market prices, and the Scottish merchants pretty well dominated the money supply on the piedmont.[13]

On the eve of the Revolution, about a third of the colony's tobacco crop was being produced in the older areas and marketed through the consignment system. The remainder was produced in the newer and more inland areas and sold for cash in Virginia. The newer planters were struggling along trying to make ends meet on inadequate prices, and were gradually sinking into debt. The older planters owed an enormous book debt, amounting to almost $10 million, to British mercantile houses. And the situation was growing worse rather than better.[14]

If circumstances should provide the opportunity, as they soon did, the philosophical value system in Virginia was admirably suited for a solution of Virginia's economic problems. The basic coloration of this system was that of rural republicanism. Under it, the ideal existence was that of the cultivated country gentleman who was occasionally obliged to devote his time to public service. (It was up to him to convince his neighbors that the time for his public service

[13] Gray, *History of Agriculture,* 1:409–33; Jacob M. Price, "The Rise of Glasgow in the Chesapeake Tobacco Trade, 1707–1775," in *William and Mary Quarterly,* 3d series, 11:179–99 (1954).

[14] *Ibid.,* Bemis, *Jay's Treaty,* 103; Jensen, *New Nation,* 16; Emory G. Evans, "Planter Indebtedness and the Coming of the Revolution in Virginia," in *William and Mary Quarterly,* 3d series, vol. 19 (1962).

had arrived.) Such cultivated country gentlemen were familiar with all the branches of useful arts and sciences, and many that were not so useful. Because it was necessary to the conduct of their semifeudal domains, they accumulated a wide variety of practical knowledge. Because there was not much else to do, they read a great deal: they read Thucydides, Virgil, and Cato in Greek and Latin, and Coke and Blackstone, Montesquieu and Bolingbroke, Locke and Hume in English; and not only could they cite this incongruous conglomerate of authorities to justify any action, they believed them all as well. More mundanely, because they often found it difficult to feed their multitudes of slaves, they embraced humanitarianism; because they were over their heads in debts to merchants who faithfully swindled them, they cursed the city and commercial life; and because it offered a way out of their material plight, they adopted, with passionate faith, rationalism and doctrinaire republican idealism. Particularly suited to Virginia's present needs was that part of the gospel of rationalism that preached the desirability of a clean break with the past.[15]

A clean break with the past meant, in immediate material terms, a complete repudiation of the debts owed British merchants. But it would be a mistake to think that that was all there was to it. On the one hand, this destructive act had to be followed by a number of positive acts, looking to the creation of a marketing system which would prevent slipping right back into debt again. On the other, a firm commitment to principles of republican idealism involved numerous political and social reforms, and once the commitment was made these secondary ends became sincere goals, equal in

---

[15] See footnote 7, above.

force to the primary end—and perhaps, because of an unconscious need to overcompensate for the original dishonest act, even superior to it.[16]

The accumulated debts were effectively repudiated during the war; the constructive economic program awaited the peace. Its outlines were fairly simple. The problem, in essence, had been that marketing had been monopolistic (or, more properly, oligopolistic). The solution was to ensure that in future marketing there would be competition, preferably between an excess of competitors. The way to do this was to build a Virginia mercantile fleet—not large enough to carry the entire crop, for unless Virginia were prepared to effect basic changes in its economy, which it was not, that would not be economically feasible because the one-crop economy dictated that the ships could make only one round trip a year. Instead the fleet should be large enough to carry about a third of the crop, and it should be guaranteed cargoes by a system of subsidies that would enable Virginia merchants to carry at extremely low freight rates. The rest would follow as of course. When British, Scottish, other American, and the expected new Dutch and French merchants came to seek cargoes or buy tobacco, there would not be enough to go around. Planters so situated as to engage in direct shipment abroad could resume the use of factors, but now on favorable terms; or better yet, they could reverse the factorage system by hiring their own com-

---

[16] The best account of the repudiation of the debts is Isaac S. Harrell, *Loyalism in Virginia* (Philadelphia, 1926), an otherwise excellent book which overlooks the need for positive supplementary action and also the underlying republicanism of Virginians. See also George Mason to Patrick Henry, May 6, 1783, in William Wirt Henry, *Patrick Henry: Life, Correspondence, and Speeches* (3 vols., New York, 1891), 2:187, and the newspaper references cited in footnotes 17 and 19, below.

mission agents in London, and market directly through them. Those not so situated could expect the greatly increased competition to bring far higher cash prices in Virginia.[17]

Enactment of the program was delayed by the unexpected appearance of its benefits without legislation. A number of Virginians—old commercial people, former lawyers, and planters who made large sums in commodity speculation—accumulated considerable loose capital during the war, and immediately afterward began to divert it into shipbuilding. In the four years following Yorktown, Virginians built about 25,000 tons of new shipping; the portion of the tobacco crop carried in locally owned bottoms rose steadily from less than ten percent in 1783 to about a third in 1786, when a saturation point was reached. And competitive buyers swarmed in, and as a result Virginia prices throughout 1783 and 1784 were upwards of forty shillings. For their entire exported production in 1784, Virginia planters received well over $4 million—roughly twice as much as in

---

[17] For contemporary suggestions regarding the desirable details of this plan, see Caroline County instructions, in Richmond *Virginia Gazette*, October 25, 1783; "To Lord North," *ibid.*, November 1, 1783; "Mentor's Reply," *ibid.*, April 10, 17, 1784; Nansemond instructions, *ibid.*, November 12, 1784; "A," *ibid.*, November 19, 1785; John Marshall to Charles Simms, June 16, 1784, in Charles Simms Papers, Library of Congress. On the progress—or lack of it—of these measures in the Assembly, the letters of Madison to Jefferson, 1785–86, in Gaillard Hunt, ed., *The Writings of James Madison* (9 vols., New York, 1900–1910), vol. 4, are useful. A brilliant summary of the commercial disadvantage under which Virginia labored before the Revolution, and a series of proposals outlining the necessary changes to secure Virginia's commercial and agricultural prosperity after the war, are contained in a series of articles written in 1783 or 1784 under the pseudonym "Columbus," and republished in the Philadelphia *Freeman's Journal*, July 11–25, 1787. In that printing, the articles are said to have been written by St. George Tucker.

the best prewar years. Norfolk, burned to the ground in 1776, was in 1784 one of the biggest and most successful American ports.[18]

Thus distracted by prosperity, Virginians could and did devote much of their political energies to disputes over various republican reforms. The main result of the state's republican enthusiasm had come in the beginning, in its justly celebrated Bill of Rights of 1776. Others followed: legislation regarding education, religious freedom, and slavery was forthcoming, and other reforms were considered and some were acted upon. Too, it became fashionable to organize societies for the guarding of one right or another, as well as general societies for the discussion and spreading of republican ideals. This practice laid the foundations for a political technique which, when matured, would loom large in national affairs.[19]

There was also another issue, even more distracting than those arising from ideology: an internal conflict of interests arising from the peace treaty of 1783. The treaty provided

---

[18] Data on shipping are derived from the Naval Officer Returns in the Virginia State Library, from which I have tabulated all pertinent information on ocean-borne commerce for all ports, 1782–89. Prices and freight rates are taken from Alexandria *Virginia Journal,* Richmond *Independent Chronicle,* Richmond *Weekly Advertiser,* Richmond *American Advertiser,* Fredericksburg *Advertiser,* Philadelphia *Evening Herald,* and New York *Daily Advertiser.* See also William Hemsley Papers Relating to the Tobacco Business, 1784–1786, in Library of Congress.

[19] William Allen Rutland, *The Birth of the Bill of Rights* (Chapel Hill, 1955), 30 ff, 83–88; Alexandria *Virginia Journal,* March 31, April 7, November 17, 1785; Richmond *Virginia Gazette,* November 1784; H. J. Eckenrode, *Separation of Church and State in Virginia* (Richmond, 1910), *passim;* Allan Nevins, *The American States During and After the Revolution, 1775–1789* (New York, 1924), 449; William W. Hening, comp., *The Statutes at Large: Being a Collection of All the Laws of Virginia, from the First Session . . . in the Year 1619* (13 vols., Richmond, 1809–23), laws of May 1781, 1782, May 1783, October 1785, chapters 34, 60, 77.

for the restitution of property confiscated, sequestered, or stolen by both sides, but given the system prevailing under the Articles of Confederation, it was up to the states to comply or not comply with the treaty. Other things being equal, Virginians who had written off their debts were not anxious to see complying legislation enacted. But British armies had confiscated about 30,000 Virginia slaves during the war, many of them from the same tidewater planters who had written off their debts, and to such planters reciprocal restitution would have been more than advantageous. In other areas, where the cash system prevailed, planters were anxious to require full payment of the debts, on the grounds (a) that it was not they who would have to pay them and (b) that massive repudiation would create a business climate which would discourage new French and Dutch merchants from coming to the state. In still others, particularly the Northern Neck, planters who marketed for cash opposed enforcement of the treaty because large numbers of them had purchased confiscated property at bargain prices. And all over the state were speculators in western lands who, like the western settlers, desired that the treaty be enforced in the hope that doing so would induce the British to evacuate the posts they held in the Northwest Territory. Finally, there were a few people—very few— who believed that national honor required obedience to the treaty. For these and related reasons, Virginians haggled with one another over the treaty for what seemed an endless period, and neglected their commercial program in the doing.[20]

---

[20] Gray, *History of Agriculture*, 2:595–96; Essex County petition, in Richmond *Virginia Gazette*, October 25, 1783; Frederick and Berkeley counties instructions, *ibid.*, December 27, 1783; proceedings of the House and Senate, *ibid.*, June 26, July 10, 1784; Harrell, *Loyalism in Virginia, passim;*

They were jarred out of their frivolity by a stimulus from an unexpected source: late in 1784 the bottom began to fall out of the tobacco market, and by late 1785 the Virginia price had tumbled to just over twenty shillings. The reasons were complex and varied, but most arose from the interplay of economic and political events that drained Philadelphia and New York of money, occasioned the troubles of the Bank of North America, and set off a chain reaction that created a money shortage everywhere. Virginia planters, however, having approximately the same amount of patience and insight concerning the mysteries of the money market as did farmers at any other place and time, looked for a tangible, personal cause of their plight. They quickly found him: Robert Morris, who in April 1785 completed his negotiations for a monopoly contract with the French Farmers-General.[21]

In truth, that contract probably worked to raise the price

Journal of the House of Delegates, May Session, 1784, p. 41, October Session, 1787, pp. 51–52; *Journals of the Continental Congress,* 32:124–25, 176–84 (March 21, April 13, 1786).

[21] Prices have been traced in the various newspapers; for example, in Alexandria the price fell from over 40 shillings a hundred in mid-1784 to 30 shillings late in February 1785, then steadily downward to 22 in December and 21 in January 1786; Alexandria *Virginia Journal,* February 24, April 14, June 30, August 4, September 29, December 1, 1785, January 12, 1786. See also Simeon Deane to Barnabas Deane, November 13, 1784, in *Correspondence Between Silas Deane, His Brothers, and Their Business and Political Associates, 1771–1795* (*Collections* of the Connecticut Historical Society, vol. 23, 1930), 205; a similar course may be seen in William Hemsley to Tench Tilghman and Company, March 21, 29, April 1, 4, May 3, 31, July 19, 1785, in William Hemsley Papers, Library of Congress; compare the curve of wheat prices in New York, steadily downward from 9s. 6d. per hundredweight in December 1784 to 7s. 6d. a year later, in *New York Packet,* December 13, 1784, March 7, June 11, October 3, December 8, 1785. Historians have generally if not invariably followed the Virginians in attributing the decline to Morris; see, for example, Jensen, *New Nation,* 203; Frederick L. Nussbaum, "American Tobacco and French Politics,

of tobacco, for because of it Morris injected a million livres (around $200,000) in cash into the market in the fall and winter of 1785–86, and the competition between him and erstwhile partners who double-crossed him, combined with an alteration of the terms by the Farmers-General and resistance by sellers, brought the price back up to around twenty-eight shillings by the fall of 1786.[22] It would have been difficult to convince most Virginians of that, however; and besides, Morris already had so many political enemies in Virginia, going back to his bitter battles with the Lees during his incumbency as superintendent, that most Virginians were prepared to believe the worst.[23]

In any event, Virginia was stimulated to complete its commercial program, and it did so by the end of 1786. When the monetary yield increased sharply in the marketing season 1786–87, Virginians could congratulate themselves

1783–1789," in *Political Science Quarterly*, 40:497–516 (1925). I did so myself in an earlier work: *We the People*, 55, 267–68. The origin of this idea is apparently Jefferson's letter to Jay, May 27, 1786, published in Jared Sparks, ed., *The Diplomatic Correspondence of the United States* (5 vols., Washington, 1832–33), 3:57–63; the contract itself is in the same, 3:64–67.

[22] The contract was signed by Morris on April 10, 1785, but it is clear that he did not enter the market on a significant scale until late summer or fall, despite having been a partner in an earlier effort to buy Virginia tobacco for the French market. Gouverneur Morris maintained that the contract broke, rather than established, a monopoly, for the Scottish merchants already had a monopoly and Morris injected new capital into the market. In any event, once he entered the market prices rose steadily, in the winter and on through the summer of 1786, resulting in considerable losses for Morris on his shipments during the winter of 1785–86 and a subsequent revision of the contract. Interestingly, prices dropped precipitously after the contract expired and Morris left the market in 1788; the causes, however, seem to have been a series of natural calamities.

[23] Sumner, *Financier and Finances*, 2:168–73; Gray, *History of Agriculture*, 2:604–5; Hemsley to Tilghman, May 31, July 19, 1785, in William Hemsley Papers, Library of Congress; Anne C. Morris, *The Diary and Letters of Gouverneur Morris* (2 vols., New York, 1888), 1:352.

on their shrewdness. That increase actually came from the rise in prices occasioned by other forces, and also from a bumper crop in 1786; but be that as it may, Virginia now had itself a marketing system that should hereafter provide maximum protection for its planters.[24] It would take powerful inducements to persuade her to part with it.[25]

In short, most Virginians were interested in and took a favorable view toward preservation of the Union; but any attempts to strengthen it that originated with the old Morris-centered nationalists, or involved surrender of Virginia's commercial gains, or violated republican principles of political theory could be expected to meet fierce resistance.

In North Carolina they had some rich soil and a lot of rednecks and a few Second Families of Virginia, and almost no way to move from place to place. The land was good and lushly forested, and it would grow tobacco about as well as the land anywhere; and it was also cheap, for once you grew the tobacco there was no way to get it out to where the money was.[26]

---

[24] Lewis C. Gray, in his *History of Agriculture in the Southern United States to 1860* (2 vols., Washington, 1933), points out that tobacco prices fell drastically late in 1788 and remained extremely low—averaging around twelve shillings—until the mid-1790s. The decline came just after the ratification of the Constitution, which necessitated the abandonment of Virginia's mercantile system; though Gray concluded that the disastrous price level was a function of natural and market causes, Virginians may well have attributed it to the political change; and whatever its causes, it may not be unrelated to the strong opposition in Virginia to Federalist governmental policies in the early nineties.

[25] Hening, *Statutes at Large,* October 1785, October 1786, sessions, *passim;* for post-1786 prices, Gray, *History of Agriculture,* 2:605.

[26] Despite the excellence of the collections of local history in the North Carolina Archives and of personal papers in the Duke University and University of North Carolina libraries, secondary works on North Carolina

Or almost none. The state was too big and too hilly and too nearly roadless to admit of transport by land, and besides, when harvest time came the rains came also and the roads became impassable troughs of mud. There were no navigable rivers to speak of, except during the same rainy reason; and so it happened that Carolinians built great plantations high in the back country, floated their tobacco and timber downstream on flatboats in late fall, and had a profitable once-a-year contact with civilization. Elsewhere, rivers bred commerce and commerce bred communication and communication bred a sense of being in the world; but in North Carolina the rivers were once-a-year rivers, and fifty weeks a year, isolated high in the hills, Carolina rednecks worked hard in the sun and Carolina gentlemen sat on their porches in the shade and had their Negroes work for them, and either way they knew not and cared not what happened on the outside.[27]

---

during this period are limited and of limited value. The most useful general published source is Walter Clark, ed., *State Records of North Carolina* (26 vols., Winston and Goldsboro, 1886–1907). For general economic and other data, see Francis G. Morris and Phyllis Mary Morris, "Economic Conditions in North Carolina About 1780," in the *North Carolina Historical Review,* 16:107–33, 296–327 (1939); Christopher C. Crittenden, *The Commerce of North Carolina, 1763–1789* (New Haven, 1936); Gray, *History of Agriculture;* Alice Barnwell Keith, ed., *The John Gray Blount Papers* (Raleigh, 1952); and Duane Meyer, *The Highland Scots of North Carolina, 1732–1776* (Chapel Hill, 1957); Lida T. Rodman, ed., "Journal of a Tour to North Carolina in 1787 by William Attmore," in *James Sprunt Historical Publications,* 27:5:46 (1922). On politics in general, see William H. Masterson, *William Blount* (Baton Rouge, 1954), which is also valuable on land speculation; Griffith J. McKee, *Life and Correspondence of James Iredell* (2 vols., New York, 1847, 1857); Blackwell P. Robinson, *William R. Davie* (Chapel Hill, 1957).

[27] Miscellaneous information about internal economic, topographic, and transportation characteristics of North Carolina are sprinkled through various sources, for example, Gray's *History of Agriculture,* 1:47–48, 355, 404,

Even the annual contact, for those who had it, was abridged, for hard as it was to get the tobacco and timber to ports, it was even harder to get the tobacco- and timber-laden vessels out to sea. North Carolina was fenced in from the sea by great chains of barrier sandbars: as the seagull flew Edenton was only thirty-five miles from the open Atlantic, but as boats sailed the safe passage out was a serpentine 180 miles. At best, it took a week and more to clear the Sound, and oceangoing ships sometimes had to wait months for a chance to make the Atlantic. Usually, only small and maneuverable sloops, ill-equipped for Atlantic crossings, dared attempt it. And thus North Carolinians sent their tobacco to Norfolk or Charleston for reexport to Europe and their timber products to the West Indies, and the more venturesome merchants and skippers went all the way to Baltimore and Philadelphia and even New York to buy foreign fineries. So it was that the scant news they got was secondhand from those places, and when they passed it on to the planters, once a year, it was thirdhand and out of date.[28]

440–43, 493, 606; *North Carolina State Records,* 24:695; Crittenden's *Commerce of North Carolina* and his three articles on internal transportation and communication, in the *North Carolina Historical Review,* vol. 8 (1931); and J. D. Schoepf's *Travels in the Confederation, 1783–1784* (2 vols., Philadelphia, 1911). An excellent general description—on which much of the following is based—is in Hugh Talmage Lefler and Albert Ray Newsome, *The History of a Southern State: North Carolina* (Chapel Hill, 1954), 17–23, 71–121.

[28] *Ibid.,* 94–105; Schoepf, *Travels in the Confederation,* 2:111; Crittenden, *Commerce of North Carolina, passim.* To gain information about North Carolina shipping beyond that given by Crittenden, I have tabulated entries, clearances, cargoes, and other data on North Carolina vessels, or vessels arriving from or departing for North Carolina, in customs office records of other ports: for Charleston, in the South Carolina Archives, Columbia;

The planters, conditioned by their annual pilgrimages to thinking in Carolinawide terms, felt allegiance to Carolina and had embraced the revolutionary cause because Carolina would gain by it, and also because their habit of emulating Virginians taught them to embrace republican idealism. The rednecks' allegiance, at the broadest, comprehended neighbors in a town or a county or a valley, and otherwise it extended no farther than their own families and farms. For no particular reason except jealousy their traditional enemies were the planters and their Enemy was authority, and so out of habit when the planters and the state became committed to the Revolution they became Loyalists, loyal to a king who, for all they knew, might have been only a rumor. When the war was over planters demonstrated their allegiance to their independent state by persecuting Loyalists, as good Whigs everywhere were demonstrating their allegiance to the Union, though there was little money in it in North Carolina because the Loyalists there had few estates worth confiscating. The rednecks, when left alone, went about their grubby business as usual, and when they were not left alone they moved west to the Promised Land of Tennessee and started secessionist movements.[29]

---

for Virginia ports, in the Virginia State Library, Richmond; for Maryland ports, in the Maryland Hall of Records, Annapolis, and in the Fiscal Section of the National Archives; for Philadelphia, in the Historical Society of Pennsylvania; for New Haven and Salem, in the National Archives; for Beverly in the Beverly Historical Society, Beverly, Massachusetts; and for Providence and Newport in the Rhode Island Archives. For all other ports, I have tabulated such data as appear in extant newspapers.

[29] Lefler and Newsome, *North Carolina,* 71–79, 161–78, 215–24, 242–43; J. S. Bassett, "The Regulators of North Carolina," in American Historical Association *Annual Report, 1894* (Washington, 1895), 141–212; W. K. Boyd, ed., *Some Eighteenth Century Tracts Concerning North Carolina* (Raleigh, 1927), 175–413; Carl Bridenbaugh, *Myths and Realities: Socie-*

The material sinews of union—public lands and public debts—existed in North Carolina, as elsewhere, and so did the quaint notion that men's loyalties would lodge at the most convenient source of lucre; but at most these could work to teach Carolinians to look to the state, not to the nation. In the postwar decade, that is just what they did.

In 1783 North Carolinians found themselves holding, as a by-product of war, a good deal of money. Most of it was not real money, but pieces of paper saying Somebody-Owes-You the equivalent of a commandeered horse or bushel of grain, and even had the paper been worth what it claimed, it would not have equaled the damage wreaked by the troops. But what was consumed or stolen or destroyed was only tangible property, and some of what was left in its place was real honest-to-God money, gold and silver. Now when the Republic was young all Americans knew what to do when they got real money: If you gave an American a dollar, he would buy something costing ten. This was only good sense, the American knew, because soon the ten would, by the sheer magic of America, become a hundred. The instrument of this magic, the touchstone, was land; and so in 1783 the North Carolinians passed a law to make themselves all rich,

ties *of the Colonial South* (Baton Rouge, 1952), 159–63; Isaac M. Harrell, "North Carolina Loyalists," in *North Carolina Historical Review,* 3:575–90 (1926); Bessie M. Steinle, "The Confiscation of Loyalist Property During and After the Revolution in North Carolina" (master's thesis, University of Texas, 1935); "A General State of the Treasury in Hillsborough District, April 1783," in Legislative Papers, House of Commons, May 1783, in North Carolina Historical Commission, Raleigh; Robert O. DeMond, *The Loyalists in North Carolina During the Revolution* (Durham, 1940), 34–52. The sum nominally realized on sales of confiscated property in North Carolina was large, £867,000; Lefler and Newsome, *North Carolina,* 242–43; but this was in greatly depreciated currency.

by selling themselves their public lands—what became the whole state of Tennessee—for a pittance.[30]

On the face of it there might seem to be no reason to expect that Tennessee lands should become valuable when the settled North Carolina lands were not particularly so, but such a view overlooked the magic. For one thing, settlers poured, of their own volition, into the Tennessee portion of North Carolina: first the rednecks, and then the Irish and Scots-Irish who spilled down the back country of Pennsylvania, down the Shenandoah Valley, and across the Cumberland Gap. A few came to buy; most came to squat, for until someone proved otherwise, the land was free. They all came in search of the mythical land of Kaintuck, which lay just over the next rise to the west, and where the soil was so rich that all a farmer had to do was throw his seed on the ground and step back out of the way of the beanstalk. (As the Spaniards had walked thousands of miles of wilderness in search of mythical cities of gold, and the French had done the same in search of mythical fountains of youth and

---

[30] House Journal, December 13, 1785, in *North Carolina State Records,* 17:341; *ibid.,* 21:144–45, 24:479; Adelaide L. Fries, "North Carolina Certificates of the Revolutionary Period," in *North Carolina Historical Review,* 9:229–42 (1932); Crittenden, *Commerce of North Carolina,* 136, 163; E. James Ferguson, *The Power of the Purse: A History of American Public Finance, 1776–1790* (Chapel Hill, 1961), 182, 186, 188, 207, 212 ff.; Lefler and Newsome, *North Carolina,* 218–21, 258–59; McRee, *Iredell,* 1:451, 472, 2:42–43; Gray, *History of Agriculture,* 2:626; Masterson, *William Blount,* 46–74. Ferguson points out that some North Carolinians complained because of the lack of certain kinds of paper; that is, paper money was abundant, but the public securities held in the state did not match the property actually taken by the armies and the Congress. So also said Richard Dobbs Spaight in a letter to the governor of North Carolina, April 30, 1784, in Burnett, ed., *Letters of Members of the Continental Congress,* 7:509. See also footnote 31.

routes to India, so would the Anglo-Americans walk in search of that mythical soil.)[31]

All the land-jobbers had to do about the first condition was make sure they had titles to the land that was being squatted, and bide their time until the season came for selling the squatters the farms that they had carved out of the wilds. This they did under the land law of 1783. As to the other condition—the vision of Kaintuck—all they had to do was spread it and exploit it. Everywhere there might be a prospective settler, the land-jobbers planted false stories of fabulous yields in Tennessee (so much wheat and so much tobacco an acre) and of the easiest possible access to market down the Tennessee and the Cumberland and the Mississippi to New Orleans, where the friendly and somewhat gullible Spaniards were paying top dollar (and hard dollars at that) for every manner of produce. And it happened that by the time these stories went the rounds and got back to their sources, they had changed enough to be new stories, and the land-jobbers heard them and believed them. And thus the price of Tennessee lands went up and up for the sole reason that everybody believed they would go up and up, and North Carolinians had themselves a long, long speculative drunk.[32]

---

[31] Gray, *History of Agriculture,* 124–26, 614, 862–63; Masterson, *William Blount,* 100; Jensen, *New Nation,* 114–15; Thomas P. Abernethy, *From Frontier to Plantation in Tennessee* (Chapel Hill, 1932), 44–63; Aaron M. Sakolski, *The Great American Land Bubble* (New York, 1932), *passim;* Henry Nash Smith, *Virgin Land: The American West as Symbol and Myth* (Cambridge, 1950), *passim.*

[32] Abernethy, *Frontier to Plantation in Tennessee,* 19, 53–55, 187; Masterson, *William Blount,* chapter iv; see also the sources cited in footnote 31. Masterson's book is a good description of how speculative fever colored men's judgment and even their "knowledge." On page 129 is a good

None of which had much to do with North Carolina and the Union, except for some trouble that developed along the way. In 1784, to ensure that the squatters played their assigned roles and got no unpatriotic ideas—such as setting up government and keeping their land for themselves—the North Carolina legislature turned over the Tennessee territory to a higher power, the United States in Congress Assembled. The condition of the cession was that all speculative titles in the ceded area be validated. Forthwith, the United States in Congress Assembled demonstrated its unbounded perfidy by passing an ordinance enabling western settlers to set up shop as separate states and full-fledged members of the Union. Forthwith, the settlers in Tennessee began to do so, proclaiming themselves the state of Franklin. There was nothing for North Carolina to do but take back its cession, which it promptly did, but it was another

---

account of one example of rumor spreading, which happens to be one reversing the earlier picture of the Spanish. This description leads one to suspect that "Letters from a Gentleman in X to His Friend in Y," common in newspapers of the period, were often bogus. For examples of such letters, see "Extract of a Letter from a Gentleman in North Carolina to His Friend in the Western Country," in *Gazette of the State of South Carolina,* November 8, 1784; "Letter from a Freelander to A. Martin, Late Governor of North Carolina," in Philadelphia *Freeman's Journal,* November 23, 30, 1785; extract of a letter from Nashville to Hillsborough dated November 3, 1785, published in the *Pennsylvania Packet* of February 17, 1786, and in a somewhat different form, republished in the *Providence Gazette* of March 4, 15, 1786. The latter is an excellent example of the way the extravagant stories were circulated. It appeared in other newspapers as well as the two cited. It claimed that Tennessee lands produced sixty to eighty bushels an acre in "common crops" and about 2,500 pounds of tobacco—each figure being about twice the actual yields in Virginia and North Carolina. It also asserted that though the Spanish would not permit trade down the Mississippi, "yet they come and trade with us. They were here a few weeks ago, and purchased all our tobacco on the river, giving us six and seven dollars per hundredweight"—almost twice the going price in Virginia.

year or two before the tempest in Franklin blew over, and inducing it to blow over involved a good deal of worry and untidy work, such as bribing the Franklin leaders to betray their followers. It even involved a brief civil war, of sorts, before the titles of the land-jobbers were secure.[33]

North Carolinians would not soon be likely to trust Congress again. Any such foolish impulses they might have had were soon dispelled. In 1786, even as they were extricating themselves from the Franklin mess, Congress was jeopardizing them again. Actually it was not Congress at all, it was one man, but to land-jobbers everywhere he came to symbolize Congress. John Jay, a brilliant and almost pathologically honest New York aristocrat, a dedicated nationalist and also a pompous and pathetically vain man, was Congress' secretary for foreign affairs. The Spanish government, perceiving with unaccustomed perception that the rush of Americans to the west might soon endanger their own holdings there, sent a minister plenipotentiary to treat with Mr. Jay on the matter. The minister, Diego de Gardoqui, flattered Jay and showered Jay's wife (whom Jay adored)

---

[33] A good brief acount of these events is that of Merrill Jensen—whose interpretation I accept—in *New Nation,* 332–34; a more detailed version of a similar interpretation is in Abernethy's *Frontier to Plantation in Tennessee,* 55–90; see also Masterson, *William Blount,* 85–99. Masterson points out that certain strong nationalists, led by Hugh Williamson, William R. Davie, Thomas Person, and Alexander Mebane, opposed the cession, largely because of the corruption of the speculators but also for other reasons. For the cession act and its passage in the legislature, see *North Carolina State Records,* 19:612–13, 621–22, 642–44, 711–14; for the repeal, see *ibid.,* 19:804–5, 814, 830–32, 24:678–79. See also Samuel C. Williams, *History of the Lost State of Franklin* (Johnson City, Tenn., 1924); W. F. Cannon, "Four Interpretations of the History of the State of Franklin," in *Publications of the East Tennessee Historical Society,* 22:3–18 (1950).

with attention and gifts, whereupon Jay agreed to ask Congress for permission to surrender American claims to rights of navigation on the Mississippi. If the Mississippi were closed, westerners would have to recross the mountains to get crops to market. Thus discouraged, perhaps not so many would be impelled to cross the mountains in the first place.[34]

The deal was by no means a bad one, for Gardoqui offered in exchange to open the port of Havana and perhaps other Spanish-American ports as well. Because Havana had hard money that America sorely needed, and because it was potentially an insatiable market for American wheat and flour, a large segment of the economy stood to gain mightily by the proposed arrangement, and few stood to lose. The few were the North Carolina speculators and their counterparts all over the South. Scarcely disposed to sacrifice their own interests for those of a nation to which they felt no particular attachment anyway, these emitted loud bellows of protest in the name of national pride and the poor folk of the back country, and the deal never came off. But the land-jobbers, twice burned, were now thrice shy.[35]

---

[34] Samuel F. Bemis, *Pinckney's Treaty: A Study of America's Advantage from Europe's Distress, 1783–1800* (Baltimore, 1926), 78–90; *Journals of Congress,* 31:574–613 (August 29–31, 1786); Burnett, *Continental Congress,* 654–55; Arthur P. Whitaker, *The Spanish American Frontier, 1783–1795* (Boston, 1927), 74–77.

[35] Bemis, *Pinckney's Treaty,* 87–89; Burnett, *Continental Congress,* 655–59; Abernethy, *Frontier to Plantation in Tennessee,* 91–102. While Gardoqui worked on Jay, he also conspired with certain speculators and Westerners to effect a separation of the transmontane South and its alliance with Spain, but western and speculator interests were basically too antagonistic to permit of that. See Whitaker, *Spanish-American Frontier,* 108–15; Archibald Henderson, "The Spanish Conspiracy in Tennessee," in *Tennessee Historical Magazine,* 3:229–43 (1920); Masterson, *William Blount,* 151. The advantages of the proposed treaty, the opening of Havana espe-

The career of the public debt—all that litter of paper saying to the farmers Somebody-Owes-You—was likewise ill calculated to gain adherents to the Union in North Carolina. Those who ran the state reckoned that the Somebody ought to be, but was not soon likely to be, Congress. So they levied heavy taxes payable in those pieces of paper, thereby giving them some currency, and raised some taxes in cash so as to pay North Carolina veterans something of what was coming to them. Sooner or later, they trusted, some fellows would come down from Congress and take a look at what North Carolina had done, learn that Congress owed the state a lot of money, and be obliged to pay it. There was no point, therefore, in sending any money up to Congress in the meantime. Besides, up North they had different kinds of pieces of paper, on which Congress regularly paid interest. True, the interest was paid in IOUs (called indents), but Congress allowed states to pay their requisitions in those, and that hardly seemed fair.[36]

Thus in practice North Carolina took on the burden of servicing the public debt held in the state, and made little or no effort to fulfill its congressional requisitions. But it was not an entirely satisfactory arrangement, for it was an expensive proposition; and though taxation was retiring the

---

cially, have often been overlooked by historians; for comments showing recognition of past and prospective importance of that trade, see the *Pennsylvania Packet,* March 29, 1785; Philadelphia *Evening Herald* (remarks of Jonathan Sergeant), September 8, 1785.

[36] *Pennsylvania Packet,* August 14, 1784; *Freeman's Journal,* December 1, 1784; *North Carolina State Records,* 17:341, 19:192, 307, 24:475–78; Fries, "North Carolina Certificates," in *North Carolina Historical Review,* 9:229–41 (1932); *Journals of Congress,* 26:312–14, 29:768; John F. Mercer to the Executive Council of Virginia, April 10, 1784, in Burnett, ed., *Letters,* 7:491; Ferguson, *Power of the Purse,* 223–25.

Somebody-Owes-You paper more or less equitably, the ex-soldiers and those who had spent money on behalf of Congress were not faring so well. Then someone realized that if Congress could print up new paper and use it to pay its interest, then so could North Carolina. The state could print $250,000 in paper money, appropriating most of it for interest payments on continental securities, but setting aside $90,000 for going into business. State agents would use the $90,000 to buy tobacco and ship it abroad at a whopping profit. Part of the proceeds would be used to pay North Carolina's fair share of the interest on Congress' foreign debt, and the remainder would go as hard cash payments to the continental creditors in the state. The debts removed, there would be no further occasion for taxes, or almost none.[37]

The execution was not half as bright as the conception. Thanks to thorough mismanagement by the local agents and to what the locals regarded as a virtual conspiracy by congressional agents, the purchased tobacco ultimately yielded only $60,000, and Congress got it all. At that, the state did not make out badly, for the tobacco had cost it nothing, and by the act it retired $220,000 in obligations. The paper depreciated and circulated at about half its face value, so for a time everyone who touched it lost a little, but the local public creditors received around $80,000 even after depreciation, and they were able to shave their losses by paying their own debts in the paper at par. In short, no one lost much and some gained much. But Congress' part in the

---

[37] The act is in James Iredell and François X. Martin, eds., *The Public Acts of the General Assembly of North Carolina* (2 vols., New Bern, 1804), 1:393–95.

episode gained it no friends in North Carolina. Nor did it gain favor a little later when the fellows from Congress finally did come down to look at what North Carolina had done, and decided that because of some highfalutin book-keeping reasons, Congress did not owe North Carolina any money after all; decided, indeed, that it was the other way around.[38]

There was one other matter that discouraged North Carolinians from concerning themselves overmuch about the fate of the nation. This was prosperity, the mortal enemy of all who would inspire men to better man's lot. Corruption and bungling and all, North Carolina was bustling and booming throughout the 1780s. Each year was better than the last, and five years after war's end almost 50,000 tons of shipping were clearing the state annually—nearly twice the total in the best prewar years, and more than two-thirds as much as sailed from wealthy South Carolina. North Carolina had

---

[38] Jensen, in *New Nation,* 319–20, has an excellent, succinct account of this episode; he asserts, however, that the legislation was the outcome of a struggle between debtors and creditors, an assertion that bears no relation to his description of the events. That assertion is so widely and uncritically made (see, for example, the brief account in Lefler and Newsome, *North Carolina,* 252) that it is almost a cliché. It may well be true, but I have never seen any evidence to support it, and I believe that the issue had at least as much to do with public debts as it did with private debts. On the fate of the tobacco marketing scheme, see also Masterson, *William Blount,* 111–12, 117, 121; Blount was one of the commissioners. Prices of the paper were reported from time to time in Philadelphia and New York newspapers; newspapers in both cities (*Pennsylvania Packet,* July 22, 1785, *New York Packet,* July 28, 1785) reported a curious story that the introduction of the paper forced "a general desertion" of British merchants, and a consequent boom in local manufactures. On the settlement of North Carolina's accounts with the Congress, see Ferguson, *Power of the Purse,* 215–16, 323–24, 333.

never had it so good. Accordingly, friends of a stronger Union would best look elsewhere for supporters.[39]

In Georgia the story was different but the outcome was much the same. That Georgia was in the United States at all was more or less an accident. It did not embrace the revolutionary cause until the last moment, a last moment delayed at least in part by Congress' hope to lure in Canada, Florida, and the West Indies as well as Georgia. It had scarcely begun participating in the national counsels when it was abruptly withdrawn from the Union by military conquest, and it remained under British control until almost a year after the battle of Yorktown. In the peace negotiations that followed, no one seemed to consider it particularly important. Negotiators on both sides, agreeing that the southern extremity of the new nation should be a straight line drawn so as to allow Britain its claims to Florida, settled on the 31st parallel. None of them had ever been within eight hundred miles of the 31st parallel, and none had but a dim notion whether there were many American patriots in its vicinity.[40]

There were, in fact, very few. The state thus created was (after others ceded their nebulous claims to territories northwest of the Ohio) by far the largest of the American states,

---

[39] Crittenden, *Commerce of North Carolina,* 161–62; Walter Lowrie and Matthew Clarke, eds., *American State Papers, Documents, Legislative and Executive of the Congresses of the United States* (38 vols., Washington, 1832–61), vol. 7, *Commerce,* 321.

[40] Burnett, *Continental Congress,* 102–21; Samuel F. Bemis, *The Diplomacy of the American Revolution* (New York, 1935); Bemis, *Pinckney's Treaty,* chapter 2; Kenneth Coleman, *The American Revolution in Georgia, 1763–1789* (Athens, 1958), 55–167, 179–83, 253.

being approximately the size of all the states north of the
Mason-Dixon line. But its settled portion occupied far less
acreage than that occupied by the inhabitants of New Jersey
or perhaps even those of tiny Delaware. It consisted of a
narrow strip, rarely more than two or three farms wide,
running down the coast from Savannah for about sixty miles
and up the Savannah River for about a hundred and fifty
miles. In it resided only six or eight thousand families, most
of whom were and all of whom aspired to be reasonable
imitations of their aristocratic, rice-planting neighbors in
South Carolina.[41]

Once its existence as a republic in the American family of
republics was confirmed, Georgia began to pursue policies
that, by their sheer lack of sophistication, worked immensely
to Georgia's advantage. At war's end, for example, not
knowing (as wiser statesmen to the north knew) that both
prudence and patriotism dictated the forceful ejection of all
British merchants, Georgia naively invited all such scoundrels in Savannah to remain after the evacuation. The result
was that after 1783 hard money did not flee the city, as it
did virtually all other American cities, but stayed, multi-
plied, and furnished the fuel for an unprecedented commercial boom.[42]

---

[41] *Ibid.*, 15, 182; Evarts B. Greene and Virginia D. Harrington, *American Population Before the Federal Census of 1790* (New York, 1932), 182–86; Stella H. Sutherland, *Population Distribution in Colonial America* (New York, 1936), 222 (map), 254–70.

[42] On the legislation against Tories and its lax enforcement and its watering-down by the legislature and governor, see Allen D. Candler, ed., *The Colonial Records of the State of Georgia* (26 vols., Atlanta, 1904–16), vol. 19, part 2, pp. 2, 100–103, 126–27, 152–66; the same editor's *The Revolutionary Records of the State of Georgia* (3 vols., Atlanta, 1908),

So, too, was it with the compound of public debts and public credits with which the state found itself at its legal birth. Like most other states, only more so, Georgia emerged from the war holding vast public properties in the form of unoccupied lands and confiscated estates. Again like most other states, only more so (on a per capita basis), Georgia emerged from the war owing a good deal of money to its citizens; for it had maintained a rump (and running) government during the occupation, and that government had managed to spend a huge amount in IOUs to pay for prolonged, if ineffectual, sniping at the British. But unlike most other states, Georgia entertained no clever ideas about subtly mixing these ingredients to produce one set of loyalties or another. It owed about a quarter of a million pounds, Georgia currency, which was about a million dollars; and the estates of eminent Loyalists, if confiscated and sold at public auction, would yield about the same amount. As it happened, most of the eminent Loyalists were members of the same families as the most eminent patriots, who in turn

---

2:348, 361–63, 3:137–38, 145, 173–79; and legislative proceedings of July 12, 24, 25, 31, August 1, 1783, February 21, 25, 1784, January 26 February 16, 18, 21, 22, 1785, all as recorded in the Journal of the Assembly, preserved in the Georgia Department of Archives and History, Atlanta. Short-lived and relatively mild anti-Tory demonstrations and petitions were reported late in 1783; see Savannah *Gazette of the State of Georgia,* September 4, October 2, 9, 1783; but these doings were far less frequent and violent than their counterparts elsewhere, and they soon disappeared; on the occasional outbursts in 1784, see the *Gazette,* February 12, May 13, and "Brutus," September–October 1784. For a good brief summary of the half-hearted anti-Toryism, see Coleman, *American Revolution in Georgia,* 183–86. On the commercial boom, see footnote 47, below. The *Pennsylvania Packet,* April 26, 1783, reported that fifty-eight British merchants had been admitted as citizens of Georgia.

were the most eminent public creditors. So the unicameral (and therefore, in theory, excessively democratic and therefore impractical) Georgia legislature passed a law confiscating the property of the state's wealthiest Loyalists, providing for its sale at public auction, the terms being annual installment payments for seven years, half in public securities and half in gold. In the same act, the public debts of the state—including its portion of the national debt—were funded. That is, the law provided that as money came in on the personal bonds posted for confiscated property purchased, it should be paid out on the public bonds. The interest rate on the personal bonds was seven percent, that on the public bonds six percent. The extra credit to the state of one percent was expected to pay the annual cost of civil government: that is, the salaries of public officials.[43]

In practice, since the forfeiters to the public were essentially the same as the creditors of the public, little money actually changed hands. Witness, for example, the case of the Houstoun family. Sir Patrick Houstoun was perhaps the wealthiest Loyalist in the state. He paid the price of being on the losing side: his estate, valued at £25,000 (about a tenth of the total confiscated in Georgia), was seized by the state. It was sold at "public" auction, but the only bidder

---

[43] The confiscation and funding act is in Candler, ed., *Colonial Records of Georgia,* vol. 19, part 2, pp. 162–66 (act of August 5, 1782). On the administration of the act, see the Sale-Books of Confiscated Estates, by counties, 1782–85, in the Georgia Department of Archives; *Gazette,* May 26, 1785, July 21, 28, August 4, 11, 1787. On the relation of the act to Georgia finance in general, see the following financial reports of the legislature: July 21, 1783, in the Journal of the House of Representatives; January 26, 1784, January 12, 1785, in the Journal of the General Assembly, both manuscripts in the Georgia Department of Archives.

was William Houstoun, his nephew. The patriot Houstouns had accumulated about £25,000 in IOUs issued for services rendered to the winning side. Since it turned out to be impractical to collect the purchase price in hard money, the state allowed them to turn their public certificates over to the state in full payment for the privilege of purchasing (acually retaining) the family property. Thereby Georgia simply canceled a debt and canceled a credit, and nobody either gained or lost in the transaction. The surplus interest of one percent was consumed by graft and inefficiency, which to the families that were at once buyers and sellers amounted to a modest annual tax. The overall workings of the system meant that, in practice, public debts and credits were thoroughly neutralized as dynamics in the postwar period.[44]

Equally naive in treatment but far more dynamic in portent were the public lands of Georgia. Trigger-happy though the state's residents were in matters of personal honor, they were more than slow in grasping the possibilities for theft that all that land afforded; and so it was a dozen years before the members of the Georgia legislature realized that it was more profitable to sell their votes and give away the public lands than it was to regard their votes as not-for-sale and sell the land. In the meantime, after almost voting to give away the vast public domain without even benefit of bribery,

---

[44] Sale-Book of Confiscated Estates, Chatham County, Liberty County, 1782–85, purchases of June 13 and June 19, 1782, in the Georgia Department of Archives. "Mentor," writing in the *Gazette of the State of Georgia,* November 27, 1783, bitterly attacked the system in general and (without naming him but clearly referring to him) Houstoun in particular. But judging from the absence of other protest, the act seems to have been popular.

the legislators did the next best thing, voted to give all comers 200 acres and sell them additional quantities at two shillings (about forty-two cents) an acre.[45]

The outcome was that settlers poured into Georgia. From the back country of Virginia and the Carolinas the rednecks came, and from everywhere the Scots-Irish came, and from the barren rocks of New England came Yankees, Yankees, Yankees; also so fast that no one had time to formulate a good sound nativist defense that would keep them from coming. The Last-Families-of-England had arrived just in time to greet a group of the Most-Maladjusted-of-Germany and another group of malcontent Scots; and then the Revolution had broken and these good and pure Anglo-Saxons had just settled in to get rich and hate all newcomers, whereupon the Revolution ended and more outsiders began to come. In the seven years after the war the population of Georgia doubled. The newcomers flocked to the uplands south and west of Augusta and began to carve out tobacco plantations, which by 1790 were yielding almost as much income as the older rice plantations.[46]

With the droves of Yankee farmers came droves of Yankee traders. By 1786, a resident of Augusta noted, New England ships and boats teemed "in every creek, river, and

---

[45] Candler, ed., *Colonial Records of Georgia,* vol. 19, part 2, 201–15, 280–84; Journal of the Assembly, February 13, 1783. The legislature got around to selling its votes in the 1790s; see Charles H. Haskins, "The Yazoo Land Companies," in American Historical Association *Papers,* 5:61–103 (1891).

[46] See the population studies cited in footnote 41, and the Census of 1790; see also Coleman, *American Revolution in Georgia,* 9–14, 217–20; Gray, *History of Agriculture,* 2:605–6; *American State Papers: Commerce,* 7:157–62; Land Grant Books, by counties, in Georgia Department of Archives.

inlet, coming here to carry our produce to Charleston, Savannah, and other markets of these states." The Yankees "open shops on board their vessels in all the cuts and channels that intersect these countries," selling goods of every description in places where "you would expect to meet with nothing but alligators, rattlesnakes, and pine trees." Overall economic expansion during the period was immense and uninterrupted. In cold figures: the population of the frontier area alone grew from less than 15,000 to more than 40,000. Annual exports from Savannah increased from about $330,000 in the last five prewar years to more than twice that by 1789, and an additional $150,000 was exported by overland transportation to Charleston. Tobacco, which was hardly cultivated at all before the war, was being produced to the amount of more than $165,000 a year by 1789. In 1784, the first full year of peace, 144 vessels, measuring about 8,700 tons, cleared Savannah; three years later 354 vessels, measuring about 24,000 tons, cleared the port. At the time of the peace almost all the state's trade was carried in bottoms belonging to Britain or the British West Indies; by the end of the decade more than a third of it—a larger tonnage than the total at the beginning—was carried in Georgia-owned bottoms.[47]

---

[47] Letter from a citizen of Augusta to his friend in Philadelphia, in Philadelphia *Evening Herald,* May 17, 1786; *American State Papers: Commerce,* 7:157–62, 321; *United States Commercial and Statistical Register,* vol. 1, number 1, pp. 4–5 (Philadelphia, 1839); *Gazette of the State of Georgia,* November 27, 1783, January 20, 1784. The data on shipping are my tabulations of entrances and clearances, as reported in the *Gazette,* 1783–89; tonnage estimates are extrapolated from these tabulations by multiplying by the approximate average tonnage for vessels of each kind of rigging, as derived from customs office records for other ports—that is, sloops at 25 tons, schooners at 50, brigs at 100, and ships at 200.

Prosperously self-sufficient as Georgia was becoming, it still contained seeds of union. For many Georgians Charleston continued to be the principal entrepôt of ideas as well as goods, and the rice planters, the Savannah merchants, and the Augustans who traded overland with it all looked to Charleston for leadership, and Charlestonians were strongly nationalistic. Too, the new Yankee settlers were mainly from Connecticut, one of the most enthusiastically (and self-interestedly) nationalist of all states. Again, the Yankee peddler-boats that crowded out the alligators carried news as well as wares, and gave frontier Georgians a more regular contact with the outside world than frontiersmen had almost anywhere else.[48]

But normally such nationalistic impulses as Georgians had were outweighed by their preoccupation with success, or negated by bickering between the state's three dominant groups, the old planters, the Yankee newcomers, and the Scots-Irish. Hence Chief Justice George Walton, who took upon himself the function of itinerant high priest of republicanism and union, soon found himself unvoiced by political enemies, deprived of opportunity to harangue grand juries and the crowds that assembled to watch them. Hence, too, the state government grew slower and slower in complying with congressional requests, and less and less precise in fulfilling Congress' desires. By 1787 experienced congressmen could have stated a good rule of thumb for Georgia: they could make any emergency request of Georgia and confidently expect that about three years later Georgia would agree to do not quite what Congress had asked.[49]

---

[48] See, for example, the *Gazette of the State of Georgia,* January 20, April 14, 21, September 1, November 24, 1785, April 30, 1786.

[49] *Ibid.,* February 6, March 13, 20, 1783, September 29, October 6, November 3, 24, December 15, 1785; Candler, ed., *Colonial Records of Georgia,*

One hint of a stimulus existed that could, under proper circumstances, divert Georgia's energies to the nation. Georgians were surrounded and outnumbered by Indians who sporadically threatened to become hostile. Should they ever do so, Georgia would scream to its neighbors for help, and immediately concede anything that appeared likely to bring it.[50]

But for Samuel Chase, Maryland's immediate postwar history would have been dull in the extreme. Not that things were not happening there, for in long-range terms vast changes were taking place. The eastern shore of Chesapeake Bay, once the seat of a wealthy and cultured aristocracy, was suffering its last gasps, and the Revolutionary generation would see it rot into the first of many American Tobacco Roads. The western shore, the frontier not long since, was booming and planters there were effecting wholesale shifts from tobacco planting to wheat, thereby becoming increasingly like their neighbors in Pennsylvania and increasingly unlike their neighbors in Virginia. And Baltimore, in colonial times only Maryland's second city, was responding to an outburst of entrepreneurial vigor by growing faster than any other American port. Artisans and mechanics flowed into it to build new ships and new wharves and new houses for new inhabitants; and every season,

---

vol. 19, part 2, acts of February 13, August 2, 1786. These acts were one to three years late, and did not precisely conform to Congress' requests. See also Coleman, *American Revolution in Georgia,* 253–57.

[50] On the Indians, see *Gazette of the State of Georgia,* May 25, June 1, September 14, 1786, May 24, June 14, October 4, 1787; Journal of the General Assembly, August 2, 3, 4, 8, 1786, January 8, 13, 15, February 6, September 22, October 6, 23, 1787; John W. Caughey, *McGillivray of the Creeks* (Norman, Okla., 1938); Coleman, *American Revolution in Georgia,* 238–52.

Baltimore's vessels grew more numerous and ranged farther and carried richer cargoes; and by 1790 only Philadelphia among American ports could clearly be counted as more important. In short, the transition that would convert Maryland from a "Southern" to a "Border" state was well under way.[51]

Yet except for the obvious bustle in Baltimore, these broad and profound social transformations, like all broad and profound social transformations, were scarcely visible as they took place. Like the United States in the late 1820s, the early 1850s, and the middle 1920s, Maryland in the 1780s was a place where big things could be seen to have happened only later, when they were done. At the time, all that seemed to be happening—or most everything with salt and spice, anyway—appeared to revolve around Samuel Chase.

Chase was a man of peculiar breed, perfectly consistent by his own standards but wildly inconsistent by any other. In his political theorizing he was a caricature of the whole nationalist mentality. He unquestioningly assumed that, since America lacked the hereditary nobility and monarchy that restrained the peoples of Europe, it was crucial that its political institutions be so shaped as to check the people against themselves. Having such checks, the harnessed energies of a free people would lead to creation and conquest of a greatness beyond any dreams men had yet dreamed.

---

[51] Barker, *Background of the Revolution in Maryland;* Crowl, *Maryland During and After the Revolution;* Craven, *Soil Exhaustion;* Gray, *History of Agriculture,* especially 2:595–613; Baltimore Import and Export Books, in the Fiscal Section of the National Archives; Miscellaneous Naval Officer Returns, in Maryland Hall of Records, Annapolis; *Maryland Journal and Baltimore Advertiser,* 1783–88.

Lacking such checks, the people would invariably fall dupes to artful demagogues, who would lead them into destructive ways and exploit them without mercy. Chase knew this to be true, for whenever he appeared in public life in the capacity of an elected official, he artfully duped the people, led them by demagoguery into destructive ways, and exploited them without mercy; and they loved him and sang his praises and repeatedly reelected him.[52]

But when he appeared in public life in a different capacity, the capacity of institution-maker or institution-preserver, he worked with sublime statesmanship to protect the people against themselves, which is to say, against the like of himself. Thus in 1776, as the principal architect of Maryland's revolutionary constitution, he created a system so fraught with checks and balances, and with its powers so distributed between aristocracy and people, that destructive radicalism seemed impossible. Less than a decade later, as a member of the state's House of Delegates, he engineered a movement to subvert that very constitution, and did so for the most flagrantly corrupt reasons and with the enthusiastic support of "the people," in whose name he did it. (Similarly, as a congressman he was no sooner in office than he at-

---

[52] There is neither a biography of Chase nor a collection of his personal papers. There is a biographical sketch in the *Dictionary of American Biography;* much information about him is contained in Crowl's *Maryland During and After the Revolution;* occasional letters are to be found in the Library of Congress, the Maryland Historical Society, the Historical Society of Pennsylvania, and Burnett's *Letters.* A great deal of information about him, including much that he said and wrote, is in the Annapolis *Maryland Gazette* and the *Maryland Journal,* throughout this period; in the *Votes and Proceedings of the House of Delegates* (Annapolis, by sessions); in the *Journals of Congress;* and in the records of Chase's impeachment trial, 1805. My own appraisal is drawn from all these, and in particular from the sources cited in the following pages.

tempted to exploit secret information for private gain and at public loss; whereas later, as a justice of the United States Supreme Court, he was so vigorous in defending the Constitution against the kind of congressman he had been that new friends of the people conspired to impeach him.)[53]

As a rogue who exploited public trust, Chase pursued private gain, but he probably did so more because he enjoyed the role than because he really coveted its fruits. Whatever his motives, he led Maryland's proud and pretentious aristocrats by the nose for nearly a decade, and in the doing executed a dazzling series of maneuvers that accounted for most of the state's major policy decisions.[54]

In 1781–82, upon being recalled to answer for the scandals attending his conduct as a congressman, Chase appeared before a hostile legislature and so charmed and manipulated them that he emerged with full exoneration. Indeed, his most vehement enemy, the great planter and celebrated Roman Catholic statesman, Charles Carroll of Carrollton, emerged from the fracas tarred with Toryism—a fate that many of Chase's enemies would suffer.[55]

---

[53] On Chase's authorship of the Maryland constitution, see the sketch of Chase in the *Dictionary of American Biography;* Charles Carroll's letter to Chase in the *Maryland Gazette,* August 23, 30, 1781; and *Maryland Journal,* November 8, 1785. For the Constitution, see Thorpe, *Constitutions,* 3:1686. On the congressional episode see, in addition to the sources cited in footnote 52, the three "Publius" essays of Hamilton, October 19, 26, November 16, 1778, in Syrett and Cooke, eds., *Hamilton Papers,* 1:562–63, 567–70, 580–82. On the impeachment, see *Report of the Trial of Samuel Chase* (Baltimore, 1805).

[54] It should be pointed out that in the following narrative, though every detail is documented the interpretation put on the events is my own. Rarely does anyone say, in the sources cited, that Chase was doing what I say he was doing. But, though untangling Chase's complex doings is sometimes a difficult process, the evidence is abundant at each point.

[55] *Maryland Gazette,* June 21, August 23, 30, September 27, October 4, 11, 1781, January 3, 10, 24, February 14, 21, 1782; *Votes and Proceedings*

In the same session of the Assembly Chase guided to passage the legislation that would form the foundation of his subsequent operations, and also organized the coalition that would participate in them. The most important pieces of legislation were two. The first established the office of intendant of the revenues, lodging in one person complete control over the state's finances and fiscal policies. (To this office was appointed Daniel of St. Thomas Jenifer, a likable, harmless-appearing, and somewhat lecherous fifty-year-old bachelor who had held a similar position under the proprietors and had shrewd talents that belied his aspect.) The second act, which had been unsuccessfully agitated in previous sessions, deprived Loyalists of their rights as citizens, confiscated their property—whose total value was well over £500,000—and provided for the sale of the property at public auction.[56]

The coalition began with Chase himself. Next came John Dorsey, Chase's partner as both a lawyer and a merchant; Dorsey was appointed clerk to the commissioners of confiscated estates. Others included Luther Martin, who had,

---

of the House of Delegates, January 11–16, 1782. Chase's pseudonym for published writings on these matters was "Censor." See also James McHenry to Hamilton, January 31, 1782, and Hamilton to McHenry, February 26, March 8, 1782, in *Hamilton Papers,* 3:1, 2, 68.

[56] On the office of intendant, see *Votes and Proceedings of the House,* January 24, 1782; *Maryland Gazette,* January 24, 1782, May 29, June 19, 1783; the records of the intendant, preserved in the Maryland Hall of Records; and the data given below. On Jenifer, see sketches in Crowl, *Maryland During and After the Revolution,* 28–29; *Biographical Directory of Congress* (1927 edition), 1148; Pierce's sketches in Max Farrand, ed., *The Records of the Federal Convention of 1787* (3 vols., New Haven, 1911), 3:93; *Biographical Cyclopedia of Representative Men of Maryland and the District of Columbia* (Baltimore, 1879); and Mary W. Williams' sketch in the *Dictionary of American Biography.* For the confiscation act and its background see *Maryland Gazette,* March 3, 10, April 21, 28, 1780; and Kilty, comp., *Laws of Maryland,* October Session, 1780, chapter 45.

through Chase's influence, been appointed attorney-general in 1778; and Jeremiah T. Chase (no kin), mayor of Annapolis, and Thomas Stone of Charles County, a pair of lawyers who between them handled most of the civil actions in Maryland courts. Still others were Captain Charles Ridgely, a rich and powerful merchant whose political prowess made him almost the "boss" of Baltimore County; John Steret and David McMechen, two more Baltimore merchants who regularly represented the city in the Assembly; Allen Quynn, an Annapolis lawyer who was regularly returned as Chase's fellow assemblyman from Annapolis; Senators John Henry and John Hall, Assemblyman Perigrene Leatherbury, and William Paca, a wealthy eastern shore planter who was soon to become governor. Through this group Chase controlled every major aspect of the Maryland government except the courts and the Senate. (Lack of control of the courts was compensated in large measure by having the attorneys on both sides of most important suits. Lack of control of the Senate was more serious, for the Senate was dominated by wealthy planters in general and by Charles Carroll in particular.)[57]

The members of the group had several aspirations in com-

---

[57] *Maryland Gazette,* March 3, 1780, January 23, December 25, 1783, May 13, October 28, 1784, September 29, December 22, 1785, and especially August 24, 31, 1786; *Maryland Journal,* 1783–87, *passim; Votes and Proceedings of the House,* 1783–87, *passim; Biographical Directory of Congress,* 804; Crowl, "Anti-Federalism in Maryland," in the *William and Mary Quarterly,* 3d series, 4:446–69 (1947), and his monograph, *passim.* I have ascertained political affiliations by tabulating all votes recorded in the *Votes and Proceedings,* throughout the 1780s. As to Martin, the only published biography is Henry P. Goddard's *Luther Martin, the "Federal Bull Dog"* (Baltimore, 1887), which is grossly inadequate. Far better is the manuscript biography by Paul S. Clarkson of Baltimore, who kindly has made parts of his work available to me.

mon, such as the promotion of Baltimore and various pet reforms, and it was also held together by mutual hostility to
various enemies and a mutual back-scratching arrangement;
but the occasion for its formation was a much more tangible
operation. Chase organized these friends into a syndicate
for purchasing confiscated estates, with a view toward obtaining certain choice plantations and town lots and a huge
and lucrative ironworks, the total value of which was at least
£ 100,000 and probably as much as £ 200,000. The group
did not have between them anything like that much ready
cash, even if they were allowed to pay on the installment
plan and in depreciated public securities. But Chase had no
intention of paying anywhere near the actual value for the
properties. Instead, the syndicate bought at trivial prices
through the execution of a clever scheme.[58]

Under the terms of the confiscation act, commissioners
(to be appointed) were required to hold auctions at certain
specified times, receive the personal bonds of the highest
bidders for each item of property, and, through the clerk
(Chase's partner Dorsey), turn over the bonds and the
records of the auction to the intendant of the revenues. The
intendant was required to inspect these documents and, if
everything was in order, formally record the transactions on
the account books of the state. At the auctions of the properties desired by the Chase group, syndicate members or
their agents bid up prices recklessly and thereby discouraged
all competitors. The commissioners—who were not a part
of the scheme—complied with the law; but invariably, some-

---

[58] Commissioners' Ledger and Journal, 186–90, in Maryland Land Office,
Annapolis; Sale-Book of Confiscated British Property, 1781–85, pp. 30–32,
in Maryland Hall of Records, Annapolis; Crowl, *Maryland During and
After the Revolution,* 47–61, 128.

where between the consummation of the sale and the inspection by the intendant, "irregularities" were committed and discovered. Jenifer, as intendant, disallowed the sale. Through liberal interpretation of the law, he then arranged for a resale to the same buyers at a readjusted price. The average price for all the property sold without "irregularities" was about ten dollars an acre. The average price for all the property sold and resold because of irregularities was just over one dollar an acre, even though much of it was in valuable town lots and manufacturing property.[59]

So far so good. But now the syndicate members had to raise the money to pay for their purchases. To some of them this was no problem; others, like Chase himself and Luther Martin, were as negligent in handling their own money as they were in handling that of the public, and had to look about for funds. Chase's own share of the syndicate's purchases was £11,000 Maryland currency, or about $30,000. To obtain the money to pay the state for property he had all but stolen from it, he now hit upon a method by which the state itself would furnish the greater part of it. The colonial government of Maryland had owned stock in the Bank of England which, with dividends accrued since the outbreak of war, was worth around $200,000. So at Chase's suggestion the state sent him to England as its agent to attempt to recover these funds. If his mission failed he would receive nothing. If it succeeded he would receive four percent of the proceeds, or about $8,000. If he used this commission to buy state securities on the open market at the current rate of

---

[59] *Ibid.; Maryland Gazette,* October 5, 12, 19, 26, and especially November 2, 1786, wherein these facts were revealed by Gabriel Duvall, one of the commissioners.

depreciation, it could be stretched to pay for two-thirds to three-fourths of his obligation.[60]

As it turned out, he was unable to recover the stock—though, through the kindness of Jenifer and Governor Paca, he was reimbursed £500 for "expenses" nonetheless—but he came back with an even hotter deal. There resided in London a young gentleman named Henry Harford, who had been heir to proprietary lands in Maryland having annual rents of some £8,518, which had been confiscated along with the property of other Loyalists and proprietors. The chances of recovery were so completely nil that no one would have thought of bringing suit; indeed, there was no court in which to bring a suit, for Harford was not a citizen. But when Chase returned he began to press Harford's claims for him, having first readjusted the figures to pad them up to almost a million dollars—all the while retaining his public stance as the vigilant enemy of Tories, and all the while seeking funds with which to pay for confiscated property, which a commission from Harford would have done many times over. Right away, he succeeded in having the House pass a general relief law for "certain" Tories, by which Harford could sue the state in the Maryland courts, where the attorney against him would be Chase's cohort Luther Martin. The bill was killed in the Senate. Undaunted, Chase prepared to press Harford's claims directly in the next legislative session, convening in November 1785.[61]

But in the meantime, if the anti-Tory, proconfiscation party was to champion the cause of a Tory, the anti-Tory

---

[60] Crowl, *Maryland During and After the Revolution, passim; Maryland Gazette,* December 1, 8, 15, 1785.

[61] *Votes and Proceedings of the House,* January 14–20, December 6, 8, 1785; *Maryland Gazette,* December 1, 8, 15, 1785, January 19, 1786.

emotional electricity in the air had to be discharged. The simplest way to do that was to recharge the air with a new emotional issue. The issue chosen was religion: the House resolved to have printed for public discussion a bill providing for taxes to support the ministers of the Christian religion. The bill was ideally suited for its purpose. In addition to secretly delighting Chase and his friends by being somewhat anti-Catholic and therefore anti-Carroll, it stirred up Baptists against Episcopalians, both against Methodists, and all three against Catholics. In 1785 more lines of newspaper and pamphlet copy were printed in argument about this "issue" than had been devoted to any subject ever considered in Maryland. By year's end everyone was thoroughly enraged at everyone else, and anti-Toryism had been all but forgotten.[62]

As soon as the Assembly reconvened in November, the House (dismissing right away the bogus religious issue) voted to honor Harford' claims, at least in part. Almost simultaneously it voted also to pass another bill which, like the religious bill, had previously been the subject of virtually no pamphlets, articles, or petitions, and which like it would inflame the popular passions.[63] Unlike it, however, this one

---

[62] *Votes and Proceedings of the House,* January 8, 1785; *Maryland Journal,* January 18, 25, 28, February 8, March–April 1785; *Maryland Gazette,* throughout 1785, especially issues of January 20 and September 29. Just before the Revolution, Chase had led a fight *against* the established church. Barker, *Background of the Revolution,* 262–64.

[63] There had been occasional agitation in Baltimore for paper money just as the war ended in 1783, and a commercial bank was discussed there in 1784 (see the Baltimore *Maryland Journal,* February–March, November, December 1784); but otherwise little or nothing appeared on the subject in either Baltimore or Annapolis until the paper bill was introduced into the House in December 1785. Newspapers of both cities were rife with discussions of the bill throughout 1786. In *We the People: The Economic*

had substance and something tangible in it for the Chaseites: it was a bill to issue £300,000 in paper money, on essentially the same plan, and designed to appeal to essentially the same interest groups, as the act recently passed in Pennsylvania and the one about to be passed in New York. The principal difference was that it would also provide additional wherewithal to Chaseites for their operations in confiscated property.[64]

But Carroll and his allies in the Senate (notably his cousin Daniel Carroll, William Hindman, Edward Lloyd, and William Perry) stood poised not only to defeat these measures, but also to open a counterattack. They blocked passage of every major House bill of the session, took a passing shot at Chase himself over the question of the compensation for his junket to London, and then fired their major volley: they managed to abolish the office of intendant of the revenues.[65]

That blast struck at the very heart of the Chase group's operations, for as the senators were beginning to perceive, Jenifer's office had been a beehive of corrupt uses of public funds. The only way to restore it was by obtaining some measure of control over the Senate itself, which would re-

Origins of the Constitution (Chicago, 1958), 155, I erroneously stated that the 1785 paper bill would not have been usable for payment of confiscated property. That is true only of the 1786–87 bill, about to be discussed.

[64] *Votes and Proceedings of the House,* November 19, December 1, 8, 13, 22, 1785.

[65] *Votes and Proceedings of the Senate,* January 14, 15, 16, 18, 1785, showing the Senate's earlier opposition to Chase, and March 2, 12, 1786, the most effective pieces of anti-Chase activity in the November 1785 session. See also the *Votes and Proceedings of the House* for the same session, and *Maryland Gazette,* April 20, June 22, July 13, 1786.

quire a net gain of four or five of the fifteen Senate seats. Senators were chosen biennially by popularly elected electors; the next such election was coming up in six months— September 1786. The campaign was bitter. The Carroll group dropped many hints, but did not openly charge, that the Chaseites had been guilty of corrupt practices. The Chaseites endorsed everything that could pass as a popular cause, but concentrated their efforts on a battle of personalities.[66]

The outcome was ambiguous, but it portended a black day for the Carroll group. The Chase faction clearly retained control of the House, and Chase himself became a senatorial elector. The electors returned the two Carrolls but also returned Chase's two staunchest supporters, and they unseated six senators, all or almost all of whom had been enemies of Chase. Some, at least, of the new senators were known members of the inner Chase clique; others were uncommitted.[67]

---

[66] That the Chase group had got in over its head and sorely needed the intendant's office is indicated by the report on confiscated property in the *Votes and Proceedings of the House,* January 10, 1786, showing that buyers of confiscated property had paid only £46,991 toward total purchases of £454,181 (after commissions and costs); and Jenifer's public notices of April 28, 1785, published in the *Maryland Gazette,* May 5, 1785, extending until July 10 the deadline for buyers to post bonds (which should have been posted years before), and making the bonds redeemable on January 1, 1790—in short, giving buyers a five-year extension. For the campaign of 1786, see the *Maryland Gazette,* August 17, 24, 31, September 7, 14, 1786, and the *Maryland Journal* for the same period.

[67] The returns of electors are reported in the *Maryland Gazette,* September 14, and the elections by the electors on September 21, 1786. To ascertain factional affiliations of the outgoing and incoming senators, I have correlated all votes recorded in the *Votes and Proceedings* for all members in both houses; and on Senate votes disagreeing with Chase-inspired House votes, compared votes in the two houses.

Immediately after the election (and two months before the new Assembly convened) the Carroll faction determined to seize the initiative and take no chances. Abandoning their policy of merely hinting that corruption existed, they began to fire charges and make revelations. That set off a powder keg. Each revelation produced another, for people who had committed minor misdeeds scurried to protect themselves by disclosing the larger misdeeds of others. By the time the Assembly convened, the air reeked with scandal, and in one way or another most of it implicated Jenifer, Chase, and their friends.[68]

To fight back, the Chaseites adopted a tactic that would forever prove useful to American politicians caught with their hands in the till. They invented a popular cause—paper money—and used it as a vehicle for denouncing their own foes as enemies of the people and defenders of entrenched privilege. The paper bill, which differed significantly from the bill of a year earlier, was brilliantly drawn. In the first place, it was "clean," offering not a hint of profits to its sponsors. (Indeed, had it passed—and they had no intention that it should—the results would have been disastrous to the Chase group.) Second, it promised something for everyone, public creditors, farmers, the state itself, and the Union. Finally, it contained certain flaws that made it impossible for the Senate to approve it. The Senate countered with a proposal virtually identical, but lacking the objectionable features. The House refused to "compromise," and took its case to the people.[69]

---

[68] *Maryland Gazette,* October 5, 12, 19, 26, November 2, 16, 23, 30, December 28, 1786.

[69] *Votes and Proceedings of the House,* December 2, 12, 15, 1786; draft of the bill, in *Maryland Gazette,* January 11, 1787; address of the House

The Carroll group refused to go for the bait: the scandals had pushed the wavering senators into their camp, and they refused to argue the secondary issue, continuing instead to lash out at corruption. Audaciously, the Chaseites determined that if the Senate would not fight, they would invent a fight. They forged a letter over Charles Carroll's signature, purporting to prove that Carroll had huge amounts out at interest and was quietly bribing senators and others to oppose paper money and thereby protect his loans, and they conveniently "intercepted" this letter and released it to the press. Then they followed this maneuver by an outlandish one. They took the issue to the grand juries (which were held in March), and though these bodies had nothing to do with the matter, several adopted resolutions demanding that the Senate follow the "popular will" and vote for the House's paper plan. A few senators publicly protested that the grand juries had no right to instruct the Senate, whereupon the Chaseites seized the moment to proclaim that the Senate was pretending that it was not responsible to the will of the people.[70]

---

of Delegates to their constituents, *ibid.,* January 25, 1787. That the Chase group did not intend for the act to pass is my inference; it seems obvious from the terms of the act, which would have been ruinous to the group. During the session they quietly took care of themselves, at least temporarily, by an act suspending executions for "public assessments" until May 1787 (*Gazette,* February 1, 1787), and by a resolution postponing executions for nonpayment of confiscated property bonds until the Court of Appeals should decide whether the obligations could be paid in certain depreciated securities (*ibid.,* January 10, 1787, and a further resolution recorded in *Votes and Proceedings of the House,* May 24, 1787). The court ruled in their favor in 1788; *Maryland Gazette,* May 29, 1788. For these reasons, Crowl's interpretation of the paper money bill of 1786–87, in his otherwise excellent book, seems to me to be untenable. See *We the People,* 154–55, and footnote 64, above.

[70] *Maryland Journal,* March 2, 1787; Maryland Gazette, February 22, March 8, 15, 22, 29, April 5, 26, May 3, 1787.

By April, when the Assembly reconvened in special session, the Chase faction had completely confused the issue.
They were unable to gain Senate concurrence to a bill designed to reestablish Jenifer in office, but they did the next
best thing: they drove through both houses a number of bills
postponing collection of obligations due on purchases of
confiscated estates and certain other debts. They also
thoroughly frustrated a series of reform measures initiated
in the Senate. As a result, the political pendulum hung at
dead center.[71]

The Earl of Cornwallis had sought, during his occupation
of South Carolina, to give the proud and ungrateful local
aristocrats their just deserts. No one, in the Earl's eyes,
deserved a comeuppance more. The great wealth of the
South Carolina planters, the material foundation of their
arrogant pride, stemmed more from the bounties of nature
and the British Parliament than from anything the South
Carolinians had done to earn it. And they had repaid the
mother country for several generations of privileged treatment by joining heartily in a move to break from the parent
and make war upon it. (Had the Earl known why they did
so, he would have been even more put out with them. Their
cardinal motive was neither idealism nor gain, but sheer

---

[71] See *Votes and Proceedings of the House,* April Session, 1787, especially
votes of May 10, 24, and 26; see also footnote 69, above, and *Votes and
Proceedings of the Senate* for the same session. After this session, various
individuals continued to air their personal feuds in the newspapers, but
otherwise the papers were strangely silent throughout the year—as if
everyone was holding his breath while the Philadelphia Convention met.
There was not even any newspaper argument over the elections to the
House of Delegates in September 1787. Chase, having moved to Baltimore
by that time, ran with his cohort David McMechen for reelection to the
House, and they defeated McHenry and Rogers by about three to one;
Maryland Journal, October 5, 1787.

vanity. Their view had been that if the other colonies were going to have themselves a revolution, it was only proper that South Carolina should furnish leaders, South Carolina planters being so much better qualified to lead than was anyone else.)[72]

Cornwallis' slap on the wrist consisted of the confiscation of the property of the forty-five leading Whig planters, the incarceration on filthy prison ships of an additional twenty-six, the pillaging and wanton destruction of plantations throughout the low country, and the theft of some 25,000 slaves, about a fourth of the state's work force. As it turned out, that was not enough, for the planters had toughness and resourcefulness to match their arrogance. Though their economy was thoroughly crushed, they were not. When the British were at last forced to move out they moved back in and resumed command of the political and social order, and did so with such easy confidence and insolent grace that one might have thought they were unaware that everything about them lay in ruin.[73]

The task of reconstruction was no easy one at best, and

---

[72] On the favored treatment of South Carolina, see Gray, *History of Agriculture*, 1:284–87, 291–92. The remainder of the paragraph is my own surmise, drawn from the absence of tangible motives and from the character of the aristocracy, as seen through study of the works cited in footnote 2, above; of David Ramsay's *History of South Carolina* (2 vols., Newberry, S. C., 1858); of a host of such works as Frederick P. Bowles' *The Culture of Early Charleston* (Chapel Hill, 1942), Alberta Lachincotte's *Georgetown Rice Plantations* (Columbia, 1955), and Elizabeth Allston Pringle's *Chronicles of Chicora Wood* (Boston, 1940); of the files of the *South Carolina Historical and Genealogical Magazine;* and of the *South Carolina & American General Gazette* for the 1760s and 1770s, the *Royal South Carolina Gazette* for the 1770s, and the *Gazette of the State of South Carolina, the Charleston Evening Gazette,* and the *Charleston Morning Post* for the 1780s; as well as the sources cited hereafter.

[73] The confiscation edicts and the imprisonment edicts are published in the *Royal South Carolina Gazette,* November 27, 1780, and the *Pennsyl-*

the immediate circumstances made it far less so. Cornwallis had little option in his departure, but had he had all the time in the world he could hardly have chosen a moment more awkward for the South Carolinians. The evacuation was completed in December 1782. When it was over, there remained in Charleston a considerable number of British merchants whose inventories included something over two million dollars' worth of goods, slaves, and provisions. As the troops were leaving, these merchants petitioned the South Carolina government to be allowed to stay in Charleston long enough to dispose of their stocks. The returning planters, whatever their feelings, were little able to refuse. It was imperative that they get provisions and materials in time for planting in March and April, for otherwise they would be without income until the harvests of November–December 1784, two full years away, and it was too late in the season to be able to order adequate stores from abroad. In the absence of the legislature Governor John Matthews and the Privy Council authorized the merchants to remain for six months (actually they remained almost a year). The merchants, being on a tenuous footing and having suffered large losses when the departing British soldiers left without paying their debts, understandably charged all the traffic would bear. It bore plenty: they sold their stocks to the planters at approximately twice their value, and for credit they charged interest as high as seventy-five percent.[74]

---

vania Packet, January 2, 30, 1781. On other losses, see Gray, *History of Agriculture,* 2:595–96. The confidence with which the planters returned is implicit in their willingness to take on huge debts, as is about to be narrated.

[74] Governor Matthews message to the legislature, published in the *Pennsylvania Packet,* April 3, 1783, and the South Carolina news reports in the same, January 13, June 19, 1783; John L. Gervais to Leonard DeNeufville, April 13, 1786, in Gervais and Owen Papers, Library of Congress; "Diary

South Carolina thus began its period of independence with its dominant class in debt more than $2 million, nearly a full year's average production. Considering the disrupted conditions attending their planting, crops that year were not bad, amounting to perhaps two-thirds of normal. Boundlessly confident, the planters imported more the next spring than ever before: they purchased about $3 million in liquors, fineries, and necessities, and more than 4,000 slaves, costing over $750,000.[75] But because they were still short of slaves, they put as many acres as possible under indigo instead of rice; and the limited rice crops turned out well but the indigo crop was a disastrous failure. The result was that by the end of 1784 the planters staggered under a tremendous burden of debt. When the spring importations of 1785 were added to the deficit, the total was more than $8 million, roughly a third of the total value of all property in the South Carolina low country. (So great were these problems that South Carolina's public debts and confiscated property, though of a magnitude that would have set off orgiastic

---

of Timothy Ford," in the *South Carolina Historical and Genealogical Magazine*, 12:193 (1912); *Acts and Ordinances of the General Assembly of the State of South Carolina* (Charleston, by sessions), acts of October 26, 1782, March 12, 1783.

[75] There has long been confusion about how many slaves were imported into South Carolina after the war; estimates have ranged as high as 25,000. My own tabulations from the customs records in the South Carolina Archives show something over 6,000 slaves imported between May 1784 and September 1787. A contemporary tabulation, that by a writer styling himself "R" (*Charleston Morning Post*, February 28, 1787), yielded the figure 8,737, but this is probably accurate, for it covers a somewhat different period, January 1783 to January 1787. The customs records for the period prior to May 1784 are no longer extant. Putting the figures of "R" together with my own tabulations, it would appear that the total number of slaves imported after the war (the importation of slaves was prohibited by South Carolina for a succession of three-year terms extending from 1787 to 1803) was about 10,000.

speculation in other states—or crushed them—simply did not enter as active political or economic elements.)[76]

Lesser folk were faring much better. The farmers and small planters in the interior had suffered relatively trivial damages at the hands of the British army, they did not take on large debts in 1783, and in the immediate postwar years they expanded production with great rapidity. Their rise was clearly visible through the growing importance of their staple, tobacco, as a portion of the total production of the state. In 1760 tobacco produced in South Carolina had been worth only 0.04 percent as much as the rice crop; by 1769 it was 0.5 percent as valuable; by 1783, 8 percent; by 1785, 11 percent; and by 1787 no less than 28 percent. In addition, back-country residents made considerable profits from increases in the prices and output of lumber, skins, and provisions. And for special reasons, South Carolina merchants found it advantageous to offer them unusually favorable marketing terms, and thereby added to their prosperity.[77]

---

[76] Books of Manifests and Entries, 1784–85, 1785–87, in South Carolina Archives, Columbia; "R," in the *Charleston Morning Post,* February 28, 1787; *Charleston Evening Gazette,* September 14, 1785, and John Rutledge's remarks as quoted in the same, September 28, 1785; *Pennsylvania Packet,* May 4, 1785. Debt is here estimated by comparing the imports, as derived from the foregoing sources, with the exports, as recorded in Port of Charleston, Account of Exports, 1782–86, in the South Carolina Archives; values were figured on the basis of price quotations in the several Charleston newspapers. On public debts and confiscated property, see the Report of the Ways and Means Committee of the House of Representatives, in *Charleston Morning Post,* February 20, 1786. As to planting indigo instead of rice, if one reckons prices, as recorded in newspapers, and figures the comparative output per slave for the two crops, as given in Gray, *History of Agriculture,* 1:284–97, indigo appears to have been twice as profitable in the 1780s.

[77] These data are drawn from the sources cited in footnote 76, and from Port of Charleston, Account of Exports, 1787, in South Carolina Archives;

The special reasons arose from the unfortunate circumstances in which South Carolina merchants found themselves at the end of the war. These were pathetic creatures in the best of times, for in South Carolina a merchant had to cow-tow to a planter's every whim, even if the merchant had money to buy and sell the planter twenty times over. And these were scarcely the best of times. The British merchants who remained after the evacuation took virtually all the lucrative business during 1783. As they left, their places were taken by the resident South Carolina factors, whose business was to act as agents for merchants in England. The South Carolina merchants, unable to extend the large credit demanded by the situation, were ill-equipped to compete, and accordingly lost an excellent opportunity for the kinds of profits that would have ensured their own quick recovery. Unsurprisingly, their bitterness toward the British, the British-connected factors, and the planters who patronized them was devout. Less expectedly, they formed a secret organization called the Marine Anti-Britannic Society, which directed a terroristic campaign against their enemies. Throughout the last half of 1783, nocturnal arson, assault, and even murder stalked the streets of Charleston.[78]

The violence abated briefly during the winter, but just

South Carolina & American General Gazette, November of each year, 1760–69. The location of tobacco planting is implicit in sites of tobacco warehouses, as stipulated in an act of March 25, 1785—three in Charleston, one each in Beaufort and Georgetown, and twelve on or above the fall line. See also Gray, *History of Agriculture,* 2:605–6.

[78] See the various Charleston newspapers, throughout 1783, especially the *South Carolina Weekly Gazette,* July–September 1783, and the *Gazette of the State of South Carolina,* August–December 1783; Philadelphia *Freeman's Journal,* October 23, 1783. See also footnotes 79 and 81, below.

then the planters took action that set it off again. They had hoped to negotiate the return of many of their slaves, but had been informed by the British in Florida that they could expect no restitution unless the confiscated property of Loyalists was restored. Accordingly, early in 1784 they caused the passage of amercement legislation. This pro-Tory stand did nothing to endear them to the merchants, and besides, a number of patriot merchants had bought confiscated mercantile property which they were now faced with losing. In April the explosive situation exploded: someone burned down the store of two prominent merchants and Society members, and the merchants assumed it had been Tories or Tory sympathizers. They retaliated with a new wave of destruction. Violence reached a peak in July, when riots occurred almost nightly, but it continued sporadically until winter.[79]

The aristocracy, having no particular love for either merchants or factors, tended nonetheless to side with the factors because they continued to need long-term credit and also because they reckoned the merchants responsible for the violence. A complex series of personal incidents drew them definitely into the conflict during the year. The merchants (styling themselves Republicans and denouncing their enemies as Nabobs) elicited and in some measure found political support from the middle- and up-country farmers. The planters could sneer at any such efforts to oppose them politically, for the constitutional apportionment of representation gave them roughly one legislative seat for every

---

[79] *Gazette of the State of South Carolina,* April 22, 29, May 6, 13, 20, 27, July 1, 15, 17, 22, August 5, 9, 12, 19, September 9, 1784; *Charleston Morning Post,* March 4, 25, 1786; *Philadelphia Freeman's Journal,* June 9, 1784; *Acts and Ordinances,* act of March 26, 1784.

fifty planter families,[80] against which the merchants were hopelessly outnumbered, even had they been able to obtain unanimous support in every city and in every district above the low country.[81]

After the crop failure of 1784, however, all but the proudest planters began to grow uneasy. If the crop of 1785 were a bumper, all would be well. If it failed, the crisis would reach emergency proportions, and in view of the fiercely hostile relations between the state's various social groups, civil war was not beyond possibility. In mid-1785 the pressure was unexpectedly eased: the merchants were suddenly thriving, largely as a result of unprecedentedly voluminous trade with the prosperous back country and with merchants in the booming states of North Carolina and Georgia. Upon the arrival of prosperity they dropped their radical activities, and upon the loss of that stimulus the back country ceased to show any interest in state politics.[82]

But then the crops failed and failed dismally. By late Au-

---

[80] The Constitution of 1778 required reapportionment in 1785, and the legislature nominally complied in that year, but the changes made were insignificant.

[81] *Gazette of the State of South Carolina,* April 29, May 13, July 15, October 7, December 6, 1784, February 24, March 3, 1785. On apportionment, the classic work is William A. Shaper's "Sectionalism and Representation in South Carolina," in American Historical Association *Annual Report,* 1900 (Washington, 1901), 245–463; see also Singer, *South Carolina in the Confederation,* 37 and *passim.*

[82] The tension and general switch in positions and moods are reflected in the various Charleston newspapers, May–August 1785. In May, for example, the Marine Anti-Britannic Society changed its name to the South Carolina Marine Society; in August, the city's merchants were meeting in the Chamber of Commerce to cooperate in dealing with national commercial problems.

gust, it was clear that they would fail, and Governor Benjamin Guerard called an emergency session of the legislature "to consider the state of the Republic." The merchants cringed, for such a session portended debtor relief legislation that would do them no good. They did more than cringe; they began discreetly to tuck their money away in safe places. Hard money all but disappeared, and prices plummeted accordingly, compounding an already bad situation.[83]

About a hundred legislators, almost all from the low country (the back country did not even bother to send representatives), gathered in Charleston on September 27, 1785. Under the leadership of the Rutledges, the Pinckneys, Ralph Izard, Pierce Butler, and others high in the aristocracy, the legislature enacted a radical debtor-relief program over the feeble protests or resignation of the merchants and back-country planters. The most important law provided for the issuance of £100,000 ($428,571) in paper money, to be lent on real estate mortgages of three times the sum borrowed. Another was the Pine Barren Act, by which debtors were privileged to tender worthless lands in payment of debts and, if the creditor refused to accept the lands, to refuse to pay until the act expired a year later. Various minor relief laws followed. Great strain ensued in the spring, when the paper money was actually issued, for rumors were rife that the planters intended to use it to pay debts at par,

---

[83] *Gazette of the State of South Carolina,* September 19, October 3, October 27, 1785; *Charleston Evening Gazette,* September 28–October 8, 1785; *Charleston Morning Post,* May 6, 1786; Journal of the House of Representatives, September 1785, in South Carolina Archives; *Maryland Gazette,* July 7, 1785; George R. Taylor, "Wholesale Commodity Prices at Charleston, South Carolina, 1732–1791," in *Journal of Economic and Business History,* 4:356–77 (1932).

but deliberately adopt a policy that would rapidly depreciate it. After a tense month during which the merchants
exerted every moral suasion within their reach to make the
planters join them in supporting the paper, it appeared and
began to circulate at or near its face value. As if by magic,
specie came from hiding, prices rose, and the worst appeared
to be over. (Meanwhile the merchants, unable to do anything more and grateful that the legal action had not been
worse, quietly took it. One of them, Alexander Gillon, a
merchant, devout patriot, and erstwhile leader of mobs,
darkly warned that the relief laws would ultimately expire,
and when they did, he said, it would "be in the power of the
merchants to sue almost the whole of the country." Uncon-
vinced, many of the richest planters went about openly
buying up their own notes at a fraction of their face value.)[84]

The crop of 1786, harvested in the late fall and marketed
during the first few months of 1787, was somewhat better
than its predecessor, and because of a considerable rise in
prices, it sold for much more. Consequently, during the
1786–87 season the state had a net favorable balance of
trade of about $800,000, the first favorable balance since
the peace. Planters began to foresee being able to retire
their debts within three years—though hardly sooner—and
early in 1787 they enacted a legislative program designed

---

[84] The debates are carried in detail in the *Charleston Evening Gazette,*
September 30–October 18, 1785; the legislation in *Acts, Ordinances, and
Resolves,* October 1785; on the matters of circulation of the paper, the
negotiations between merchants and planters over supporting it, and the
return of specie, see *Charleston Morning Post,* April 25–27, May 2, 6, 8,
23, July 12, August 4, 1786; the Gillon quotation is in both the *Post* and
the *Evening Gazette,* March 23, 1786; for a description of planters buying
their own notes, see Arthur Bryan to George Bryan, April 9, 1788, in
George Bryan Papers, Historical Society of Pennsylvania.

with that in mind. They prohibited the importation of slaves for three years, prohibited the effective collection of debts during the same period, and otherwise geared the law to South Carolina's complete recovery in 1790. And to no one's surprise, that was the way it worked out.[85]

The history of South Carolina in the half-decade after the war had many causes but few effects. It settled no problems, it changed nothing. But it illustrated something: that now, as before the war and for as long in the future as anyone could see, the South Carolina aristocrats would do as they pleased, come what may. And unless someone on the outside should rub them the wrong way—as the king had in the 1760s—they would please to work for a stronger Union.

[85] Port of Charleston, Account of Exports, 1787, and Book of Manifests, 1785–87, in South Carolina Archives; comparative prices in *Gazette of the State of South Carolina,* December 22, 1785, January 30, August 7, October 16, 1786; John Drayton, *A View of South Carolina, As Respects Her Natural and Civil Concerns* (Charleston, 1802), 168, 173; *Charleston Morning Post,* February 28, March 15, 29, 1787; *Acts, Ordinances, and Resolves,* March 1787.

Chapter Four

Completion
of the Revolution:
The Eastern States

Clichés about the South seemed especially valid when viewed from the vantage point of New England. In return, Southerners could have cited some clichés about Yankees. Most were variations on a theme of littleness: Yankees were puritanical, stern, brittle; stingy, greedy, shrewd; vulgar, mean, democratic. They were the negation of magnanimity, of elegance, of taste: they drove sharp bargains, were too busy, talked too fast and through their noses, built fences of stone as if man's days on earth were not numbered. And above all, there were so many of them.

These things were about as true as what New Englanders thought of Southerners, which is to say, not very; for Yankees differed from one another almost as much as Southerners did. And yet, if you placed a group of Yankees together—any Yankees—side by side with a group of Southerners—any Southerners—you could distinguish the two groups at a glance, and see that somehow the Southerners were all alike, and so were the Yankees. However difficult it may have been to define or even to demonstrate the difference, it was there.

The difference and the sameness were equally visible in

the countrysides from which Southerners and Yankees came; so nearly did the men reflect their environments that they might have been vegetation. This could be true partly because man had not yet learned the tricks that would convince him he was master of his environment. It could also be true because Anglo-Americans had set out to fashion themselves and their societies in the image of God, and that image was shaped (whatever the Scriptures might say) by the tangible evidence of Him in Nature. As it happened, Nature had been as generous in the South as she was parsimonious in New England. Accordingly, to the Southerner the evidence said that God was a decent, easygoing chap; to the Yankee, it said that God was a harsh, vindictive old man who was always putting people on trial. The identity of New Englanders lay in sharing the same problem with Nature. The differences between them lay in their different institutional compromises with that problem.

From the 1760s to the 1790s, most of New England had nothing but trouble. Now, to say that anybody's troubles are "basically" this or that is a tricky business, but if the Yankees' problems were basically anything, it was that in each of the four communities—Connecticut, New Hampshire, Rhode Island, and Massachusetts—the institutional compromises had ceased to work. There was every material reason for them to change their ways, for a transition to manufacturing from a life based upon tilling the soil and sailing the seas could have been relatively simple. But when ways become institutionalized they become invisible, and lead men to solutions that worsen problems instead of solving them. Roots and habits ran too deep in New England, and doing things differently—leaving one's land or the sea, even changing towns or occupations—involved a wrench painful

in the extreme. So painful, indeed, was its mere contempla-
tion that for two generations New Englanders were willing
to effect political revolutions to avoid facing it.

For a hundred years people in Connecticut had made
their living by selling one another land. The life cycle of a
settlement began with the sale of a large tract by the General
Assembly to a group of two or three dozen proprietors.
Normally a few proprietors held their land in absentia and
sold it off piecemeal without ever seeing it, but most became
actual settlers. The settling proprietors kept far more than
they could ever farm, and sold the remainder in large parcels
to other settlers. The proprietors thus became men of surplus wealth and their customers became great landowners,
and thereby the first generation was prosperous and har-
monious. In subsequent generations the land was further
divided until it became crowded with small farms; and then
the descendants of the original proprietors and settlers, using the surpluses earned by their forebears, moved away to
become proprietors and early settlers elsewhere. And so on,
ad finitum.[1]

The system had finite limits because the supply of land
was finite and the birthrate was just barely so. The birthrate
in Connecticut would have sent a Malthusian into raptures

---

[1] There is no good general treatise on the land system in Connecticut, but
an excellent recent monograph, though intensively focused on a single
town, provides a general education in the subject: Charles Grant's *Democracy in the Connecticut Frontier Town of Kent* (New York, 1961). See
also Roy H. Akagi, *The Town Proprietors of the New England Colonies*
(Philadelphia, 1924), which has been corrected by Grant's study; and
A. L. Olson's "Agricultural Economy and the Population in Eighteenth-
Century Connecticut," vol. 40, and various others of the *Tercentenary
Publications in the History of Connecticut* (60 vols., New Haven, 1936).

of pessimism: a Connecticut family with eight children was small, twelve to fifteen was the norm, and twenty was not unusual. At that pace, original proprietors could watch their towns fill to overflowing in their own lifetimes.[2]

By the middle of the eighteenth century large blocs of Connecticut towns had become overcrowded. Such vacant land as remained in the colony was eaten up in another generation or two by the lucky ones who could continue to play the proprietors' game. Those who stayed at home, instead of changing their ways in the face of a steadily declining amount of land per family, adapted so as to be able to continue as farmers and yet continue to live. This was possible because of the nature of the colony's soil: only about a sixth of it was arable, and perhaps a third was unimproved and unimprovable rock and brush land. The remaining half, while too poor for the plow, was adequate for grazing, and in the decade or two before the Revolution Connecticut changed from a colony of plow farmers into one of stock farmers, their specialty being the raising of horses for export to the West Indies. Only in the rich lands of the Connecticut River Valley, where good crops of tobacco and wheat were grown, did the plow continue to yield appreciably; and even there, because population was greatest (the arable land being less than one acre per farm inhabitant), only supplementary horse-raising made continued survival possible. Survival, however, was conditional upon the market, for by the 1770s Connecticut no longer grew enough foodstuffs to feed its inhabitants. Thus it preserved the form of rural life, the one-family farm, but lost its psychological substance: the insular security derived

[2] Grant, *Town of Kent, passim;* Olson, "Agriculture and the Population." The generalization on the birthrate is based also on calculations made from *Census of 1790, Heads of Families: Connecticut.*

from the belief that however bad outside economic conditions become, one can always live from the food and shelter of one's own land.[3]

Merchants and traders adapted to this transition. It was easy enough to do so; all that was involved was a minor adjustment of markets and sources of supply. But the doing necessitated one physical change that rendered future adaptability extremely difficult. Conventional hulls—whether of sloops, schooners, brigs, or ships, the standard American forms of rigging—were suitable for almost any kind of cargo except live animals. Transporting of horses required specially built bottoms that were ill-designed for any other kinds of cargo save possibly slaves, and Connecticuters no longer had the stomach for that branch of commerce. When the transition was complete, Connecticut merchants seemed doomed to be horsetraders forever.[4]

---

[3] These generalizations are drawn from tabulations and study of Property Evaluation of 1785, in Finance and Currency, vol. V, page 229a, and Trade and Maritime Affairs, series 1, part 2, p. 183a, both manuscript volumes in Connecticut Archives, Hartford; New Haven port records, 1760s and 1780s, National Archives; Jacob Sebor to Silas Deane, November 10, 1784, in *Deane Papers,* 204; annual reports of exports published in the various Connecticut newspapers (e.g., Hartford *Connecticut Courant,* January 6, 1786; *The Middlesex Gazette,* January 22, 1787; and New London *Connecticut Gazette,* January 4, 1788); and the descriptions of the Connecticut economy in the series of articles by "Phil-Pat" and "Policy of Connecticut," published in the *Connecticut Gazette* beginning late in 1783 and running to mid-1784. See also William B. Weeden, *Economic and Social History of New England* (2 vols., Boston, 1891), vol. 2, *passim.*

[4] The adjustment is implicit in the commercial documents cited in footnote 3. The statement regarding hull design was partly inferred from the same sources, but the problems of design were kindly and excellently explained to me by James D. Phillips of the Essex Institute. No Connecticut vessels appear in the Books of Manifests and Entries in the South Carolina Archives, which record virtually all slave importations into South Carolina after the Revolution—and that was the only place, with small exceptions in Savannah, which imported slaves after the war.

By mid-century in some towns, and by the 1770s in most of them, even this palliative was exhausted. Social tension mounted accordingly, often to the exploding point. The most common form of explosion (not unexpectedly, considering Connecticut's origins and traditions) was religious frenzy of one sort and another.[5] Revivalism, awakenings, and embracing of radical sects cropped out sporadically until they had gathered enough momentum to set off a colonywide religious controversy, the celebrated battle of the New Lights and the Old Lights.[6]

So much for the common folks. The less common, who likewise grew restive, were of two kinds: those who believed that relief lay in the acquisition by Connecticut of lands elsewhere, and those who sought broadened commercial opportunities. The first would seek to validate the colony's tenuous charter-derived claims to vacant lands (in Pennsylvania, New York, and what became Vermont and

---

[5] It was long supposed by historians that it was in the newer, frontier areas that religious radicalism was most manifest, but the reverse now appears to have been true—that is, that it appeared primarily in the most thickly populated towns. Charles Grant, in his *Democracy in the Connecticut Frontier Town of Kent* (New York, 1961), suggests this, and his work implicitly offers a reason: that overpopulation bred idleness and the kind of restless insecurity that goes with it, and religion offered the easiest available outlet.

[6] See Clarence C. Goen, *Revivalism and Separatism in New England, 1740–1800* (New Haven, 1962); Oscar Zeichner, *Connecticut's Years of Controversy, 1750–1776* (Chapel Hill, 1949); and various of the pamphlets in the *Tercentenary Publications in the History of Connecticut,* particularly Olson's "Agricultural Economy and the Population," vol. 40, and Mary H. Mitchell's "The Great Awakening and Other Revivals in the Religious Life of Connecticut," vol. 26. Mr. John Bumstead, a graduate student at Brown University, has made sample studies of towns all over southern New England and found a high correlation between density of population and age of settlement on the one hand and religious (and to some extent political) radicalism on the other.

Ohio), and promote land companies to resettle local inhabitants, thus doing a service to Connecticut and, in the
process, earning the promoters a tidy profit. The second
saw relaxation or dissolution of the commercial system of
the British Empire as a means to an end, the transformation
of Connecticut into a manufacturing center. The groups
shared two characteristics. Both sought goals that ran directly counter to policies and laws laid down in London.
Both, like the common people they led, rationalized their
material aims into spiritual values—the difference being
that they embraced radical republicanism rather than radical religious movements.[7]

Upon the winning of independence, Connecticut's leaders
pressed forward in search of solutions to the local problems
that had brought them into the Revolution. The reasons

[7] Primary sources on Connecticut's land operators and their efforts to
obtain lands are abundant; see particularly Julian P. Boyd's edition of the
Susquehanna Company Papers (4 vols., Wilkes-Barre, 1930–34); Archer
B. Hulbert, ed., *The Records of the Original Proceedings of the Ohio Company* (2 vols., Marietta, 1917); the Pickering Papers in the Massachusetts
Historical Society; the various Connecticut and Philadelphia newspapers,
1785–86, especially the articles in the *Connecticut Courant,* beginning
January 4, 1785, and the issues of March 6, April 3, and September 18,
1786. See also Boyd's articles, "The Susquehanna Company," in *Connecticut Tercentenary Commission Publications* (New Haven, 1935), "The
Susquehanna Company, 1753–1803," in *Journal of Economic and Business
History,* vol. 4 (1931), and "Attempts to Form New States in New York
and Pennsylvania, 1786–1796," in the *Quarterly Journal of the New York
State Historical Association,* 12:258–63 (1931). More on this and other
subjects dealt with in the foregoing paragraph is to be found sprinkled
through Leonard W. Labaree, ed., *The Public Records of the State of
Connecticut,* vols. 4 and 5, and the various Connecticut newspapers
throughout the years from the 1760s to the 1790s. For a good example
of those who thought manufacturing was the answer, see the "Phil-Pat"
articles in the *Connecticut Gazette,* cited in footnote 3. For a debate on the
subject, see the proceedings of the General Assembly, as reported in the
New Haven Gazette, October 19, 1786.

were all the more pressing for solving them by changing the economy, for switching from agriculture and a land-selling system to manufacturing. To the basic ingredients— an abundance of convenient sources of water power and a surplus of skilled and semi-skilled labor—was now added a potential catalyst, the relatively huge continental and state debt held in Connecticut. Except for one obstacle, the time was ripe for promoting manufacturing through protective duties, bounties, and other mercantilist devices, and for making it financially possible by funding both forms of debt. The one drawback was that because of the design of the state's fleet, local merchants had to import through New York instead of from abroad, and so Connecticut was no more able to control its own commerce than it had been in prewar days. The public debt, unsupported by convenient and regular revenue from import duties, was thus a burden instead of an asset. The state attempted to levy and collect direct taxes on land to support the debt, but the effort was vain. Indeed, many public creditors suffered the absurd experience of having their farms sold for nonpayment of taxes that had been levied to pay them interest on their securities.[8]

The way out was obvious: the creation of a national government that would change the burden into a boon. For a

---

[8] The foregoing is drawn from a manuscript volume in the Connecticut Archives, Finance and Currency, 5:180, 190, 194a, 200, 204, 226, 245, 265, 273, 277; and from a series of letters by Erastus Wolcott in the *Middlesex Gazette,* February 5–21, 1787, and in the *Connecticut Courant,* February 9, 23, 1787; "Policy of Connecticut," in the *Connecticut Gazette,* April 23, 1784; advertisements for tax sales in all three newspapers, 1786–87; and Labaree, ed., *Records of Connecticut,* 5:37, 131, 278, 327, 375, 432–33, 6:11–18, 36, 152, 174, 291, 292. See also the sources cited in footnote 3.

moment toward the end of the war it appeared that persons so believing would prevail in Connecticut. The number and wealth of such persons—primarily merchants and entrepreneurs—had grown through the business of privateering and profiteering in army supply. They also had some cohesiveness, being connected in various ways with Jeremiah Wadsworth, and they had strong support among the many officers and men that Connecticut had furnished for Washington's armies. But this prospect died in the wake of the fiascoes of 1783, thanks to the feverish popular reaction against the formation of the Society of the Cincinnati and against the army revolt, the commutation of officers' pensions, and the revenue plan of 1783, which Connecticuters considered to be all of a piece.[9]

The nationalists being discredited, the state reverted to the hands of diehards who would preserve the Old Way against the wave of the future. Two movements ensued, one spontaneous and popular, the other planned and led. For themselves, the people started to move out, began an exodus that would fill Vermont and Georgia and New York

---

[9] On Wadsworth and the group around him, see Platt, *Jeremiah Wadsworth, passim,* and East, *Business Enterprises,* 80–100. On the reaction to the events of 1783, see the *Connecticut Gazette,* the *Middlesex Gazette,* the *Connecticut Courant,* and the New Haven *Connecticut Journal,* April 1783–June 1784, but especially February and April 1784, and November 20, 1786; Oliver Ellsworth to Samuel Holten, October 28, 1783, in Emmett Collection, New York Public Library; Jonathan Trumbull to George Washington, November 15, 1783, in Francis Wharton, ed., *The Revolutionary Diplomatic Correspondence of the United States* (6 vols., Washington, 1889), 4:53; Peter Colt to Wadsworth, February 28, 1784, in Wadsworth Papers, Connecticut Historical Society; Daniel Humphreys to Henry Knox, September 25, 1786, in Knox Papers, Massachusetts Historical Society. Despite the to-do, the Connecticut Assembly ultimately granted Congress the impost requested in April 1783; Labaree, ed., *Records of Connecticut,* 5:326–27 (May 1784).

and Pennsylvania and Ohio with Yankees, and spill them over half a continent before its momentum ended.

As for the leaders, they sought to direct and exploit what the people were doing on their own. Some of them thought and operated independently: Oliver Phelps, for example, who with Nathaniel Gorham acquired a million acres of Massachusetts-owned land in western New York. Most, however, worked in groups and concentrated on one prime object: acquiring lands in the Ohio country. Particularly, they tried to obtain all or part of the Western Reserve, the tract which Connecticut had continued to claim after ceding all of its other alleged land titles to Congress. It was rivalry over the means of validating title to the Western Reserve— and of disposing of the land once it was obtained—that set off, in 1785–86, the major political battle of the postwar decade.[10]

One faction took what was operationally a nationalistic stance. It proposed to work through Congress until Connecticut's claims were guaranteed beyond question, and then have the state sell the land in large blocs and for state or continental securities, at par. (Simultaneously, many men in this faction tried an alternate tactic. They joined with promoters in Massachusetts to form a huge private land company, engaged the Reverend Manasseh Cutler as the first professional congressional lobbyist, and sought thereby to acquire vast acreage and incidentally shaped the creation

[10] William G. Sumner, *The Financier and the Finances of the American Revolution* (2 vols., New York, 1891), 2:253 ff.; Journal of the House of Representatives of the General Court of Massachusetts, March 31, 1788, in the Massachusetts Archives; Hulbert, ed., *Records of the Ohio Company,* vol. 1, *passim;* Payson J. Treat, *The National Land System, 1785–1820* (New York, 1910), chapter 3. See also the sources cited in footnotes 7 and 11 in this chapter.

of the American public land system.) The other group took a state-oriented position. It proposed to act as if the title were already secure, and successfully insisted that the state pass a law providing for sale of the land in blocs of any size, and only for state securities, at par. For obvious reasons, continental creditors joined the first group and state creditors joined the second.[11]

The dispute grew bitter and loud, but it came to nothing, for the rival groups were like so many ants on a log drifting down a river: all thought they were directing it but in actuality it was driven by a current beyond their control. Within five years after the peace the vast majority of people in Connecticut had become archnationalists—not because of anybody's arguments, nor even because of specific events, but simply because the state went so quickly and thoroughly to seed. Many had, at war's end, entertained high hopes of a new prosperity in the expanded markets of the world; but by 1787 Connecticut was importing annually twice what it exported. Government fared even worse, for the state government almost completely disintegrated as a result of a ludicrous scandal. The state treasurer, John Lawrence, had been repeatedly returned to office out of sentimentality and force of habit, though he was old, feeble, and nearly blind.

---

[11] Labaree, *Records of Connecticut,* 6:36, 104–5, 155–56, 237–38; *New Haven Gazette,* August 12, 1786; *Connecticut Gazette,* October 9, 26, and throughout December 1786; *Connecticut Courant,* November 26, 1786; *Journals of Congress,* 28:375–81, 33:334–43, 399–401 (May 29, 1785, July 13, 23, 1787); Jensen, *New Nation,* 354–59; Hulbert, ed., *Records of the Ohio Company, passim;* and the correspondence between Samuel Holden Parsons and Henry Knox, 1786–87, vols. 19 and 20, in the Knox Papers, Massachusetts Historical Society. The leaders of the nation-oriented faction were Parsons, Jeremiah Wadsworth, Roger Sherman, and others; the leaders of the state-oriented faction were James Wadsworth, Joseph Hopkins, and William Williams.

Toward the end of 1787 the General Assembly, not having had a report from Lawrence since 1778 (and having levied taxes all the while without having the faintest notion as to the state of the treasury, or even whether taxes were being collected), asked him for an accounting. He protested, delayed, and finally resigned. It took a legislative committee two full years, working under the direction of the brilliant financier Erastus Wolcott, to figure out what had been happening.[12]

For Connecticut this brief taste of independence was enough, for its fruits were bitter.

At a glance, New Hampshire might have seemed quite another matter, for its commerce boomed throughout the postwar decade, and nearly half its land, far from being crowded, was unoccupied and almost unexplored. But the state was so maladjusted that groups of its citizens periodically gathered—after the New England fashion—with a view toward shooting other groups of its citizens. The maladjustment was between a niggardly Nature on the one hand and, on the other, an ignorant breed of men incongruously characterized by lethargy and volatility.

Nature's inhospitality was most obvious in three ways: the climate, the soil, and the terrain. Winters in eighteenth-century New Hampshire were uncommonly long and cold: so cold that all men save the most industrious stayed in-

---

[12] The transition is most strikingly seen in the attitudes of the newspapers in New London, Hartford, New Haven, and Middlesex for 1786–87. On the economic plight of the state, see the sources cited in footnote 3, above. On the Lawrence episode, see the manuscript volume Finance and Currency, vol. 5, pp. 284–87, and the Wolcott letters in the *Connecticut Courant,* February 9, 23, 1787.

doors, making their wives pregnant and praying to a Fundamentalist, Calvinist God to make it warmer; and so long that when spring finally broke, all men save the most industrious got fiercely drunk and made other men's wives pregnant. The soil was stubborn: except in the river valleys, where it was fertile enough to grow almost anything the climate allowed, it could be made to yield little beyond what it had yielded for thousands of years before man came— weeds, brush, birches and beeches, and magnificent forests of towering white pines. The terrain seemed one transportation barrier after another: mountains and hills and forests and rocks, so distributed as to make road-building impracticable, and to leave the three river systems as the only passable highways.[13]

The sensible way to have compromised with Nature would have been to build an economy on the forest resources: fell the choice trees and sled them to river banks in winter, raft them to the lowest falls (which happened to be near ports) in early spring, process them in late spring, make things from them during the summer, and export the

---

[13] For an excellent contemporary description of the climate, soil and terrain of New Hampshire, and of the mores of its inhabitants in the eighteenth century, see Jeremy Belknap, *The History of New Hampshire* (3 vols., Boston, 1792), vol. 3. The physical and economic characteristics of the Piscataqua region are well described in William G. Saltonstall, *Ports of Piscataqua* (Cambridge, 1941), chapter 1. For primary materials supplementary to Belknap's account, I have drawn on the Microfilm Collection of Early Town Records in the New Hampshire State Library, Concord; the correspondence and public records scattered through Isaac W. Hammond, Charles S. Batchellor, and others, eds., *State Papers of New Hampshire* (40 vols., Concord and Manchester, 1885–1943); and the various newspapers, including the Portsmouth *New Hampshire Gazette, Fowle's New-Hampshire Gazette,* the *New-Hampshire Mercury and General Advertiser,* and the *New Hampshire Spy.*

finished products in the fall. That, in fact, is the general way the New Hampshire economy operated, and as a whole economy, it operated rather well. The difficulties were that as individuals all but a handful of persons fared rather badly, and that as a state New Hampshire existed only legally—and even its legal existence was touch and go.[14]

In the first place, nearly half the inhabitants declined to take part either in this "economy," or for that matter, in the state's political life. None of the towns between rivers or north of Lake Winnipesaukee engaged in the lumber business or held any more than token trade with any other towns, and the same was true of about two-fifths of the towns that bordered the Merrimack and Connecticut rivers. Men there rarely left their farms except for an occasional trip to the miller's, the church, or the town hall. Trips to the miller's were as frequent as necessity dictated; trips to the church, except for perhaps a fourth who attended regularly, were as frequent as the occasions for hiring or firing a minister or for voting against some new heresy. Most men went to the annual town meetings, being likely to vote there for town officers and against collecting current state taxes, against the latest proposed state constitution or congressional ordinance, and against sending representatives to the legislature this year.[15]

In the second place, in the two interior areas where the

---

[14] On the New Hampshire economy in general, see Belknap, *History of New Hampshire,* 3:210–22, 261; Salstonstall, *Ports of Piscataqua, passim;* James E. Defebaugh, *History of the Lumber Industry of North America* (2 vols., Chicago, 1906, 1907), 2:138 and *passim;* Weeden, *Economic and Social History of New England,* 2:766 and *passim.* See also Brentwood Town Records, 1:391 ff., 520, in the Microfilm Collection, New Hampshire State Library.

[15] These generalizations are drawn from study of the Town Records, *ibid.* I have worked out the geographical distribution of commercial lumbering

inhabitants were more nearly a part of the world, it was not the New Hampshire part of it. In the Merrimack valley most of the towns did export lumber regularly, and some of them (notably Londonderry, where a thriving linen business was established) produced semifinished manufactures for export; but their avenue of commerce led to Massachusetts, and they looked there for leadership and ideas as well as trade. When they were not ignoring their own state's economic center, Portsmouth and environs, they were doing battle with it politically. Along the Connecticut River most towns were populated, in the main, with former inhabitants of Connecticut; and for that reason as well as the fact that their most accessible market was Hartford, they looked to Connecticut when they looked outside at all. So pronounced, however, was their isolationism that at one point sixteen of the valley towns seceded to join the renegade state of Vermont, changed their minds, flirted with the idea of setting up a separate republic, and then drifted back to New Hampshire, though not so far back as to participate regularly in its government.[16]

---

by ascertaining, from these records, whether towns annually elected inspectors of lumber, and by transferring that data to a map. See also Belknap, *History of New Hampshire,* 3:207–8. On each of the other points in the paragraph, countless examples could be cited. For illustrations, see the records of Acworth, 1:20, 128; Gilmantown, 1:454–55, 2:16, 17, 29, 34, 42, 52; Alsted, 1:347; New Ipswich, 3:20; Wilton, 1:450; Winchester, 1:639–44; Hampstead, 1:283–84; Dover, 4:555.

[16] *Ibid.,* with such additional examples as Bedford Town Records, 3:454; Belknap, *History of New Hampshire,* 3:207, 216–18, 262, 283; *The History of New Ipswich* (Boston, 1852), 221–23, 330–33; Franklin B. Sanborn, *New Hampshire: Epitome in Popular Government* (Boston, 1904), 241. The Newburyport newspaper was styled the *Essex Journal & the New-Hampshire Packet.* On the Vermont episode, see Microfilm Collection of Town Records: Alsted, 1:230; Chesterfield, 1:292; Cornish, 1:70–74, 170; *New Hampshire Gazette,* 1781–82; Richard F. Upton, *Revolutionary New Hampshire* (Hanover, 1936), 188–98.

In the third place, that portion of New Hampshire which was thrivingly alive, the Piscataqua region (Portsmouth and the surrounding towns in the southeastern part of the state), had developed an economic system that bred continuous social discord. Of the roughly 4,600 adult males in the area, about 900 were farmers who earned a respectable livelihood, about 750 were artisans and craftsmen who earned good wages, largely in shipbuilding and related industries, and perhaps 180 were merchants and professional men. But 800 more were rootless and seasonally unemployed, being sailors, and 2,000 or more were common laborers in the lumber camps. The lumber workers, most of whom had once been farmers, were tempted into their labor by the promise of cash, but entering it precluded continuing to farm, for "the best season for sawing logs is the spring, when the rivers are high; this is also the time for ploughing and planting." Once in, mill owners extended them long-term credit, and most soon fell into inescapable dependency. Habitually drunk, unemployed half the year, and lacking "necessities . . . education or morals," these men contributed to political life mainly by selling their votes and furnishing the manpower when mob action (for whatever purpose) was desired. What was worse, they showed no more inclination to change their lot than did their apathetic country cousins, though they were likely, in the off-seasons, to erupt into mob violence out of sheer boredom.[17]

---

[17] Occupational distributions are reckoned as follows: estimates of all commercial personnel except traders and shopkeepers are made on the basis of tabulation of all such persons advertising merchandise or services in the *New Hampshire Gazette* (1781–84), *New Hampshire Mercury* (1785–88), and *New Hampshire Spy* (1788). Shopkeepers and traders are estimated at the rate of one for every town not immediately on a river, and two for each town on a river, exclusive of port towns. All ministers in

In short, most New Hampshireites had already achieved the taxless, shiftless utopia which most Americans cherished as a secret dream, and for which "republicanism" and "unalienable rights" were merely euphemisms.

Yet New Hampshire did have members of that creative minority who, along with a handful of statesmen, would make America great: those impelled by an irresistible and illimitable compulsion to get more. In this state the group was small, numbering well under two hundred, and what they got was considerable: the lion's share of $150,000 a year from exports and, on the average, half that much again from seagoing craft built locally and sold elsewhere. But not even these were the actuating forces in New Hampshire politics. To the extent that it can be said that New Hampshire politics was actuated at all, it can be said that the moving forces were two men.[18]

the state are listed in Belknap, *History of New Hampshire,* 3:300 ff.; the number of lumber workers is estimated from data given in the same, 210 ff., 261; and in the same, 3:227, is an estimate of the number of seamen in the various branches of the state's trade and fishing. The number of workers in shipbuilding is reckoned from data supplied in Saltonstall, *Ports of Piscataqua,* 51–54, 102, 117–23. All other persons are assumed to have been farmers. The quotations are from Belknap, *History of New Hampshire,* 3:210 ff., 261. See also the *New Hampshire Spy,* October 24, 1786, and the account of the Exeter Rebellion, chapter 5, herein.

[18] On the state's commerce during the period, the earliest complete accounts of exports are for October 1789 to October 1791 and are to be found in Belknap's *History of New Hampshire,* 3:219, with a table of prices on pages 221–22. A search in the Portsmouth Customs Office and the National Archives revealed that each agency thought the other had records for the period; they may be extant, but none were found. However, I have tabulated ship movements from the *Gazette,* the *Mercury,* and the *Spy* for the entire period, and these tabulations indicate that commercial activity throughout the 1780s was about 95 percent as much as in 1789–91. On this basis it is assumed that imports and exports during 1783–89 were not significantly different from those in 1789–91. As to shipbuilding, see

The first, John Langdon, was a lovable chap and most everyone in the state loved him. He devoutly cherished popular acclaim and won it largely by practicing and preaching his favorite principle, that everyone, and particularly government, should mind his own business and leave everyone else alone. His generosity was most visible on election days, when he was likely to buy drinks for everybody. It was not visible at all on other days, for it did not exist then. On other days—until he made his fortune—Langdon was busy praising the New Hampshire system and bleeding it unmercifully. After he made his fortune, he praised and bled the system some more. And the people loved him, and elected him president of the state, and cheered as he rode down the streets.[19]

The other man, General John Sullivan, was tough, austere, and serious, and almost no one in the state loved him. Because he commanded respect outside the state and because he had a reputation as a military hero (neither of which anyone could quite explain), his fellow citizens regularly elected him to some high office. The office was never too high, however, because he gave people the uneasy (and well-founded) feeling that he was a martinet, and that given half a chance he would start enforcing laws and making people pay taxes and start working a lot more and

Belknap, *History of New Hampshire,* 3:209–10; Saltonstall, *Ports of Piscataqua,* 51–54, 95, 102, 117–23; Weeden, *Economic and Social History of New England,* 2:766; W. S. Robertson, ed., *The Diary of Francisco de Miranda, 1783–1784* (New York, 1928). The political observations are documented in subsequent paragraphs.

[19] Generalizations about Langdon are derived from study of the John Langdon Papers in the Historical Society of Pennsylvania; the sketch of Langdon by his grandson, John Langdon-Elwyn, in *State Papers of New Hampshire,* 21:804 ff.; Lawrence S. Mayo, *John Langdon of New Hampshire* (Concord, 1937); and comments about him in the several Portsmouth newspapers, 1783–88.

drinking a lot less. So the people did not love him, and did not elect him president, and did not cheer as he rode down the streets.[20]

The political history of the state until 1786 can be summarized in three words: not much happened. Though Sullivan was a dedicated nationalist (being on reasonably close terms with Hamilton, Knox, and Washington), his dedication moved his home state not at all; and though Langdon paid lipservice to nationalism (it was good business to do so, for he was the Portsmouth agent of the Bank of North America), he did little for the Union beyond making speeches about how glorious it was. Indeed, most citizens of New Hampshire were so local-minded and politically apathetic that to get them to become loyal to the state and conscious of its problems would have constituted a vast broadening of their horizons.[21]

The history of the establishment of the state constitution

---

[20] Charles P. Whittemore, *A General of the Revolution: John Sullivan of New Hampshire* (New York, 1961), *passim*, especially 180–203; William Plumer, "John Sullivan," in *State Papers of New Hampshire*, 21:819 ff.; Otis G. Hammond, ed., *Letters and Papers of Major-General John Sullivan, Continental Army*, vol. 3, 1779–95 (*Collections of the New Hampshire Historical Society*, vol. 15, Concord, 1939), especially 385 ff., 407 ff.; *New Hampshire Gazette*, March 4, September 30, 1785, June 22, 1786; *New Hampshire Mercury*, August 12, 1785, March 8, 1786; William Plumer to John Hale, October 22, 1786, in Colonial Society of Massachusetts *Publications*, 11:402; Jeremy Belknap to Ebenezer Hazard, March 9, 1786, in *The Belknap Papers*, 1:433 (Massachusetts Historical Society *Collections*, 3 parts: 5th series, vols. 2, 3, and 6th series, vol. 4, Boston, 1877, 1891).

[21] See all the sources cited in footnotes 15, 19, and 20, above, together with the William Plumer Papers in the New Hampshire Historical Society (5 volumes of biographical sketches of leading New Hampshire figures) and "Journal of the House of Representatives," in *State Papers of New Hampshire*, vols. 20, 21. From the latter, I have tabulated all votes cast in the House, 1784–88, matching each delegate's votes with those of each other delegate; and from the town records I have tabulated every recorded popular vote on state and national issues.

epitomizes New Hampshire politics. Doing so took three years, from 1781 to 1784. Many towns refused to send delegates to the constitutional convention, and those elected did not regularly attend, with the result that the convention usually lacked a quorum. Those present knew little of what they were about, half the towns did not take the trouble to vote on various questions referred to them, and the other half were divided in several ways. The convention finally completed a constitution largely by copying clauses from the Massachusetts constitution. The document was never actually ratified; the convention, anticipating that most towns would take no action, submitted it to them with a notice that failure to vote on it would be construed as approval. Only by this means was the state constitution brought into existence.[22]

There seemed, in fact, little reason for New Hampshire to have any state government. Business worked well without it, for on the one end, town governments were perfectly adequate to the task of regulating lumber production; and on the other end, the world was wide open, for the Revolu-

---

[22] See the running summaries of the activities of the convention, published in the *New Hampshire Gazette,* 1781–84, especially the issues of February 3 and June 28, 1783; see also Upton, *Revolutionary New Hampshire,* chapter 13. I have also traced, in the town records, the constitution through the three referendums held on it, November 1781 to April 1782, the fall of 1782, and the fall of 1783. A few samples will suffice. In Hillsborough County, Amherst neglected to vote on the first referendum, voted no in the second, and yes in the third (Amherst Town Records, 1:414, 430); Merrimack did not vote on the first, voted a conditional yes with amendments on the second, and sent the third to a committee that never reported (Merrimack, 175, 181); Nottingham West voted no, yes, and then refused to act (Nottingham West, 3:352, 363, 368); Peterborough voted no, no, and a split vote that did not answer what was put to the towns (Peterborough, 1:69, 74, 84). Towns in the other counties behaved similarly.

tion had resulted in the opening of the French West Indies to American shipping and these islands furnished an insatiable market for New Hampshire lumber and lumber products. The state had a war debt, but it was relatively small, about $2.50 per capita; and besides, most of it was owned by citizens of Massachusetts, and thus not many locals were particularly anxious that it be paid. True, the state government had somehow acquired $137,000 in continental securities, and Langdon himself owned $26,500 of such securities, and accordingly, the state was regularly quick to approve amendments to the Articles of Confederation that would vest Congress with a revenue from import duties. Otherwise, however, few in New Hampshire could think of much for a government to do.[23]

Then one day it was decided that John Langdon should stop being president for a while, and Sullivan was elected. As many had dreaded, Sullivan immediately attempted to put into practice his belief that a government should govern; he started enforcing laws and making people pay taxes and insisting that people work a lot more and drink a lot less.

---

[23] On commerce, see footnote 18, above. For a translation of the French *arrêt* which established the commercial regulations that made trade with the French West Indies lucrative for American lumber and livestock exporters, see the Annapolis *Maryland Gazette,* March 24, 1785. The observations on public debts are drawn from the following volumes of the Records of the Loan of 1790, in the National Archives: vol. 242, Journal of the Domestic Debt, 1791–96, and vol. 249, Subscription Register, Assumed Debt of New Hampshire; the figure on the total amount of continental securities held in New Hampshire is from Summary Volume 174A, Treasury Department; for Langdon's holdings, see vol. 249, folio 35, vol. 242, folio 4, and vol. 495, folio 128. New Hampshire's responses to congressional requests for amendments are recorded in *Laws of New Hampshire* (5 vols., Bristol, New Hampshire, 1916), acts of April 6, 1781, January 2, 1784, June 23, 1785.

By chance, or perhaps not by chance, this happened in the spring of 1786, at a moment when all hell was about to break loose, all over New England.[24]

Rhode Island was different. The state had been created as a haven for the otherwise-minded, and throughout the eighteenth century it had produced, even more than it had attracted, men with a passion for the untried. Its citizens were as alert as New Hampshire's were dull; in dealing with changing conditions, they were as flexible as Connecticut's Yankees were doggedly conservative. Yet such was the weight of postwar problems for all New England that even Rhode Islanders found it difficult to cope with them. Or so they said, and so it seemed. But that is what they always said, and that was the way it always seemed.[25]

Noisily complaining about hard times was the Rhode Islander's most apparent trait; quietly succeeding against heavy odds was his most persistent trait. Nature had been as stingy in endowing Rhode Island's land as it had been with the rest of New England, so Rhode Islanders learned to live on and from the sea. They had no staple, so they grew

---

[24] On Sullivan's election and administration, see Whittemore, *John Sullivan,* 195 ff.; *State Papers of New Hampshire,* 20:614. See also chapter 5, herein.

[25] In making my analysis of Rhode Island, I became deeply indebted to Messrs. James B. Hedges and Franklin Coyle of Brown University, who have for several years studied the Brown Papers and the Arnold Papers, respectively, in the John Carter Brown Library, and have shared with me their intimate knowledge of the psyches of the state's merchants. Professor Hedges' *The Browns of Providence Plantations* (Cambridge, 1952) is by far the most valuable account of eighteenth-century American merchants; another excellent analysis, overlapping this period, is Peter J. Coleman's *The Transformation of Rhode Island, 1790–1860* (Providence, 1963).

what they could and processed it and reprocessed it and processed it again until they had a little something to trade. The something was still very little, so they learned to trade their own products for those of New York, and to trade those for South Carolina products, and those for Philadelphia products, and those for products of the West Indies, making a profit on each and returning home with handsome sums. They, like all Americans, suffered a chronic shortage of hard money, but this too they turned to advantage, by carefully following the local price variations it engendered and profiting accordingly.[26]

This shrewd opportunism was by no means owned only by a special few: it characterized the whole population, from the lowliest farmer or mechanic to the richest international merchant. Farm families pooled their savings and bought thirty- or forty-ton vessels for marketing their produce and trading during the off-season, and every doctor, watchmaker, cooper, or carpenter was likely to own all or part of a trading vessel. In the years 1781–83 alone, about a third of Providence's adult males registered as owners or masters of new vessels of more than twenty tons burden, and perhaps another third were proprietors of smaller craft. In the entire postwar decade, roughly nine-tenths of the

---

[26] This general picture is put together from study of the Maritime Papers, Petitions to the General Assembly, records of the paper money issues of 1750 and 1786, Reports to the General Assembly, and collections of Rateable Lists, all in the Rhode Island Archives; the Moses Brown Papers and the Rhode Island Historical Society Manuscripts, both in the Rhode Island Historical Society; the various newspapers of the state; and assorted town records, in the several city and town halls. For a good general description, see Coleman, *Transformation of Rhode Island,* chapter 1; for rich illustrative matter see Hedges, *Browns of Providence Plantations, passim.*

men in Providence owned all or part of or captained at least one commercial vessel, and the portions in other towns were almost as high.[27]

The Rhode Islanders' skill as traders matched their ability as seamen. One spectacular voyage epitomized this skill. In 1784 the ship *Hydra* cleared Newport with about $3,500 in assorted local goods. After two years and trading stops at Charleston, Philadelphia, St. Eustatia, Cape Verde, Bengal, and St. Eustatia again, it returned with a cargo worth almost $60,000—which was sold in several American ports over the next two years for more than $100,000. More typical, but likewise immensely profitable, were the voyages of the forty-ton brig *Britania,* owned by a pair of farm families, the Arnolds and the Rices of Warwick. These farmers acquired the vessel only for the increased profits of marketing directly, but soon their annual marketing voyage regularly involved four or five ports and sharp trading that doubled or trebled the value of their farm production.[28]

Given total social acceptance of opportunism as the proper key to economic success, other unorthodox attitudes necessarily followed. Two were of prime moment: the views

---

[27] Ownership of vessels tabulated from *Ship Documents of Rhode Island* (6 vols., mimeographed, Providence, 1938–41); for occupations of ship-owners who were not merchants, I have traced individual owners in the town tax records and through newspaper advertisements.

[28] The voyage of the *Hydra* was commented on at some length in the *Newport Mercury,* the *Providence Gazette,* and newspapers of New York and Philadelphia in May and June 1786; its trading stops were mentioned in newspapers of Charleston, Philadelphia, and New York; its arrival, cargo, and some details of the voyage are recorded as an entry of June 8, 1786, in Maritime Papers: Manifests of Import Cargoes, in Rhode Island Archives. The registration and ownership of the *Britania* is in *Ship Documents of Rhode Island,* Providence Register 450, December 22, 1777; its voyages are recorded in the Maritime Papers in the Rhode Island Archives.

of Rhode Islanders toward the function of government and their general system of business ethics.

The prevailing view toward government was as practical as it was novel: it held that the function of government was to serve as a business agent of the people, especially in their dealings with other, more conventional governments. Quite in character were the manipulations that attended the state's refusal to ratify the impost amendment of 1781 and its subsequent easy ratification of the 1783 revenue plan. Equally so was the matter of ship registration; the state issued registration papers of whatever description permitted most profitable use of the world's ports. For example, after 1785 vessels in the Irish tobacco trade were required to measure at least seventy-five tons. John Brown's brig *Hope,* actually about 120 tons but registered as sixty, received a new registration of eighty tons for this trade. Again, under certain conditions vessels of less than forty tons could enter French ports duty-free; Rhode Island craft of more than a hundred tons circumvented French duties by showing local registrations of forty tons. Other vessels carried papers falsifying cargoes or ownership. (Such accommodations were available to all; so close was the Rhode Island government to its citizens that its all-powerful legislature rotated among five towns in the tiny state, that all might watch its sessions.)[29]

---

[29] Registration of John I. Clark's ship *Providence,* June 1783, in Register of Rhode Island Vessels, 3:199, and the clearance of the same ship on October 5, 1784, in Bonds, Masters of Vessels, 11:13; manifest of ship *Hope,* in Manifests of Export Cargoes, 1784–90, vol. 4, p. 14; John Brown to Henry Ward, undated note (1785) in Manifests of Export Cargoes, 4:29; clearance of the brig *Prudent,* October 21, 1784 (with a cargo that would have required a vessel of at least 75 tons, but under 25-ton registration), in Newport Outward and Inward Entries, 1776–87, p. 221; all

The prevailing code of business ethics had only two essential positive aspects. One cardinal rule was that, in dealing with one another, Rhode Islanders were required to keep their word: a reputation to the contrary ostracized a man for life. The other was that one stuck by one's group—friends, neighbors, associates, or clan—against all comers and at all costs, even if doing so meant personal ruin.

Otherwise, no holds were barred. The only restraints upon trickery and sharp trading were those imposed by a prudent regard for future dealings. No avenue of commerce was too unsavory, neither smuggling, nor slaving, nor even profiteering in supplying soldiers who were protecting one's own property. And most notably, Rhode Islanders were unconscionable liars in their business dealings, with one another as well as with outsiders.[30]

This system worked with striking effectiveness. From 1760 to 1790, while calamity befell the rest of New England, Rhode Island complained of calamity but actually underwent a huge boom. In midcentury, Providence had but two seagoing vessels, measuring about fifty tons; by

---

manuscripts in the Maritime Papers, Rhode Island Archives; John Brown to David Howell, October 23, 1783, and Nicholas Brown to Howell, March 26, 1785, in Rhode Island Historical Society Manuscripts, 14:27, 53; *Providence Gazette, Newport Mercury,* 1780s, *passim.*

[30] These comments on the Rhode Island "code," positive and negative, summarize long study of the Moses Brown Papers, the Rhode Island Historical Society Manuscripts, and the Frederick S. Peck Collection, all in the Rhode Island Historical Society; the Brown and Arnold Papers in the John Carter Brown Library; and the Maritime Papers in the Rhode Island Archives. See also Hedges, *Browns of Providence Plantations,* 329–32. For specific examples that are delightful (if one finds delight in observing clever scoundrels), see John Brown to Moses Brown, November 27, 1786, in Peck Collection, 8:10; and the statement of Benjamin Remington, in Jamestown folder, Property Inventory, 1783, in the Rhode Island Archives.

1790 it owned shipping registered at 10,000 tons and actually measuring perhaps twice that. Newport sent out 140 or so vessels annually before the war; it was razed during the war and was able to send out only half a dozen during the first year of peace, but bounced back and had more than 200 new craft ranging the seas by 1790. The smaller towns, combined, matched either of the larger ports. By the 1780s Rhode Islanders were able to import almost $2 million worth of goods annually—most of which were soon re-exported to other American ports—though total exports were little more than $500,000. With just over a fourth as many people as Connecticut, Rhode Island imported and exported almost ninety percent as much; with less than half the population of New Hampshire, Rhode Island did three times as great a volume of business.[31]

But for a time after the war it appeared that the whole mechanism might grind to a halt, the works gummed by an insupportable tax burden. Toward the end of the war, moved by a war-inflated treasury to a momentary state of euphoria, Rhode Islanders committed themselves to supporting the entire public debt held in the state, congressional obligations included. For a year or two this occasioned no problem, partly because revenues were large and partly because, in

---

[31] *Providence Gazette,* September 6, 1783, April 29, 1786; *United States Chronicle* (Providence), March 2, 1786; from *Ship Documents of Rhode Island,* Newport, 1:791 ff., Providence, vol. 1, part 2, pp. 1497 ff.; tabulations from Maritime Papers in Rhode Island Archives: Outward and Inward Entries, 1776–1787; Bonds, Masters of Vessels, vols. 7, 8, 9a, 9b, 10, 11; Manifests of Export Cargoes, vols. 1–4; Manifests of Import Cargoes, vols. 1–5; Book of Manifests, 1785–89; Light Money Accounts; and Registry of Rhode Island Vessels, 1782–83; gaps in the customs records filled from ship news items in the *Newport Mercury* and the *Providence Gazette;* Samuel Hazard, ed., *United States Commercial and Statistical Register,* 1:232, 332, 359 (1839).

the disarranged state of the finances, few claims had been audited and no one suspected how large the public debt was.

It was staggering. When the various kinds of securities were audited and consolidated in 1784, the state of the various forms of public debt in Rhode Island was as follows:

> 566 six percent notes issued for money advanced to the state, held by 354 persons, amounting to $166,500.
>
> 2,416 four percent notes issued of the same character, held by about 2,300 persons, amounting to $153,180.
>
> Continental Loan Office certificates, two-thirds of which were owned in Providence and more than half by twelve men in that city, amounting to $524,000.

(Also floating around were several hundred thousand dollars' worth of individual claims against Congress for goods and services supplied. But these were widely held and unaudited until 1789; they were thus politically impotent, and no payments were made on them until after 1789.)[32]

Even after the auditing and consolidation, the state continued to try to support the interest on the debt. But the tax burden soon became unbearable. Five thousand, then ten, twenty, and thirty thousand pounds annually were levied in direct taxes. The towns complained, yet most kept trying to collect. But the situation soon became absurd, for there was simply not enough money in the state to support taxes on that level. The plight of the town of South Kingstown epitomized the plight of private citizens. That small town gradually fell behind in tax collections: $1,650 in arrears

[32] List of Notes Issued for Consolidating the Securities Issued from the General Treasurer's Office, September 1782 to June 1784; Ledger A, Accounts of Rhode Island Against the United States, folios 200–203, pp. 500–501; Proceedings of the General Assembly, 13:689; all in the Rhode Island Archives; E. James Ferguson, *The Power of the Purse: A History of American Public Finance, 1776–1790* (Chapel Hill, 1961), 332–33.

in 1783, twice that amount by 1785, and twice that again a year later. Most of these taxes were levied to support interest payments on continental and state debt, yet the town government itself owned about $12,000 of the continental and state obligations, and residents of the town owned more than $65,000. But there was not that much money in all South Kingstown, and so the town tax collectors went to jail for failing to collect the taxes.[33]

For once Rhode Islanders had a normal human reaction: they sought and found a scapegoat. They also had another: they sought and found a panacea. The scapegoat was the handful of holders of Continental Loan Office certificates. Throughout 1784 and 1785, increasing numbers of persons —especially politicians outside Providence—began to realize that something like two-thirds of the tax burden was being levied to support these securities, and that almost a third of the total was levied for the benefit of but a dozen men in Providence. Moreover, increasing numbers began to suspect (what was true) that this same dozen men had hoodwinked the state for their own benefit during the to-do over the impost amendment in 1781–82.[34]

---

[33] Proceedings of the General Assembly, 12:134–46, 137–39, 160–63, 475, 685–86, 13:109–10, 288, 360; Reports to the General Assembly, 1778–88, pp. 63, 74, 90, 94; Papers Relating to the Adoption of the Constitution, 105; Ledger A, Accounts of Rhode Island Against the United States, folios 29–154, 155–64, 167–82, 200, 500; Notes Issued for Consolidating Securities, 1782–1784, *passim;* Impost Accounts, *passim;* all in the Rhode Island Archives.

[34] Reports to the General Assembly, 1778–88, pp. 94, 116; Papers Relating to the Adoption of the Constitution, 101–105; Notes Issued for Consolidating Securities, 14; all in Rhode Island Archives; Moses Brown to Champion and Dickason, September 6, 1786, in Moses Brown Papers, 5:73, and Nicholas Brown to David Howell, March 26, 1785, in Rhode Island Historical Society Manuscripts; *Newport Mercury,* September 17, 1786; and the *Mercury* and the *Providence Gazette,* 1785, *passim.*

The panacea was paper money. By coincidence, a group of western shore politicians led by Jonathan J. Hazard had occasion to study the records of the last colonial issue of paper money. From that study they devised a scheme for abolishing the public debt burden. To take care of its own creditors, the state would issue, on loan at interest to anyone who wanted to borrow it and who could furnish the required security, a sum of paper money roughly equal to the outstanding state debt. The annual interest received by the state would match the interest the state had to pay. To ensure that the paper did not depreciate, high taxes would continue, but the burden would be lessened because of the vastly increased circulating medium. As the paper came in, it would be used to retire the principal of the state debt. As it continued to come in, it would be removed from circulation.

As to the continental creditors, they would be disowned, but in a thoroughly honorable manner. The state would simply reverse its earlier stand and ratify the 1783 revenue amendments to the Articles of Confederation, and then inform continental creditors that thenceforth they should look to Congress, the rightful debtor, for the state would no longer be responsible for another government's debts.[35]

At a plebiscite held early in 1786, the proposal met with enthusiastic popular support. Unsurprisingly, Providence

---

[35] Reports to the General Assembly, 1778–88, pp. 16, 39, 100, 111, 117. A writer in the *Newport Herald,* June 19, 1788, asserted that Hazard was only the nominal leader of the paper faction, and that an unnamed Providence merchant and speculator was the real leader. If so, the writer could have been referring only to Clark and Nightingale; see footnotes 39 and 40, below. The Providence merchant-speculators did not oppose ratification of the 1783 amendments, for that was to their advantage; Nicholas Brown to David Howell, March 26, 1785, in Rhode Island Historical Society Manuscripts, 14:53; but disowning them was another matter.

voted against it, but not by an overwhelming margin. Two other towns, Portsmouth and Newport, also voted against it by small margins; these towns had huge, albeit tenuous, claims against Congress for war damages they had suffered, and the new scheme left them unsupported. All others, port towns and country towns alike, approved the plan by votes that ranged from lopsided to unanimous. Accordingly, the system was enacted into law in May 1786.[36]

The plan did not differ significantly from the successful paper money and debt-funding programs adopted in New York and Pennsylvania—except in two respects. First, the Rhode Island plan contemplated only public finance, and was not designed primarily as a circulating medium for private debts and commercial transactions. Thus, the size of the issue (£ 100,000 Rhode Island current, or $333,333), while just right for the public debt and tax structure, was much too large to be absorbed in regular commerce. Second, whereas the New York and Pennsylvania systems accommodated or deliberately split the interests of the continental creditors, that of Rhode Island abandoned them. The first flaw was manageable. The second was lethal.[37]

---

[36] Records and Proceedings of the General Assembly, 13:262–66; Papers Relating to the Adoption of the Constitution, 47, 50, 58–60, 63; Petitions to the General Assembly, vol. 25, part 1, p. 59; all in Rhode Island Archives; Town Meeting Records, in town halls of the several towns, as follows: Tiverton, 1754–98 volume, p. 170; Middleton, 1743–1808 volume, p. 161; West Greenwich, 2:121; Cranston, 1:99; *Providence Gazette,* February 25, 1785, and the winter of 1785–86, *passim.* Unfortunately, the three towns which opposed paper neglected to record their votes in town meetings, but judging by the votes there for governor in 1787, as recorded in Providence Town Meeting Records, 7:89–91, and New York *Daily Advertiser,* April 30, 1787, the majority against paper was not lopsided. Governor John Collins, outspoken champion of the paper plan, received from a fourth to 40 percent of the vote in each of the three towns.

[37] Everything in this paragraph except the statement that the primary aim of the paper was public debts is implicitly documented in the fore-

The great holders of Continental Loan Office certificates
—Nicholas and John Brown, Phillip and Zachariah Allen,
Joseph and William Russel, Jabez Bowen, John I. Clark,
and Joseph Nightingale—set out to defeat the plan.[38] They
had little choice, for their commercial lifeline, their personal
credit, was at stake. At war's end they had made a rare and
serious blunder: they had grossly misjudged the postwar
demand for British goods. Between them, they had imported
huge amounts on credit, and four years later £100,000 in
goods remained on their shelves, unsold and unpaid for.
Their Continental Loan Office certificates thus became

going and following notes. Contemporaries clearly recognized the purpose
of the plan; see, for example, Providence Town Meeting, April 30, 1787;
in Providence Town Meeting Records, 7:99–105; *Newport Mercury,* September 17, 1787; *Newport Herald,* May 3, 1787; William Ellery to Benjamin Huntington, in Ellery-Huntington Papers, Rhode Island Archives;
Moses Brown to Champion and Dickason, September 6, 1786, in Moses
Brown Papers, 5:73.

[38] The role of Clark and Nightingale is not clear. There is strong, albeit
indirect, evidence that they were the instigators and designers of the paper-
money plan: (1) J. P. Brissot de Warville, in his *New Travels in the United
States of America, Performed in 1788* (London, 1796), records that it was
well known in Rhode Island that a pair of Providence merchants promoted
the paper issue as a means of relieving themselves from the burdens of their
land speculations; his description could only refer to Clark and Nightingale.
(2) A writer in the *Newport Herald,* June 19, 1788, said that the man behind the movement was the fifth representative from Providence, and a
merchant and speculator. Inasmuch as Joseph Nightingale was the fourth
representative from Providence and there were only four, the reference
clearly is to John I. Clark. (3) Clark and Nightingale, as a firm, were the
largest borrowers of paper money in the state, taking out £2,625 of the
£96,000 actually loaned; Grand Committee Office, Account Books A and
B, 1786–1803, pp. 15–16, in Rhode Island Archives. (4) Clark and Nightingale did not use the money to repay private debts against the wishes of
creditors; see the public notices of such transactions as required by law to
be published in the *Providence Gazette,* beginning in August 1786 and
summarized in the issue of January 27, 1787. Whatever their part in
creating the issue of paper, however, they joined their fellow merchants in
driving down its market value.

pivotal investments. Payment would surely save them, re-pudiation might ruin them. Accordingly, they were prepared to go as far as destroying the entire fiscal machinery of the state, and they had the tools for so doing: money, connections, and brains.[39]

Their means were subtly ingenious in detail but simple, even gross, in general. They undermined faith in the paper through a fierce and palpably false propaganda campaign. Agrarian radicals, they charged, had seized control of the state and issued paper money that was designed to depreciate and enable dishonest debtors to defraud their creditors. (The charge had the interesting secondary effect of giving the propagators an excuse for continuing to forestall their own creditors in London.) To give substance to their words, they audaciously borrowed $10,000 of the new paper and used that as a fund for manipulating its value downward in the open market. The efforts were successful. In thirty months the paper depreciated, at an approximately steady rate, to about twelve or fifteen for one—that is, until its market value was about eight cents on the dollar. Along the way, whatever reputation "Rogue's Island" had among its sister states was destroyed. A New York newspaper, for example, ran a column called "The Quintessence of Villainy; or, Proceedings of the Legislature of the State of Rhode Island." Ironically, the only Rhode Islanders who emerged

---

[39] For the holdings of Continental Loan Office certificates of these men, see Notes Issued for Consolidating Securities, 14; on their postwar mercantile problems, see Moses Brown to Champion and Dickason, June 26, 1785, September 6, 1786, and Champion and Dickason to Moses Brown, August 10, 1785, in Moses Brown Papers, 5:38, 42, 73; Agreement of Providence Importers, May 14, 1784, and John Brown to Moses Brown, November 27, 1786, in Peck Collection, 7:43; Nicholas Brown to David Howell, March 26, 1785, in Rhode Island Historical Society Manuscripts, 14:53; Hedges, *Browns of Providence Plantations,* 287–98, 314–23.

with reputations untarnished were the Providence operators who undermined the currency.[40]

Despite the depreciation, however, and despite the widespread conviction that Rhode Island had run amuck, the system worked. The state debt was retired, to the advantage of the creditors, and the economy-crippling tax burden was abolished. The state's trade, far from being destroyed, as the enemies of the paper shouted, was liberated and thriving: Rhode Island's interstate and foreign commerce increased every year the paper-money plan was in operation. During the melee John Brown informed his London creditors that hard times, aggravated by financial disorder, prevented his being able to pay his debts; the while, he built fifteen new schooners and a mansion and outfitted slaving and whaling vessels in addition to conducting his usual business. His case was unusual only by its magnitude; otherwise it was typical.[41]

Yet in the broad view what happened was not so significant as what outsiders thought was happening. What

---

[40] The propaganda regarding the paper, pro and con, may be traced in the Rhode Island newspapers, 1786–88. The *Providence Gazette* and the *Newport Mercury* started out being, and in the main remained, impartial; accordingly, the foes of paper started two new newspapers, the *Newport Herald* and the *United States Chronicle* (Providence), which published only antipaper materials and did so with great enthusiasm. The "Quintessence of Villainy" piece is in the New York *Daily Advertiser* of April 6, 1787. At least twenty-three Providence merchants, apart from Clark and Nightingale, borrowed paper, as did at least twenty-three Newport merchants; Grand Committee Office, Account Book A, pp. 15–16. As to the falsity of the propaganda against the paper, see the detailed analysis of "lodge money" payments in McDonald, *We the People,* 332–33. On the depreciation, see price quotations in the various newspapers, Grand Committee Office, Account Book A, pp. 61–110, and Account Book B, *passim;* Records and Proceedings of the General Assembly, vol. 14.

[41] In the main, this generalization is based upon the commercial sources cited in footnote 31, above. But see also the *New York Journal,* December

happened was, in effect, that the price of Rhode Island's prosperity was partial secession and partial ostracism from the Union. What people thought was that wild-eyed levelers had taken over the state. This impression added force to another one: that an eighteenth-century form of bolshevism had swept New England, and threatened to engulf the entire country.

That fear derived chiefly from the tumults in Massachusetts. Throughout the war, and at its end, no state was more dedicated than was Massachusetts to the proposition that the Union should be preserved forever—but only as a league of sovereign republics. Upon the signing of the peace that belief was strengthened. A scant three years later, most of its leaders were ready to part with sovereignty, and many were ready to forgo republicanism as well.[42]

Massachusetts was like a sick man in the hands of a

11, 1788; *Providence Gazette,* January 17, 31, February 21, 1787, March 28, April 18, 1789; and advertisements in the several newspapers, 1787–89. On Brown, see the correspondence cited in footnote 39, above, and the registrations of his fishing vessels as recorded in the Maritime Papers, Rhode Island Archives; the mansion is currently the home of the Rhode Island Historical Society.

[42] The attitudes of Massachusetts' republican leaders during and at the end of the war, as well as the transition in the mideighties, emerge most clearly from study of the letters of its congressmen (the Adamses, Lovell, Gerry, Higginson, and so on), published in Edmund C. Burnett, ed., *Letters of Members of the Continental Congress* (8 vols., Washington, 1921–36), and from such collections of writings as Harry A. Cushing, ed., *The Writings of Samuel Adams* (4 vols., New York, 1904–08); Charles F. Adams, ed., *The Works of John Adams* (10 vols., Boston, 1850–56); James T. Austin, *The Life of Elbridge Gerry, with Contemporary Letters* (2 vols., Boston, 1828, 1829); J. Franklin Jameson, ed., "Letters of Stephen Higginson, 1783–1804," in American Historical Association *Annual Report,* vol. 1 (1896); and Charles R. King, ed., *Life and Correspondence of Rufus King* (6 vols., New York, 1894–1900). See also *Connecticut Courant,* November 20, 1786.

quack, genuinely ill but sicker yet for the medicine he has taken. The Revolution had been welcomed as a cure-all; but so thoroughly had it dislocated the state's economic and social order that, troubled as the sixties and seventies were, they could seem like golden years before a generation had passed. The old problem—too many people, too little good land, considering everything—remained unsolved. The many new problems each aggravated the old, and aggravated one another as well.[43]

Massachusetts had long since reached the point of being unable to support itself except by shrewd trading. Its first postwar problem was that it now had less to trade. Farm production remained about the same, because declining crops were compensated by increased raising of livestock, as in Connecticut, and by increased elementary manufacturing of farm products, as in Rhode Island. Even so, Massachusetts' commercial centers had less to export. They had less from the land because, as a by-product of political doings, the farmers of the central and western parts of the state abandoned ancient trade habits and began to export through Hartford and New York, rather than Boston and Salem. They had less from the sea because the war resulted in the

---

[43] There is no adequate general account of Massachusetts during the period. The first two chapters of Samuel E. Morison's *Maritime History of Massachusetts* (Boston, 1921) contain some data, but this well-told sea story is sadly lacking in useful economic analysis. Robert E. Brown's *Middle Class Democracy* has immense amounts of useful data, but it ends in 1780. Oscar and Mary F. Handlin's *Commonwealth, A Study of the Role of Government in the American Economy: Massachusetts, 1774–1861* (New York, 1947), 1–112, contains much useful analysis, as do John A. Worsley's "Massachusetts in the 1780s" (MAT Thesis, Brown University, 1963) and vol. 2 of Weeden's *Economic and Social History of New England*. The following analysis is based upon manuscript sources, particularly those in the Massachusetts Archives, Boston, and upon newspapers.

destruction of most of the state's whaling and fishing fleets, and also because the Atlantic whales, once near at hand, migrated during the war without telling the whalers where they were going. This left Boston roughly in the position Norfolk would have been in had Virginia's tobacco production been cut by a third.[44]

And not only did Massachusetts have less to trade; it soon had fewer places in which to trade it. Simultaneously in 1784 the British West Indies were closed to American bottoms and a prohibitive duty was placed on American whale oil imported into England. The French West Indies remained open to American shipping and offered a boundless market for lumber, horses, and fish. Massachusetts had neither lumber nor horses, and before it could profit much from the fish market, the French islands were (in 1785) abruptly closed to American fish. Furthermore, markets in

---

[44] Production data are derived from "An Account of Exports from Boston in the Year 1787, with Their Current Values at the Place of Exportation," compiled and published by the Northampton *Hampshire Gazette* in July 1788 and subsequently republished in the Boston *Massachusetts Centinel,* August 2, 1788; Customs Office Records, Port of Salem: Abstract of Exports Previous to 1792, in the National Archives; Beverly Customs Records, Book 44 (Entrances and Clearances, 1784–88), in the Beverly Historical Society. On the loss of the interior sources of exports, see the *Boston Gazette* of February 9, 1767, for evidence that most of the wheat of the Connecticut Valley was at that time exported to Boston by sled and thence to foreign markets. Postwar wheat exports from Boston, as indicated in the "Account of Exports," were only a fraction of what they had been before 1776. My tabulations of ship movements from newspaper notices indicate that clearances from early spring through December were, in the postwar period, about what they had been before the war, but that clearances in the early months, formerly a busy exporting season, were now small. The number of small manufacturing establishments has been tabulated from *Evaluation and Taxes,* 1788, vol. 163 in the Massachusetts Archives. On whaling, see Elmo P. Hohman, *The American Whaleman* (New York, 1928), 34 ff.

the Mediterranean, politically opened by the success of the Revolution, were soon physically closed by the activities of Algerian corsairs who demanded either tribute, which Americans could not pay, or annihilation, which Americans, lacking a navy, could not mete.[45]

Not even these difficulties needed to spell disaster, for Massachusetts had long rectified an unfavorable balance of trade with profits from the transportation business. But the carrying trade, too, grew less easy as a result of the Revolution. The closing of the British West Indies scarcely helped. Worse, American ports were thrown open to Dutch and French shipping without a counterbalancing exclusion of British vessels. Finally, the two most lucrative kinds of American cargoes were subjects of unprecedented competi-

---

[45] For a good summary of the development of the British regulations, see Jensen, *New Nation,* 160–64; for their effects on whaling, see Hedges, *Browns of Providence Plantations,* 295–96, and Curtis P. Nettels, *The Emergence of a National Economy, 1775–1815* (New York, 1962), 52–53; for the French regulations and their effects, see *Maryland Gazette,* March 24, 1785, *New York Journal,* July 5, 1787, and Henri Sée, "Commerce Between France and the United States, 1783–1784," in *American Historical Review,* 31:732–52 (1925–26); James Warren to John Adams, April 30, 1786, and Adams to Warren, July 4, 1786, in *Warren-Adams Letters,* 2:271 ff., 276 ff.; on Algiers, see *Massachusetts Centinel,* December 17, 1785; *Maryland Gazette,* April 28, 1785, January 12, 1786; *Providence Gazette,* June 25, 1785 (by a writer who thought the Algerian scare was a "bugbear"); Jefferson to Adams, May 11, July 11, 1786, to John Jay, May 12, 23, August 13, September 26, 1786, November 3, 1787, to William Carmichael, June 20, 1786, Carmichael to Adams and Jefferson, February 3, 1786, and John Lamb to Jefferson, May 20, 1787, all in Jared Sparks, ed., *The Diplomatic Correspondence of the United States* (5 vols., Washington, 1832–33), 3:20, 21, 33, 48, 74, 108, 126, 138, 257, 320; "Report of the Secretary of State Relative to the Mediterranean Trade, December 28, 1790," in *State Papers of the United States* (10 vols., Boston, 1817), 1:41–47; Nettels, *Emergence of a National Economy,* 67. The province of Maine, then a part of Massachusetts, had an abundance of timber, but the shippers of Massachusetts proper were no yet profiting from it.

tion: South Carolina rice because of crop failures and Virginia tobacco because of the state's mercantile policy.[46]

Had Massachusetts' dislocations been merely economic, they might have been manageable, but these were almost trifling compared to the social and political problems that beset the state. Nearly half of this difficulty was that nearly half of the state's population was endemically disloyal to it. Most inhabitants of the towns west of Worcester—like most back-country folk in the rest of New England and in North and South Carolina—were anarchists at heart, or aspired to such an extreme form of local self-government that it amounted to the same thing. While the Revolution was coming on, they opposed their eastern brethren as usual and remained Loyalist. After war began they (unlike their Southern counterparts) embraced the Revolution, but only as a vehicle for effecting their narrow local ends. From 1776 to 1780, by repeated mob actions in the name of Whiggism, they hampered the creation and working of a state government, and to that extent hampered the prosecution of the Revolution. Upon the firm establishment of the state government under the Constitution of 1780, they rioted regularly to prevent the sitting of the courts, and thereby to prevent the effective working of government. In 1784 and 1785 they temporarily stopped fighting the government and simply ignored it, that being possible because the lax administration of Governor John Hancock amounted, in the western part of the state, to no administration at all. Inhabitants of the

---

[46] These generalizations are based largely upon study of the statutes of the several states; Jensen, *New Nation,* chapters 8, 12, 17, and 20, contain much valuable information; on South Carolina and Virginia, see chapter 3, herein. See also Albert A. Giesecke, *American Commercial Legislation Before 1789* (Philadelphia, 1910).

western towns continued to complain that they were over-taxed and underrepresented, but few of the towns bothered to send any representatives, and fewer still paid any taxes. In short, for a couple of years they were free to pay allegiance to the only government they really recognized, that of the towns.[47]

No aristocrat would have approved such bumpkins, but had one taken a look at their opponents, he might at least have been sympathetic. Boston's merchants, who dominated the state's postwar politics, were as incompetent a ruling class as was likely to be seen anywhere, anytime. Most of Boston's leading colonial merchants—men with the wits and the daring to thrive in a hostile world—had been Loyalists, along with the more seasoned lawyers, public officials, and intelligentsia. They were, as they deserved to be, banished from the state when British troops were expelled. The departed professional public officials were not replaced at all. The departed lawyers, with a handful of outstanding exceptions, were replaced by mediocrities. The merchants, with even fewer exceptions, were replaced by submediocrities.[48]

The last loss was the most telling, for along with mercan-

---

[47] Robert J. Taylor, *Western Massachusetts in the Revolution* (Providence, 1954); Lee N. Newcomer, *The Embattled Farmers: A Massachusetts Countryside in the American Revolution* (New York, 1953); Worcester *Massachusetts Spy; Hampshire Gazette;* Springfield *Hampshire Herald;* Journal of the House of Representatives of the General Court of Massachusetts, 1780–1788, in the Massachusetts Archives; Handlin and Handlin, "Radicals and Conservatives in Massachusetts After Independence," in *New England Quarterly,* 17:343 ff. (1944), and their *Commonwealth,* 267–68. My running summary is put together from all these sources.

[48] The list of banished Loyalists is in "An Act to Prevent the Return to This State of Certain Persons Therein Named," published in the *Boston Gazette,* September 1, 1783; see also John Adams to James Warren, March 21, 1776, and Warren to Adams, June 13, 1779, in Burnett, ed., *Letters of Members of Congress,* 1:402, 4:269; Paine to Gerry, April 12, 1777, in Austin, *Gerry,* 1:221.

tile problems that would have challenged the most able and experienced traders, the new merchants inherited an ill-fitting mantle of leadership. One could be harsh and recite their blunders in detail; or one could be kind and merely point out that the new merchants, most of them sons of artisans or packet-boat operators who stumbled onto riches through privateering, did not measure up to their postwar tasks.

A few details are necessary. One is that some ports were not so thoroughly enervated as was Boston. Hence the whalers of Nantucket, virtually wiped out by the war, plodded and persisted until they had reestablished an industry that would thrive for another half-century, until technological change exacted its toll; hence the merchants of Salem, old pros all, faced the new adverse conditions, studied them, and then roamed the seas and unlocked the treasures of the Orient; and hence a few grubby new-rich artisans, unable to shake their old ways, returned to making things, and thereby laid the foundations for New England's future greatness.[49]

A second is that these exceptional men, by finding their way through private initiative rather than governmental action, abandoned the political arena to the bungling Bostonians. The greater number of these ignored the changed world commercial conditions, slavishly imitated their predecessors and betters, and thereby soon dissipated their fortunes. The first step on their path to ruin was that taken

---

[49] Hohman, *The American Whaleman, passim;* Morison, *Maritime History,* 154, 156–59, 314–26; *Salem Mercury,* April 21, 1787; *Massachusetts Centinel,* June 27, 1787; *New York Journal,* August 2, 1787, January 15, 1789; Weeden, *Economic and Social History of New England,* 2:776–78, 821–26; James D. Phillips, *Salem and the Indies* (Boston, 1947), *passim;* Victor S. Clark, *History of Manufactures in the United States* (3 vols., New York, 1929), vol. 1, *passim.*

by the merchants of Providence, overimportation of British goods in 1783–84.[50] There was one difference: the Bostonians erred on a much larger scale, and ended up holding and being in debt for several times as much in unsalable goods.[51]

[50] Historians have generally recognized that Bostonians greatly overimported in 1783–84, but they have also asserted, repeatedly and uncritically, that these goods were passed along, on credit, to retailers who sold them on credit to back-country farmers, thus creating a chain of debts which led to the troubles of 1786–87. I have never seen a shred of evidence that this was the case.

[51] That the Bostonians greatly overimported in 1783–84 is abundantly evident; see, for example, advertisements in Boston newspapers, 1783–85; George Benson to Nicholas Brown, March 15, 1782, in Brown Papers, John Carter Brown Library, cited in Hedges, *Browns of Providence Plantations,* 362; Jacob Sebor to Silas Deane, November 10, 1784, in *Correspondence of Silas Deane,* 201; Moses Brown to Champion and Dickason, June 26, 1785, in Moses Brown Papers; London *General Evening Post,* August 19–21, 1783; Warren to Adams, June 24, October 27, 1783, in *Warren-Adams Letters,* 2:219, 232; Higginson to Adams, August 8, 1785, in Jameson, ed., "Higginson Letters," American Historical Association *Annual Report,* 1:723 (1896). For evidence that the Boston merchants were unable to sell the imported goods and were, as debtors, in a desperate plight by 1785, see, for example, Moses Brown to Champion and Dickason, June 26, 1785, as cited above, stating flatly that this was the case; Christian Febiger to J. Sobotken, June 15, 1785, in *Magazine of American History,* 8:352, in which a Danish mercantile agent reports that the Boston merchants had been unable to sell their English importations because "they have no back country to consume their goods"; the manuscript volume *Evaluation and Taxes,* 1786, vol. 163 in the Massachusetts Archives, which shows that the entire back-country debt was only about £25,000, whereas Boston merchants had imported several hundred thousand pounds of British goods; James Swan's *National Arithmetick* (Boston, 1786), 25, 82, indicating that Boston merchants had been able to pay for much of their imported goods with war-accumulated specie, but still owed well over £100,000; Weeden's reference to the papers of the Boston firm of Amory and Amory (*Economic and Social History,* 2:819), showing that that house was proving unable, as early as 1784, to sell the English goods it had imported; the advertisements in the Worcester *Massachusetts Spy,* January 5, 1786, showing attempts of Boston merchants to sell British goods; the Christopher Gore Papers, Baker Library, Harvard, showing the efforts of a Boston merchant, hired by the London firm of Champion

The third and salient detail is that the Bostonians, again like the Providence merchants, turned inward and tried to save themselves by bleeding their neighbors. Their means was gross, as befitted the new rich. Like the other states, Massachusetts had, after the continental money collapsed in 1779–80, issued its own securities for the payment of war goods and services; but unlike the others Massachusetts tied the fate of its public bonds to that of the continental paper, and soon the bonds also collapsed. During the next three years the now all-but-worthless securities gravitated toward Boston. In 1784, when most of the paper had come to rest, the owners in Boston induced the General Court to fund these debts at their war-inflated face value. Massachusetts was thereby saddled with a debt of about $5 million, an enormous sum for the day. If the public debt were paid in time, the new rich would be secure in their fortunes for life, and the taxpayers of Massachusetts would be impoverished.[52]

and Dickason, to collect debts owed by Boston merchants; "A Return of Excise and Dutied Articles Which Were on Hand or Brought into the Several Towns Herewith Annexed," in the Sedgwick Papers, Massachusetts Historical Society, indicating the general volume of trade in Berkshire County—fifty-nine purchases of outside goods in two years, 1788–90, totaling only about $5,200, and none of the transactions being with Boston. The total amount of debts owed by Bostonians to London firms, unsupported by sales on credit to Massachusetts consumers, cannot be reckoned. Professor James B. Hedges, in an interview, stated that his estimate (based upon the correspondence of the Browns of Providence with Champion and Dickason, and particularly on the records in the Brown Papers of the visit in 1790 of Thomas Dickason, Jr., to New England to collect the debts owed his firm) was between £200,000 and £300,000.

[52] *Acts and Resolves of Massachusetts,* 1784, chapter 25; Journal of the House of Representatives, February 20, June 8, 1784; *Massachusetts Centinel,* September 21, 1785, February 8, 1786; Bates, *State Finances of Massachusetts,* 85–93; Ferguson, *Power of the Purse,* 245–46, 273–75; Jensen, *New Nation,* 307–8.

After a while the taxpayers, especially those to the west who professed no love for the Bostonians anyway, began to get other ideas. Like their counterparts in Rhode Island, they began to entertain the notion of writing off the public debts with an issue of paper money. Governor Hancock, his celebrated gout serving, as always, as a reliable barometer of political storms, saw fit to retire. His replacement was more to the Bostonians' liking, and less to that of the westerners: James Bowdoin, an upright and otherwise intelligent man who believed that just now, more than anything else, Massachusetts needed an energetic government. The westerners did not like this. They liked it so little that they saw fit to resist, to resume their belligerent ways.[53]

In this resistance some opportunists saw opportunity, and their doings led to civil war. In the civil war other opportunists saw larger opportunity, and their doings led to the creation of the American nation.

---

[53] See chapter 5, herein.

Chapter Five

The Critical Period of American History

In the early spring of 1787, after the most violent winter but one in almost a decade, ominous calm descended upon the land. The very life of the Republic was on trial. (No external enemy threatened its shores, and no enemy agents conspired to destroy it from within, but it was in mortal danger nonetheless, for the freest people in the world had ceased to care whether the Republic lived or died.)

Or so it had seemed for four years and more, and especially for the last two. During those four years, and especially those two, everywhere one looked closely the Union seemed to be coming apart. When one took the broader view, say from the vantage point of a European capital, the visible events were different but their portent was the same.

From that distance, in one respect only did the America of 1785–87 resemble the one which, ten years earlier, had struggled so mightily to be born. The similarity was that significant things seemed to be happening—or significantly failing to happen—in just three places: the Congress, Massachusetts, and Virginia. All else was different. Congress, far from leading as it once had led, was reduced to begging its own members to attend its sessions. In Massachusetts the popular rage and enthusiasm that had once terrified British generals was now aimed by the people one against the other. And in Virginia statesmen were piddling away their considerable talents on inconsiderable matters of money-changing.

During those two years the shows in the three arenas began like so many circus rings populated by has-been performers, competing with unrelated acts for the attention of bored spectators. Actually the various acts were intimately related at all times, and soon they vitally affected everyone present. But before this could become apparent, and before people could be brought to care again, an improbable combination of violence, coincidence, and leadership had to coalesce.

In Congress, the Year of Our Lord 1785—and of the Independence of the United States the Tenth—began as if there would be no action at all. For three months there were never more than seven states represented; and that, as the Articles of Confederation dictated, meant that Congress could do no more than adopt resolutions on picayune subjects, and even then only by unanimous vote. When, during the next six months, larger numbers occasionally attended, their doings were dreary in the extreme.[1]

But in its tedious and ineffectual manner, Congress dealt with three subjects during the year: public debts, public lands, and the regulation of commerce. And however ponderously it handled them, it did so in a way that had consistent implications.

---

[1] Burnett, *Continental Congress,* 638–41 (see also index, reference to Continental Congress, decrease in attendance).

As to the public debts, it would have seemed that all talk was meaningless unless Congress could lay its hands on some money. In March Congress examined the prospects by surveying the status of the revenue amendments that had been proposed two years earlier. The results were not encouraging. The amendments concerning land taxes and requisitions had got nowhere. Ten states had, in one way or another, ratified the amendment giving Congress power to tax imports, but Georgia, New York, and Rhode Island had not, and no one was optimistic about Rhode Island. (Actually, Rhode Island had ratified conditionally in February, but Congress had not yet received the news.) [2]

These facts upset the republicans who dominated Congress not at all. The national debt, Robert Morris had preached, was the makings of a tangible web that could be spun to create a strong national government. Very well then, the republicans said—but only with actions, not with words—let them be dissolved. Increasingly the states were starting the process by assuming payment of interest and principal on the national debt. Now Congress could hasten things along: it established a Board of Treasury to replace the departed superintendent, and entrusted to it the task of auditing all claims so as to render them more easily abolished. The persons appointed to the board clearly reflected the intentions of Congress. One of its members, Walter Livingston of New York, was a lukewarm nationalist who viewed the office as a vehicle for private speculations; the other two, Samuel Osgood of Massachusetts and Arthur

---

[2] *Journals of Congress,* March 15, 1785 (28:162); for a good summary of state actions, see Jensen, *New Nation,* 407–17.

Lee of Virginia, were archrepublicans who viewed it as a
means of destroying the possibility of the permanent concentration of national power.[3]

The companion task was to make the audited certificates
of public debt convertible into public lands, thereby using
one adhesive of union to cancel the other. In 1784 Congress
had taken the first step, passing an ordinance providing for a
large measure of local self-government by the settlers in the
western territory, and their ultimate admission to the Union
as states equal to the original members. Now, in May 1785,
it passed an ordinance providing for the survey of the lands
in the territory. Soon the actual process of sale could
begin.[4]

And while thus preparing to reduce itself to perpetual
impotence, Congress fretted over its impotence. A young
and devoutly republican delegate from the back country of
Virginia, James Monroe by name, proposed a new series of
amendments to the Articles of Confederation. The amendments—vesting Congress with power to regulate interstate
and foreign commerce—were little different from proposals
someone else had made a year earlier. Nothing came of
either, save two days of debate in July, after which the
subject was dropped for yet another year.[5]

---

[3] *Journals of Congress,* 26:356–57, 27:437–43, 469–71, 28:18, 29:582;
Jensen, *New Nation,* 262–63, 371–74; Osgood Papers, New York Public
Library; Wadsworth to Hamilton, November 11, 1785, in *Hamilton
Papers,* 3:633–35. On the work of the Board of Treasury, 1785–89, see
Ferguson, *Power of the Purse,* 186, 189, 195–227.

[4] *Journals of Congress,* 26:275–79, 28:375–81.

[5] *Ibid.,* 28:201–5; Monroe to Jefferson, July 15, 1785, and to Madison,
July 26, 1785, in Burnett, ed., *Letters of Members of Congress,* 8:166,
177–72; Burnett, *Continental Congress,* 634–35.

Commerce, debts, and lands: stir them one way and the Union would be cemented, stir them another and it would be dissolved. True to the latter formula throughout, Congress dealt with one more matter that involved all three ingredients. It received the minister plenipotentiary from Spain, Diego de Gardoqui, and authorized superintendent of foreign affairs John Jay to negotiate a commercial treaty with him. In August, however, it explicitly instructed Jay not to yield America's claim to free navigation of the Mississippi—in short, that he should not betray the interests of western land purchasers, real and potential, for the sake of commercial concessions.[6]

In Massachusetts the play was the same but it was far more interesting, if only because there were more actors. On stage, as 1785 began, were only the merchants of Boston, looking for all the world as if the Day of Judgment were at hand. As other characters entered and the action started, the shadows of this illusion deepened. In January, farmers sledded their products to market and found farm prices at record peacetime highs. The prices of British goods, which Boston merchants had imported in unparalleled quantities for the preceding eighteen months, were at record lows. British creditors were beginning to grumble: the merchants had taken on debts of around a quarter of a million pounds sterling to buy these goods, and no remittances were forthcoming, for the goods proved entirely unstable. The fledgling Bank of Massachusetts, thrown into panic by the plight

---

[6] *Ibid.,* 654; *Journals of Congress,* 29:658 (August 25, 1785).

of its mercantile customers, stopped discounting and thereby threw its customers into even further panic.[7]

General frenzy, born of this panic, pervaded the Massachusetts elections in the spring of 1785. The Boston merchants, or most of them, clamored for payment of the public debts due them so that they could pay the more legitimate private debts they owed. They also clamored for the enactment of various commercial laws in their behalf, most notably laws prohibiting the further importation of British goods. The artisans and mechanics of Boston added to the din, hoping with the merchants that legislation could somehow remove the destructive competition of British manufactures, retroactively.[8]

Governor John Hancock, being unwilling to alienate the consumers, producers, and taxpayers at whose expense such laws would be enacted, and yet being unwilling to disappoint the Boston merchants and mechanics who had so long looked to him for leadership, hit upon a compromise: he would let someone else have a turn at the governorship. But Hancock was consistent. Not wanting to resolve the situation himelf, he did not want anyone else to resolve it either. He therefore fiercely opposed his logical successor, James Bowdoin, who let no one doubt that he would seek to resolve matters decisively in favor of the Bostonians. Hancock's efforts were as shrewd and as vicious as usual, but

---

[7] *Pennsylvania Packet,* January 7, 24, 1785; Weeden, *Economic and Social History of New England,* 2:898–903; *Massachusetts Centinel,* January–March 1785; James Warren to John Adams, January 28, 1785, in *Warren-Adams Letters,* 2:249; see also the sources cited in footnote 51, chapter 4, herein.

[8] *Massachusetts Centinel,* March 30, April 2, 9, 16, 20, 23, 30, May 7, 11, 21, 25, 1785; Boston *American Journal,* May 10, 1785.

by no means as successful, for Bowdoin easily defeated Hancock's man Thomas Cushing.[9]

(The name-calling and backstabbing were, indeed, totally insignificant but for one thing: it introduced a new minor politician whose petty personal grudges would spark vast events. Benjamin Austin, Jr., a young mechanic who aspired to be the Sam Adams of his generation, attempted to defeat Hancock's bid for a seat in the state House of Representatives by campaigning and maneuvering in behalf of his father, Benjamin Austin, Sr. Young Austin was driven by his hatred for Hancock, for the Massachusetts court system, and for the judges Hancock had appointed to the courts. None of these had anything to do with the outcome of the election; they all, however, had to do with what followed a year later.)[10]

If sound and fury would solve commercial problems Massachusetts would have been booming by September. In response to assorted mass meetings, as well as to Bowdoin's leadership, the General Court passed laws and resolutions excluding foreign vessels from the Massachusetts export trade and establishing protective tariffs and a system of bounties and other subsidies for the promotion of the local economy. It issued a ringing manifesto for other states to do the same. It also instructed the Massachusetts congressmen to ask Congress to call a general convention to revise the

---

[9] *Massachusetts Centinel,* as cited in the previous note, and May 28, 1785; *Boston Gazette,* May 16, 1785; returns of the election in the manuscript volume, Votes for Governor and Lieutenant Governor, 1785–88, and Journals of the House of Representatives, May 21, 1785, both in Massachusetts Archives; James Warren to John Adams, September 4, 1785, in *Warren-Adams Letters,* 2:262–63.

[10] See footnotes 23 and 24 in this chapter.

Articles of Confederation—particularly, to endow Congress
with power to shut the British out of American ports. Boston
mechanics did their part, too. In July they engaged in several bloody brawls with crewmen of British vessels and in
August they formed a committee of correspondence and
sent a circular letter to their counterparts in Philadelphia,
Baltimore, and Charleston, pleading with them to join the
crusade.[11]

It was all an exercise in futility. The circularized mechanics wrote back their polite condolences. The anti-
British navigation acts proved unenforceable and useless,
and the only state that was moved to enact similar legislation was New Hampshire, which did no trading with Britain
anyway. As to the call for a "constitutional convention," it
did not even reach Congress. The state's archrepublican
delegates refused to present the resolution because, as they
wrote Bowdoin, they feared its "aristocratical" implications,
and also feared that such a convention might go far beyond
the subject of commercial problems and attempt to establish a national government.[12]

---

[11] *Massachusetts Centinel,* July 13, 16, 23, and throughout August 1785;
Boston Gazette, June–July 1785; *Acts and Laws of the Commonwealth of
Massachusetts* (13 vols., Boston, 1781–89, republished in 1890), acts of
June 23, July 2, 11, November 28, 30, 1785, and messages of Bowdoin to the
legislature in the same, June 2, 10, 16, July 2, October 25, 1785. On all these
doings, see also the letters to and from Bowdoin during the period in *The
Bowdoin and Temple Papers* (Massachusetts Historical Society *Collections,*
series 6, vol. 9, series 7, vol. 6, Boston, 1897, 1907), 2:50 ff.; and Samuel
Adams' letters in Cushing, ed., *Writings of Adams,* vol. 4.

[12] Burnett, *Continental Congress,* 636–37; King, Gerry, and Holten to
Bowdoin, September 3, 1785, in Burnett, ed., *Letters of Members of Congress,* 8:206–10; Bowdoin to Gov. Nicholas Van Dyke of Delaware, July
28, 1785, in Van Dyke Papers, Library of Congress, and Van Dyke to Bowdoin, March 15, 1786, in Emmet Collection, New York Public Library;
Laws of New Hampshire, act of June 23, 1785; *Pennsylvania Gazette,* Sep-

Somewhat more effective, if only in stirring people up, were the efforts to pay off the state debt. The legislature enacted a new excise tax, an increase poll tax, and an unprecedented stamp act. Governor Bowdoin himself saw to it that the town tax collectors became a more energetic lot than had been their predecessors under Hancock. Money thus began to trickle steadily into the state treasury, and thereby the strain under which the Boston merchants labored was reduced. Thereby, too, the strain under which all others in the state labored was increased. The excise tax angered all who bought imported goods, for it was laid on top of already high import duties; but those so angered were not particularly numerous, for those so buying were few. The poll tax enraged those upon whom it bore the hardest, the subsistence-and-barter farmers who, rarely seeing a dollar from one year to the next, now had to come up with three dollars every year for every male over sixteen. The stamp tax was the least popular of all, for it recalled the hated Parliamentary taxes, which a lot of common folks thought they had fought a revolution about; and it also struck at the pocketbooks of those with the loudest voices in America, the newspaper owners.[13]

All was unquiet on the northern front.

Far to the south, the doings were less turbulent but equally destructive. Virginia, leisurely pursuing its dream

---

tember 14, October 5, 1785; *Massachusetts Centinel,* August 20, October 26, 1785.

[13] *Ibid.; Boston Gazette,* May–June, October–November 1785; *Acts and Laws,* acts of March 18, July 2, 1785; Bowdoin's message to the legislature, in Journal of the House of Representatives, June 2, 1786; Bates, Finances of Massachusetts, 103, 118–20, appendix.

of a tobacco-planter's heaven, started to work on its state commercial policy. To that end it appointed commissioners to deal with commissioners from Maryland and draw up a bistate compact relating to the use of the Potomac and Pocomoke rivers and Chesapeake Bay.[14]

The implications of this conference scarcely favored a stronger union.[15] For one thing, because the commissioners were empowered to settle interstate commercial problems outside the framework of the Confederation, it was an overt flaunting of the Congress. For another, the commissioners appointed were five of the nation's least enthusiastic friends: Samuel Chase, Daniel of St. Thomas Jenifer, and Thomas Stone of Maryland, and Alexander Henderson and George Mason of Virginia.

At the invitation of George Washington, the commis-

---

[14] Hening, ed., *Statutes of Virginia,* 12:50–55; *Votes and Proceedings of the Senate of Maryland,* March 8, 11, 1786; "Resolutions Touching the Navigation and Jurisdiction of the Potomac," December 28, 1785; Madison to Edmund Randolph, July 26, 1785, Madison to Jefferson, October 3, 1785, January 22, March 18, 1786, Madison's notes for a speech on commercial regulations, November 1785, Madison to Monroe, December 9, 1785, January 22, May 13, 1786, Madison to Washington, December 9, 1785, November 8, 1786, all in Gaillard Hunt, ed., *The Writings of James Madison* (9 vols., New York, 1900–1910), 3:152, 178, 194, 196, 201, 214, 222, 224, 242, 279, 283.

[15] Accounts of these events are numerous; see, for example, Edward Channing, *A History of the United States* (6 vols., New York, 1905–25), 3:469–73. Conventional accounts, however, disregard the antinationalist implications of the conferences, and treat them as if they had led inevitably to the Philadelphia Convention of 1787. Not even Washington viewed them as steps toward a stronger union; his part in the doings was apparently confined to promoting the interests of two internal navigation companies in which he had investments, the Potomac and James companies, though he was also interested in seeing to it that western trade went eastward instead of down the Ohio and Mississippi, until western settlers were numerous enough to be a threat to Spanish-held territory; see Washington to Richard Henry Lee, December 14, 1784, February 8, March 15, June 22, August 22, 1785, in Lee, *Life of R. H. Lee,* 2:26–34.

sioners removed the seat of their deliberations from Alexandria to Mount Vernon, where they completed their negotiations on March 28. The awesome presence of the Father of his Country did not, however, make the compact any the more nationalistic. The commissioners agreed to bistate control of navigation of the waterways in question, and also recommended to their state governments that another convention be held to arrange for the establishment of a state navy on the Chesapeake and the scheduling of uniform, state-enacted tariff duties for the area.

In October Virginia ratified the Mount Vernon compact. A month later Maryland also ratified and, flushed with the success of one local conference, proposed another. This one would include Pennsylvania and Delaware, and would be instructed to deal with the remaining minor interstate commercial problems in the area. On that not particularly meaningful note, winter descended and the year was over.

(At year's end on the other major fronts nothing much happened save a general drift from bad to worse. Things in Boston grew portentously quiet. Things in Congress grew quiet also, but not portentously: it was only that congressmen almost entirely ceased attending. Between October 1, 1785, and January 31, 1786, Congress had a quorum on only ten days, and never were more than seven states represented. Between October 1, 1785, and April 30, 1786, nine states— the minimum required to do any serious business—were represented on only three days.)[16]

But the new year had hardly dawned when the silence was shattered by explosive activity on all fronts. For three months events seemed to be popping simultaneously and

---

[16] Burnett, *Continental Congress,* 640, 647.

everywhere. *In January:* On the second, Congress heard a
new report on the fate of the impost amendment of 1783
that suddenly reversed the way it had been thinking for
many months past. Only Georgia and New York had failed
to comply with the amendment, and both now had it under
consideration. Lethargic as Congress was, none could but
tremble at the potential energizing effect of an independent
revenue, now apparently just around the corner. On the
twenty-first, Virginia responded to Maryland's proposals
for an enlarged commercial convention. But a handful of
nationalists in the Virginia Assembly maneuvered through
a resolution broadening the call still further to include all
states, thus changing the charter of the proposal entirely.
On the twenty-fifth, Benjamin Tuppen and retired general
Rufus Putnam issued a call to their fellow veterans in Massachusetts to flee crowded and troubled New England with
them, by joining in a vast resettlement and enrichment
scheme, through the formation of an organization to be
called the Ohio Company.[17]

In February: On the third, Congress again had a quorum.
Partly in hope and partly in despair it determined to go, on
bended knee if necessary, to the legislatures of Georgia and
New York and get them to ratify the impost amendment.
On the eighth, and on many of the days that followed, Boston witnessed agitation to substantially repudiate the public
debt by paying it off at market value instead of face value.
Many means were proposed for so doing: Governor Bowdoin thought it might be practicable for the state to acquire
a shipload of local products and sell them abroad, using
the proceeds toward retiring the debt, as was being tried in

---

[17] *Ibid.*, 642; *Massachusetts Centinel*, January 25, 1786; Madison to Jefferson, January 22, 1786, in Hunt, ed., *Writings of Madison*, 2:218.

North Carolina.[18] More radical voices urged that paper money be printed and the debt paid with it, as was about to be done in Rhode Island. Bowdoin's scheme would take too long, however, and Massachusetts' marketing farmers had been too badly burned by the depreciation of continental paper to think seriously of the latter suggestion. The most common and the most practical demand came to be that state securities, whatever their market value, be accepted at par in payment on taxes. On the twenty-third Governor Patrick Henry of Virginia, following the instructions of the Assembly, sent out a circular letter to his fellow governors, recommending that all states send delegates to a commercial convention to be held in Annapolis on the first Monday in September.[19]

In March: Congress learned that its life or death depended upon the action of one state. All hope of gaining power to regulate commerce appeared gone, for a survey revealed that three states had declined to grant the power and the others had complied in ways that largely canceled one another; and few believed that if the proposed Annapolis convention yielded anything, Congress would be any the more powerful for it. Prospects of replenishing its empty treasury through requisitions from the states, never very bright, were now dimmed to the vanishing point, for New Jersey flatly refused to comply with the most recent requisition, and it appeared inevitable that other states would do

---

[18] The Bowdoin plan had been presented earlier; see Bowdoin's message of May 31, 1785, in the manuscript Journal of the House (Massachusetts Archives), 42–46, and his message of June 2, 1785, in *Acts and Laws of the Commonwealth of Massachusetts* (13 vols., Boston, 1781–89; republished in 1890).

[19] Burnett, *Continental Congress,* 642–43; *Massachusetts Centinel,* September 21, 24, 1785, for earlier agitation, and February 8, 15, 22, and March–May 1786; *American Herald* for the same period.

likewise. But prospects for revenue from import duties appeared immeasurably brighter, for Georgia ratified the necessary amendment and Rhode Island removed all conditions from its ratification. That left only New York. Until this very March, New York had had a consistent record of supporting Congress; and its legislature was now in session.[20]

In that same March giant steps were taken toward the liquidation of the national domain. On the eleventh, the Ohio Company was officially organized in Boston and shares were sold (the most enthused subscribers proved to be from Connecticut, and soon that state dominated the company). On the twenty-fourth, Congress appointed a committee to revise the 1784 Northwest Ordinance. The revision did not materialize for more than a year, but it was clear from the beginning that the changes would be designed to ease the path of such organizations as the Ohio Company. Specifically, they would lodge political control of the West in the hands of Eastern promoters instead of Western squatters, and they would saddle Congress with the cost of Western government until Western states matured, thereby freeing land companies from taxes during developmental periods.[21]

And in the same month of March Benjamin Austin, Jr.,

---

[20] Burnett, *Continental Congress,* 643–44; *Journals of Congress,* 30:93–94 (March 3, 1786); Richard P. McCormick, *Experiment in Independence* (New Brunswick, 1950), 208–9; *Providence Gazette,* March 4, 1786; Allen D. Candler, ed., *The Colonial Records of the State of Georgia* (26 vols., Atlanta, 1904–16), vol. 19, part 2, act of February 13, 1786; *Gazette of the State of Georgia,* April 20, 1786; *Votes and Proceedings of the Assembly of New York,* January Session, 1786.

[21] *Massachusetts Centinel,* March 11, 1786; Burnett, *Continental Congress,* 651; *Journals of Congress,* 32:334–43, 33:399–401 (July 13, 23, 1787); Jensen, *New Nation,* 355–59.

of Boston renewed his campaign for power and vengeance. As a means to both ends he chose an issue so explosive that no other Massachusetts politician, however reckless, had dared touch it: the cost of justice. Under Massachusetts' archaic legal system even the pettiest transactions had to be recorded in some court or other, an encumbrance not lightened by the Yankees' habit of hauling one another into court over the most trivial grievances. The fees charged by courts and lawyers were, on paper, modest enough; but the abundance of actions earned lawyers and clerks and judges a good deal better living than that of their neighbors, and Massachusetts was normally so short of money of any kind that even nominal sums, if cash were required, were hard to raise. Unsurprisingly, the areas in which money circulated most slowly were the areas in which the cost of justice was most painful. The issue was a dangerous one because, on the one hand, it was only through the administration of justice that the state, as state, was held together; and on the other, the interior portions of the state had, through the Revolution, witnessed the periodic gathering of armed bands, which prevented the courts from sitting. Moreover, it was doubly dangerous because fees bit hardest in the same places where taxes bit hardest, among the isolated and essentially lawless countrymen of Worcester, Hampshire, and Berkshire counties. These men wanted nothing in the world so much as to be left alone, and they would band together only to protect what they regarded as an unalienable right to be left alone.[22]

---

[22] *Massachusetts Centinel,* March 25, April 15, 19, 26, May 10, June 24, September 9, 1786, January 9, 1788; *American Herald,* May 8, 1786; item dated May 31, 1787, in the Knox Papers, Massachusetts Historical Society, identifying Austin as "Honestus"; Boston *Independent Chronicle,* March 9, May 11, 1786; Robert J. Taylor, *Western Massachusetts in the Revolu-*

Whether Austin knew what he was doing is beside the point. He probably did not. He does not appear to have been the most balanced of young men; his pique against the courts stemmed from a costly and unfavorable decision in a suit he had brought for questionable motives. Too, what was pique in most could become blind rage in Austin. In any event, he fanned embers that were long smouldering but far from dead. The issue became a principal one in the spring elections in Boston, and then the agitation spread to nearby towns in Essex County on the north, and in Plymouth and Bristol counties on the south. From there it spread gradually but surely westward until, by fall, it had reached forest-fire proportions.[23]

As the flames of discontent spread across Massachusetts in the summer of 1786, events on the other major fronts swept toward climaxes. On each, hopes were suddenly raised and as suddenly dashed or dissipated. The state legislatures responded with unexpected speed to the call for the commercial convention at Annapolis, and even New York and Rhode Island chose delegates. But the momentum soon died, and when the legislative season was over, four

---

tion (Providence, 1954), 80, 126–27, 134–36; Caleb Strong to Theodore Sedgwick, June 24, 1786, in Sedgwick Papers, Massachusetts Historical Society, and scattered scraps in the same collection. Hostility to lawyers in central and western Massachusetts is commented on by scores of authors of local histories, for a bibliography of many of which see the footnotes in McDonald, *We the People*, 191–99.

[23] Reports of conventions and instructions of legislators in *Massachusetts Centinel*, 1786: in Roxbury and Lynn, May 10; eight towns in Bristol County, July 29, August 12; thirty-seven towns in Worcester County, August 26. See also the Northampton *Hampshire Gazette, the American Herald*, Worcester *Massachusetts Spy*, May–September 1786.

states had failed to act. If the elected delegates ran true to form, half of them would show up in September.[24]

On the matter of obtaining a desperately needed revenue, the word came that New York had ratified the impost amendment. But any nationalist enthusiasm was short-lived; it lived only until the fine print could be read. New York had required that the collections be made by the state, had stipulated that the state's paper money be acceptable for duties, and had otherwise hedged its ratification with such conditions that, even had Congress been disposed to accept them, they would have canceled the grants of several other states. Congress, facing utter bankruptcy, urged Governor George Clinton to call a special session of the legislature to ratify the amendment in acceptable fashion. Clinton flatly refused. The issue would have to hang in suspense until January—if the nation could hang together that long.[25]

In its land dealings Congress seemed about to resolve many long-standing problems when a related issue arose that almost tore Congress itself apart. As the summer began, John Jay showed up with a request that his instructions be changed so as to allow him to surrender navigation rights on the Mississippi to Spain. As the summer progressed congressmen showed more energy than they had shown in a decade, and they used it all to fight one another over this question. As the summer ended, the matter came to a vote:

---

[24] The elections of delegates to the Annapolis convention are summarized in the convention's "Address," which is published in many places, e.g., *Hamilton Papers*, 3:686–90.

[25] *Laws of New York*, 2:320 ff.; New York *Daily Advertiser*, February 1787; *Journals of Congress*, 30:439–44, 31:513–14, 559; *Votes and Proceedings of the Assembly of New York*, April 13, 15, 1786; Clinton's message to the legislature, January 13, 1787, in the same; Burnett, *Continental Congress*, 659, 662.

all seven states north of the Mason-Dixon line voted to grant Jay's request, and all five states from Maryland south voted against it. Besides foreboding ill for the upcoming Annapolis commercial convention, the bitterness of this battle opened a sectional conflict of interests that would not soon be healed. (Off and on during the debates men began to talk of giving up on the Union, and trying to salvage something by creating several regional confederations. Such talk was heard in and out of Congress, in high places and low.)[26]

But from mid-August onward, Massachusetts held the center of the stage. Word came to Boston that the inhabitants of Bristol County planned to rise in arms to prevent the sitting of the county court when it convened the following month. On the twentieth—too late, as it turned out—Samuel Blackden wrote to Superintendent of War Henry Knox from London, warning Knox that the British were about to attempt some form of counterrevolution, presumably military, in New England. On the twenty-sixth a convention of delegates from thirty-seven towns in Worcester County met and drafted a petition of grievances. No one said so, but the air was full of hints that the delegates intended to stop the sitting of the Worcester County Court until their demands were met. Three days later, the Hampshire County Court attempted to convene for its fall session

---

[26] *Ibid.*, 656–59; *Journals of Congress*, 31:574–613 (August 29–31, 1786); *New Hampshire Spy*, December 26, 1786; *Charleston Morning Post*, March 15, 29, April 3, May 19, 1787; Theodore Sedgwick to Caleb Strong, August 6, 1786, in Burnett, ed., *Letters of Members of Congress*, 8:415; Benjamin Rush to Richard Price, October 27, 1786, in "Price Letters," Massachusetts Historical Society *Proceedings*, 17:353 (1903).

in Northampton, only to find the path blocked by a mob of 1,500 men, 500 of them armed. The court prudently adjourned without sitting and—in a fit of wishful thinking—resolved to convene in Springfield on September 25.[27]

The complaints of the Worcester County convention and the action of the Northampton mob were aimed at an assortment of petty grievances and two major ones: the cost of justice, and the unbearable tax burden levied in cash to pay off at par the state's depreciated public securities. More than a month earlier, the General Court had passed a law streamlining the court system and effecting other reforms designed to speed up and reduce the expense of civil actions. This law was long and complicated, however, and somehow it was never published in the back country until the shooting was over.[28] At the same time, the General Court had passed a law that might have cut the tax burden by seventy-five percent, for it made public securities receivable at par in payment of taxes. But this did not become known in the hinterlands either; those shrewd and energetic tax gatherers the Bowdoin administration had ushered into office, quickly perceiving the opportunity for personal profit thus afforded, suppressed the news of the changed law. Then they demanded and continued to collect taxes in hard money, bought and delivered the necessary securities, and pocketed the difference between the par and market value of the

---

[27] Blackden to Knox, August 20, 1786, in Knox Papers, Massachusetts Historical Society; Shays' Rebellion Papers, vol. 190, Massachusetts Archives, reports of August 29 and September 5, 1786; *Massachusetts Centinel,* August 12, 26, September 2, 1786.

[28] A more extravagant act regulating the practice of law was passed by the House but defeated in the Senate; see Robert J. Taylor, *Western Massachusetts in the Revolution* (Providence, 1954), 135–36.

paper. Thus a mixture of ignorance and greed and opportunism set off the spark that would become Shays' Rebellion.[29]

On the second of September Middlesex County towns
held a convention that was essentially the same as the one
held earlier in Worcester. On the fifth Judge Artemus Ward
attempted to convene the county court at Worcester, and
was prevented by a mob of two to four hundred men. Four
days later a Hampshire County convention met, following
the examples of Worcester and Middlesex. On the eleventh,
or so Judge Ward reported to Governor Bowdoin, about a
dozen men, said to be British emissaries, were seen riding
from town to town and county to county calling men to
arms. The next day, three county courts attempted to sit
and were preventing from sitting: the Middlesex County
Court was stopped at Concord by 300 men and seventy-five
horse, the Bristol County Court was stopped at Taunton by
182 men, and the Berkshire County Court was stopped at
Great Barrington by seven to eight hundred men. On the
twenty-fifth the adjourned Hampshire County Court attempted to sit in Springfield and was prevented by a mob
estimated at five hundred to two thousand men. South and
west of Boston the government of the Commonwealth of
Massachusetts had entirely ceased to function.[30]

During the same month of September the Congress of the

---

[29] *Massachusetts Centinel,* July 12, August 26, 30, September 13, November 8, 1786; Springfield *Hampshire Herald,* September 5, 12, 1786; *Acts
and Resolves,* 1786.

[30] Shays' Rebellion Papers, Massachusetts Archives: entry of September
5, 1786 (vol. 190, pp. 226, 231–37); Thomas Clarke to Bowdoin, September 8, 1786 (190:238); Bowdoin to Moses Gill, September 8, 1786
(190:239); Artemas Ward to Bowdoin, September 12, 1786 (190:252);
190:249–51, 253–61; Bowdoin to General Court, September 28, 1786
(190:267–74). See also *Massachusetts Centinel, Hampshire Herald,* and
Boston Gazette, September 1786.

United States had likewise ceased to function. On the eleventh the Annapolis convention had opened. No "quorum" was present and almost immediately it became clear that those in attendance had no intention of allowing one to become present. Instead, a small band of long-time and devout nationalists did what they had previously decided to do: meet, declare that efforts to patch up a commercial agreement were hopeless, and request Congress and the several states to call a full-fledged constitutional convention to meet in Philadelphia the next May. In retrospect Hamilton, who drafted the resolutions of the convention, and his principal fellow "conspirators," James Madison and John Dickinson, would appear by this action to have been shrewd political operators and men of great vision. In context, what they did was merely visionary. Congress was peopled by members who did not trust one another, who feared a stronger general government but despised the states, and who jealously guarded their prerogatives even though they had no power. This Congress was no more disposed to call a general convention to revise the Articles of Confederation than it was to vote funds for the exploration of Canada. It referred the proposals to a committee of three, which referred them to a committee of thirteen, which Congress never appointed. In short, the grandiose proposal was not even allowed to lie and die on the table.[31]

---

[31] Thomas A. Emmet, *Annapolis Convention Held in 1786 with the Report of the Proceedings Represented to the States by President John Dickinson* (New York, 1891); "Annapolis Convention. Address of the Annapolis Convention," September 14, 1786, in *Hamilton Papers*, 3:686–90; *Journals of Congress*, September 20, 1786; Rufus King to Bowdoin, September 17, King to Adams, October 2, 1786, and Henry Lee to St. George Tucker, October 20, 1786, in Burnett, ed., *Letters of Members of Congress*, 8:468–69, 475, 489–90; Burnett, *Continental Congress*, 668–71, 673. That Hamilton had no intention of allowing the convention to meet for the purposes

In the same September the disaffections in Massachusetts threatened to spread to New Hampshire. On the twentieth a mob of 1,500 men, many of them lumberworkers fortified with courage from demon rum, gathered to do battle against their state in Exeter. They were approximately as well informed as were their counterparts to the south; indeed, their main stimulus was apparently a rumor that all Loyalists were about to be returned and that New Hampshire, along with the other states, would be taxed to compensate them for their confiscated estates. They were dealt with, however, much more decisively than were the insurgents in Massachusetts: Governor (and ex-general) John Sullivan stamped them down, and only in an unexpected fit of leniency refrained from hanging the whole lot.[32]

Governor Bowdoin was scarcely able to emulate Sullivan's example. On September 27, the legislature convened and heard Bowdoin's plea for, on the one hand, measures to secure the safety of the state and, on the other, laws to rectify the grievances complained of. Throughout October and early November the General Court did both, and it

---

for which it was called seems clear from his letter to his wife, September 8, 1786, in which he indicated that he only planned to stay a few days; and his taking action to adjourn quickly, ostensibly because there appeared no likelihood of a quorum, but in full awareness that the delegates from Rhode Island and Massachusetts, at least, would show up within a day or two (Thomas Cushing, Francis Dana, and Samuel Breck to Alexander Hamilton and Egbert Benson, September 10, 1786); both documents in *Hamilton Papers*, 3:684, 685.

[32] *New Hampshire Spy*, October 24, 1786, January 5, 1787; *New Hampshire Mercury*, October 4, 1786; documents reproduced in Hammond, ed., *Sullivan Papers*, 3:483–85; Whittemore, *John Sullivan*, 200–203. See also William Plumer to Samuel Plumer, Jr., July 22, 1786, and to John Hale, August 13, September 18, 20, 21, 26, October 6, 1786, in Colonial Society of Massachusetts *Collections*, 11:385–98 (1906–07), which indicate various aspects of the insurrection.

went a few steps further. It also passed laws making farm products legal tender for past-due taxes levied before 1784, suspending judgments against private debtors for eight months, and making various kinds of goods as well as money legal tender for the payment of private debts. The latter two measures were designed for those few who had complained about private indebtedness. Another was designed for the many who were complaining that, quite apart from the cost of justice and the cost of supporting the state debt, the state government was too expensive, being bloated by high salaries for every state official from Bowdoin down. To meet this complaint, the General Court published a detailed financial statement showing that the cost of government in Massachusetts—even when salaries were paid, which was not always—was relatively modest. Finally, the legislature legally closed the Hampshire and Berkshire courts for a time, and granted indemnity to all those who had participated in stopping the courts.[33]

The while, the malcontents bided their time, but not idly. Every town in Massachusetts, like every town everywhere, had its ne'er-do-wells. Some hung around the inns and drank, and some hung around the general stores and whittled, and some worked from time to time, for others or on their own farms. Most had never left their town and most were without influence in their towns, but a few were seasoned veterans of service in the continental line who had fallen to their shiftless state by abandoning their private

---

[33] *Massachusetts Centinel,* November 4, 1786; *Hampshire Gazette,* October 18, December 13, 20, 1786; Knox to Samuel Holden Parsons, November 19, 1786, in Knox Papers; Journal of the House of Representatives, seventh court, second session (September 1786), *passim; Acts and Resolves,* 1786–87, pp. 87 ff., 90 ff., 111 ff., 102 ff., 113 ff., 166 ff., 391 ff.

affairs while fighting to make their country free; and of these, some had the plausibility that makes for leadership in troubled times. Massachusetts also had a number of well-heeled Tories who had swallowed their pride and checked their bitterness and waited and prayed for the moment of counterrevolution to come. Somehow (nobody knows how) some of these men (nobody knows how many or, for sure, exactly which) got together and began to think of turning local turbulence to much grander account.[34]

Henry Knox, as was his wont, reacted to what he learned of this with the poise of an old maid who has heard a burglar. On the strength of little more than his imagination, he shouted to all who would listen that a full-fledged rebellion was under way, that huge bands of armed men were about to seize the federal arsenal at Springfield, and that, for good measure, an Indian uprising was about to appear from somewhere. Among others, Congress heard, and authorized Knox to raise 1,340 men for defense against Indians in those portions of Massachusetts and Connecticut where no Indian had been seen in a quarter of a century. And then, as was also his wont, Knox shrewdly perceived that even if his fears were entirely unfounded, it might be advantageous to have everyone think they were rooted in truth. Accordingly, he sat himself down to compose a letter, out of the whole cloth, and addressed it to George Washington; a letter which, in one form or another, reached and was believed by almost everyone of influence in the several states. There were, Knox said, 12,000 to 15,000 well-disciplined men under arms in western Massachusetts. They were talking of high taxes and an unjust court system, he

---

[34] See footnote 36, below.

added, but that this was their real cause was "as remote from truth as light from darkness." Their real aim was nothing less than a common division of all property. They would march upon Boston and, if they succeeded there, would be reinforced by malcontents in New Hampshire, Rhode Island, and Connecticut, and spread anarchy and bloodshed the length of the land.[35]

Knox knew how wrong he was, but he did not know how nearly right he was. Two weeks after he wrote Washington, he received a letter from ex-General Samuel Holden Parsons that must have caused him to lose several of his 280 pounds: Parsons had learned that upwards of two thousand men were drilling almost daily; that their officers, being former junior officers in the continental army and present officers in the state militia, knew what they were about; and that the men were being paid three shillings a day in cash. Parsons did not know the source of the money, which amounted to between five hundred and a thousand dollars a day. Where it came from was never learned. Some of the men through whom it was disbursed did become known: John Hulbert of Alford, Samuel Willard of Uxbridge, William Whiting of Great Barrington, James Freeland of Sutton, Marshall Spring of Watertown, and Samuel Kittridge of Groton. All, coincidentally, were doctors; all, perhaps coincidentally, were flaming Tories. The same John Hulbert also went to Sharon, Connecticut, and hired an agent to

---

[35] Knox to Joseph Williams, October 16, 1786, to Congress, October 18, 1786, to Washington, October 23, 1786, James Swan to Knox, October 26, 1786, Major North to Knox, October 29, 1786, all in Knox Papers; Burnett, *Continental Congress,* 671–72; *Journals of Congress,* October 21, 1786. I have traced the coverage of Shays' Rebellion in newspapers in every major city from Savannah to Portsmouth, and some variation of the Knox letter to Washington appears in virtually all.

begin drilling rebel troops there, and the same Samuel Willard went to Rhode Island for similar purposes. (As the insurgents drilled and the instigators instigated, the legislatures of Virginia and New Jersey voted to send delegates to the proposed Philadelphia convention, whether Congress approved or not.)[36]

The insurgents did little more than drill until the General Court adjourned on November 18. Three days later two hundred of them—well armed, well drilled, and well captained—marched into Worcester and stopped the proceedings of the Court of Quarter Sessions. After that action and after efforts to do the same in Middlesex County miscarried, things grew quiet—temporarily.[37]

They also grew confused. A goodly number of the men began to wonder why they were drilling, since most of what they thought they had been complaining about seemed to have been taken care of by the General Court. Few walked out, for the pay was too good to turn down, but those in Worcester took advantage of the inactivity to draw up and publish a disavowal of any sympathies with the British or with Tories. More important than money in keeping them together, however, was a great and general fear that seized

---

[36] Parsons to Knox, November 6, 1786, and Knox to Parsons, November 19, 1786, in Knox Papers; Shays' Rebellion Papers, Massachusetts Archives, 189:75 ff., 81–82, 83–84, 100, 171–82, 369–74, 190:150, 297, and, in the same (190:238), Thomas Clarke to Bowdoin, September 8, 1786; Larabee, ed., *Public Records of Connecticut*, 6:295 n; *Massachusetts Centinel*, December 13, 1786, January 16, May 16, 1787. See also Max Farrand, ed., *The Records of the Federal Convention of 1787* (3 vols., New Haven, 1911), 3:559–65.

[37] *Hampshire Gazette*, November 29, 1786; George R. Minot, *History of the Insurrections, in Massachusetts, in the Year MDCCLXXXVI, and the Rebellion Consequent Thereon* (Worcester, 1788), 73–76.

the countryside. Many feared reprisals; their leaders had kept from them the news that participants in the earlier court stoppages had been forgiven by the General Court, the leaders themselves fearing that the indemnity did not extend to them. Others feared fantasies and rumors, as the Exeter rebels had in New Hampshire, and still others feared God or the devil. But almost all were afraid of something, even if they knew not what. Ignorance had taken them this far, and fear would take them a lot further.[38]

As to the leaders, befuddled and afraid as they might be, they knew only that they had gone far enough so that it was not possible to go back. On December 9 a group of them met in Pelham and, while not yet knowing what they sought, organized themselves into efficient units for seeking it. They grouped their men into six regiments and formed themselves into a "Committee of Seventeen." (One of their number was a Pelham farmer and ex-captain named Daniel Shays. For reasons as obscure as all the other reasons, the rebellion soon bore his name.) And yet, except for dispatching 300 men to stop a Yuletide sitting of the Hampshire County Court, the rebels still did nothing but drill and grow more impatient and more restless and more afraid. (As they did so Pennsylvania and North Carolina voted to send delegates to the proposed Philadelphia convention.)[39]

---

[38] Address of the Insurgents in Worcester, December 7, 1786, in Shays' Rebellion Papers, 190:297, Massachusetts Archives, and 189:52, in the same; Rufus Putnam to Bowdoin, January 8, 1787, in Shays' Papers, American Antiquarian Society. Much of what is said in this paragraph is inferred from the various documents previously cited.

[39] Shays' Rebellion Papers, December 9, 1786 (190:297), in Massachusetts Archives; Taylor, *Western Massachusetts,* 156–58; Farrand, ed., *Records of the Federal Convention,* 3:565–71.

And now, as the new year began, the fear spread eastward. On January 4, 1787, Governor Bowdoin decided to raise 4,400 men to suppress the rebellion. It was hardly practicable to do so by leving new taxes, but it was hardly necessary to do so either. Few rebels had any idea of what they were about, but all Bostonians knew: they were going to do what Knox had said they were going to do. In panic, the Bostonians contributed £ 5,021 in private subscriptions to field the army. They had only one immediate aim, to get their private army to Worcester before January 23—when, they were convinced, the other private army would move in to prevent the sitting of the proposed county court. The governor and his council, emboldened by the apparent success of law and order, issued warrants for the arrest of the "Committee of Seventeen." On the twenty-third, the court, backed by a "loyalist" army under General Benjamin Lincoln, sat and no one appeared to stop it. (Meanwhile, New Hampshire elected delegates to the proposed Philadelphia convention.)[40]

The climax—which is to say, Shays' Rebellion—happened on January 25. It had been extremely cold for several days, with temperatures twenty and thirty below zero and snowdrifts higher than the head of the tallest rebel. Benjamin Lincoln and his fat and well-clothed mercenaries were marching westward from Worcester. General William Shepard, with about five hundred warm and loyal militia troops, sat in Springfield trembling, nonetheless, out of fear. Insurgent Captain Luke Day sat with four hundred men on

---

[40] Bowdoin to General Brooks, December 7, 1786, and List of Subscribers, in Shays' Rebellion Papers, 189:56, 64–66, 73, 105, Massachusetts Archives; Taylor, *Western Massachusetts,* 159; Farrand, ed., *Records of the Federal Convention,* 3:571–73.

the other side of the river in West Springfield, warmed by more rum than good fighting men could carry and still fight. Upriver on the east side were Eli Parsons and his 400 rebels in Chicopee, warmed by neither clothes nor rum nor even courage. On the east side also were Captain Shays and 1,200 men, encamped in the town of Wilbraham. Shays, bewildered and afraid and anxious to get out from under the rebellion that bore his name, did not know what to do. He sent two messages, both of which miscarried. The first, addressed to General Shepard, asked for amnesty for the rebel leaders and a release of the prisoners captured in the recent abortive actions in Middlesex. It closed with a hollow request that the General Court settle the grievances that had been complained of for months. Hearing nothing from Shepard—because Shepard had heard nothing from him—Shays sent a message ordering Day to back him in an attempt on Springfield on the twenty-fifth. Day's men, perhaps because of an excess of rum, were unable to march until the twenty-sixth, but his message so advising Shays was intercepted by Shepard's forces. Parson's men went home where it was warm. The result was that on the twenty-fifth Shays and his men marched into Springfield without support.[41]

Shepard's men opened fire upon the appearance of the first Shaysites. On the first volley four Shaysites were killed and the others broke ranks and fled for home. Minor "battles" took place for another month, and as late as May, rebels were conducting sporadic raids from Vermont and upstate New York; but for all practical purposes Shays' Rebellion was over by sundown, January 25. (As the mopping

---

[41] *Ibid.,* 160–63; Minot, *Insurrections in Massachusetts,* 108–60; *Massachusetts Centinel, Boston Gazette,* January–February 1787.

up actions took place, Delaware and Georgia elected delegates to the proposed Philadelphia convention.)⁴²

On February 4, the rebellion safely quashed, Governor
Bowdoin declared that a state of rebellion existed in Massachusetts, and sent a dispatch to New York so advising Congress. After a week Congress decided that maybe it should
consider the proposed convention after all. It had hardly
sat down to think about it when the tidings came from the
New York legislature: New York would not now or in the
foreseeable future consent to granting Congress an independent revenue. (Paradoxically, the New York Assembly
voted two days later to send delegates to the proposed
Philadelphia convention.) At the end of its limited wits,
Congress voted on the twenty-first to ask the states to send
delegates to Philadelphia.⁴³

Everything else was anticlimax. The only question remaining that seemed worth answering was whether it was
worthwhile to hold one's breath until the convention met. In
the ensuing two months four more states decided favorably.
If the delegates elected should bother to attend, the convention would become a reality.

It was a critical moment only for the United States as
United States, not for the several states or their inhabitants.
In the short range—the range in which every living person
lived—it made little difference whether the convention met

---

⁴² *Ibid.* (all sources cited in footnote 41); *Maryland Gazette,* June 7, 1787;
Farrand, ed., *Records of the Federal Convention,* 3:574–78.

⁴³ Shays' Rebellion Papers, 189:105 ff.; New York *Daily Advertiser,* Feb-
ruary 26, 1787; *Votes and Proceedings of the Assembly of New York,*
February 17, 1787; *Votes and Proceedings of the Senate of New York,*
February 20, 1787; *Journals of Congress,* 32:71 ff. (February 21, 1787).

or not. Congress had gone to hell, and so had the principal bonds of union and so had the mottoes around which the Union had rallied in the first place. But rebellion had blown its course and so had depression, and most Americans had it better than they had ever had it before. It was the Critical Period of American history only to those who thought that the American Republic was worth creating and saving.

Chapter Six

The Philadelphia Convention

The appointed day—Monday, May 14—was hardly promising. It rained: the coldest winter in memory had turned into one of the wettest springs, and any delegates who chose to come had either to come by sea or by mud, for there was scarcely a dry road in the United States. So far, only two had come, both by way of the mud. How many more would make it, no one could predict.[1]

The list of distinguished Americans certain not to come was large. Only one of the great diplomats of the Revolution, Franklin, would be there; John Jay of New York and Henry Laurens of South Carolina had not been chosen, and

---

[1] Observations on the weather are from scattered newspaper references and from the diary of delegate William Samuel Johnson. That it rained on May 14 is only highly probable, not certain; it rained in Philadelphia almost every day in late May and early June 1787; Johnson's Diary, in Max Farrand, ed., *The Records of the Federal Convention of 1787* (3 vols., New Haven, 1911), 3:552; Madison's Journal, May 25, and Madison to Jefferson, May 15, 1787, *ibid.*, 1:4, 3:20; Freeman, *Washington,* 6:87, 88. In this chapter, references to the various diaries or journals will be made by person and date, with pages from Farrand's *Records.* Farrand's volumes contain every known record of the convention except the journal of John Lansing, which was edited by Joseph R. Strayer and published as *The Delegate from New York* (Princeton, 1939).

Thomas Jefferson and John Adams were in Europe as ambassadors. Most of the great republicans would likewise be missing. Thomas Paine ("Where liberty is not, Sir, there is my country") was also in Europe, hoping to spread the gospel of republican revolution. Neither Sam Adams and John Hancock of Massachusetts nor Richard Henry Lee and Patrick Henry of Virginia chose to come[2] (Henry did not because, he said, "I smelt a rat"; the others offered no excuses).[3]

Furthermore, it seemed distinctly possible that three states would send no delegates at all. Rhode Island had flatly refused. New Hampshire had authorized its delegates to Congress to double as delegates to the convention, but the legislation, typically, was defective; and besides, there was probably not enough money in the state treasury to send anyone as far south as Boston. The Maryland legislature had elected five delegates but every one of them had declined to serve. The New Hampshire and Maryland legislatures, now in session, were considering whether to try again.[4]

Those already in town were a distinguished lot, far more distinguished, in fact, than those to come. Pennsylvania's nationalist faction, temporarily in control of the Assembly,

[2] Henry and Lee had actually been elected but had declined to serve; Hancock and Adams had not been elected but doubtless could have been had they so chosen.

[3] Delegates and their credentials are in Farrand, *Records,* 3:557 ff. The Henry story is from Hugh Blair Grigsby, *The History of the Virginia Federal Convention of 1788 with Some Account of the Eminent Virginians of That Era Who Were Members of the Body,* edited by R. A. Brock (2 vols., Richmond, 1890–91), 1:32.

[4] Farrand, *Records,* 3:571–73, 586; Annapolis *Maryland Gazette,* April 26, May 31, 1787; *Votes and Proceedings* (of both Senate and House in Maryland), April 23–May 26, 1787, and (of the House only) January 15, 1787.

had chosen an eight-man delegation. Two (George Clymer and Thomas Fitzsimons) were important merchants who had served in Congress, but as statesmen they were little more than Morris party hacks; and two others (Thomas Mifflin and Jared Ingersoll, the former a popular figure and the latter a son-in-law of Charles Pettit) had been chosen as sops to the Constitutionalists.[5] But the remainder of the delegation was loaded with nationalist powers. The senior man was Benjamin Franklin, who had proposed a national union, in a colonial congress, before many of the delegates were born; Franklin, now eighty-one and approaching senility, might add little that was constructive to the convention, but he would add enormously to its prestige. The other three were none less than Robert Morris and his brilliant henchmen, James Wilson and (though he was actually a New Yorker) Gouverneur Morris.[6]

---

[5] On Clymer, see Henry Simpson, *The Lives of Eminent Philadelphians* (Philadelphia, 1859), 211, and John Sanderson, *Biographies of the Signers of the Declaration of Independence* (3 vols., Philadelphia, 1831), 3:147 ff. On Fitzsimons, see John B. McMaster and Frederick D. Stone, *Pennsylvania and the Federal Constitution, 1787–1788* (Philadelphia, 1888), 705 ff.; and Simpson, *Eminent Philadelphians*, 372–73. On Mifflin, see Kenneth R. Rossman, *Thomas Mifflin and the Politics of the American Revolution* (Chapel Hill, 1952). On Ingersoll, see Simpson, *Eminent Philadelphians*, 1137–38; Charles Warren, *The Supreme Court in United States History* (2 vols., New York and Boston, 1922), 1:545; and scattered references in Lawrence H. Gipson's biography of Ingersoll's father, *Jared Ingersoll: A Study in American Loyalism* (New Haven, 1920). On all four men, see *Pennsylvania Packet,* Philadelphia *Evening Herald,* Philadelphia *Independent Gazetteer,* Philadelphia *Freeman's Journal,* 1783–89, *passim;* Brunhouse, *Counter-Revolution in Pennsylvania, passim;* and sketches in the *Biographical Directory of Congress.*

[6] The Franklin bibliography is huge; my own view of him is derived largely from Albert H. Smyth, *Writings of Franklin* (10 vols., New York, 1905–07). On Robert Morris, the biographies are Oberholtzer's *Robert Morris,* Sumner's *Financier and Finances of the Revolution,* and Ver Steeg's *Robert*

The two out-of-state delegates were George Washington and James Madison. Washington, at fifty-four (or at any other age), could have added little to the intellectual average of any convention, and his knowledge of what to do in one barely extended beyond rules of order. But that was all he needed to know, for any assembly he attended was likely to elect him presiding officer. He had two attributes that, even without his unparalleled prestige, prompted men to choose him The Leader; and it mattered not that one of the attributes was trivial and the other he carried to the point of triviality, nor did it matter that for the last third of his life he was largely (and self-consciously) playing a role. The first attribute was that he looked like a leader. In an age in which most Americans stood about five feet five and measured nearly three-fourths of that around the waist, Washington stood six feet and had broad, powerful shoulders and slim hips; and he had learned the trick, when men said something beyond his ken, of looking at them in a way that made them feel irreverent or even stupid. The other attribute was personal integrity. At times, Washington's integrity was bewildering, for his artlessness and his susceptibility to flattery led him to endorse actions that less scrupulous but more cagey men might shun; and at times it could be overbearing, stifling. But it was unimpeachable,

---

Morris, all previously cited (chapter 2, footnote 3); see also chapters 1 and 2, herein. On Wilson, see Page Smith's *James Wilson,* previously cited (chapter 1, footnote 2), and the Wilson Papers in the Historical Society of Pennsylvania. On Gouverneur Morris, the bibliography is sizable but disappointing; it includes Jared Sparks' *Life of Gouverneur Morris* (3 vols., Boston, 1832); Theodore Roosevelt's *Gouverneur Morris* (Cambridge, 1888); Howard Swigget's *The Amazing Mr. Morris* (New York, 1952); and Anne Cary Morris, ed., *Diary and Letters of Gouverneur Morris* (2 vols., New York, 1888).

and everyone knew it, and that, above all, made Washington useful. Others would do the brain work and the dirty work; Washington needed only to be there, but if there was to be a national government he absolutely had to be there, to lend his name to the doings.[7]

Madison, at thirty-seven (or at any other age), was Washington's opposite. Few men looked less like a leader: scrawny and pale, a bookworm and a hypochondriac, he owned a physical presence as uncommanding as one was likely to meet. But his knowledge of what to do in a convention was vast, and his talents for doing it matched his knowledge. True, it was easy, and in retrospect it became easier, to overrate his intellectual power. He had read so much and remembered so much that he could sound wise when actually he was only quoting somebody wise. Nor was his knowledge, in any general sense, practical: he could recite the principles of navigation and quote the latest developments in "scientific" farming, but he could no more sail a boat than he could hitch a plow. And because he had read the right books—notably the works of Harrington, Hume, and Montesquieu—he sounded for all the world like a man with a flexible brain, whereas at base he was a brittle, doctrinaire theorist. But these very attributes were useful (practical, freewheeling politicans can always use a good theoretician, much as practical, freewheeling businessmen

---

[7] The Washington bibliography is enormous; see vol. 6 of the more or less definitive biography, that of Douglas Southall Freeman (New York, 1954), 393–502. Doubtless Freeman would not have agreed with my appraisal; my view coincides more nearly with that expressed by Hamilton in a letter to Philip Schuyler, February 18, 1781, in *Hamilton Papers,* 2:563–68. The anecdote about Gouverneur Morris and Washington, repeated in Farrand's *Records,* 3:85, captures Washington's personality and demeanor well.

can use a good lawyer); and together with persistence, shrewdness, and devotion to the nation, they made him a priceless member of the nationalist group in the convention.[8]

Four more delegates arrived the next day, Tuesday the fifteenth. All were from Virginia, and none added much. One might have: George Wythe, chancellor of Virginia and beloved old mentor of Jefferson, Madison, and enough other Founding Fathers to populate a small standing army, was a man whose devout and learned republicanism never wore off onto his pupils. But Wythe's wife fell ill just as the convention began, and he went home to watch her die, and never returned. Judge John Blair of York was a tolerably good judge and Dr. James McClurg of Williamsburg was a tolerably good doctor, but neither was much at altering Articles of Confederation to make them adequate to the exigencies of the Union, and neither did much more than ensure that the Virginia delegation had a quorum. The fourth, Edmund Randolph, was and would ever remain an enigma. He was a doctrinaire republican, but also espoused the national cause, if it could be made compatible with an acceptable republican formula. As either, no one knew how gifted he was, or whether he was gifted at all. He had a proud name and he was the governor of Virginia, and both name and rank dictated that all sides reckon with him; but no one was ever sure what side he was on. (Some speculated

---

[8] Irving Brant's *James Madison* (6 vols., New York, 1956–61) is the most ambitious biography to date; a new edition of Madison's writings, supplanting the Gaillard Hunt edition (9 vols., New York, 1900–1910), is being published by the University of Chicago Press. The appraisal of him here is my own. I disagree to a considerable extent with Brant's interpretation of Madison's role in the convention, but I agree with much of his analysis of the convention itself and believe that much of it is the best work yet done on the subject.

that Randolph, having more slaves than he could support and few scruples that he had to support, would cast his modest talents and immodest pretensions on whichever side offered him the most.)[9]

On Thursday of the first week three more arrived in town, and all were men who counted. One rounded out the Virginia delegation: George Mason, the celebrated author of the Virginia Bill of Rights and, in a practical sense, the author of the whole modern idea of a bill of rights, had prestige not drastically beneath Washington's and talent that far outweighed Madison's. (He differed from both in one salient: his eyes were on the ground, theirs on the skies. Bill of rights or no, he knew that if Virginians had to pay off their prewar debts or to surrender control of their commerce to Yankees, the Revolution would have been pointless.)[10] The other two had sailed up from South Carolina. John Rutledge, wartime state governor and one of the most able, successful, and distinguished lawyers in America, moved in with another such lawyer, James Wilson; in Wilson's home they began to lay plans for "managing" the convention. (Wilson probably did not tell Rutledge, but he had likewise conspired with Madison and with the two Morrises; and

---

[9] Farrand, *Records,* 3:94–95, 587–90; Sanderson, *Biographies of the Signers* (1845 edition), 4:172 ff.; *Biographical Directory of Congress* (1927 edition), 1734; sketches of Wythe, Blair, and Randolph in *Dictionary of American Biography;* Warren, Supreme Court, 1:38 and *passim;* Howard A. Kelly and Walter L. Burrage, *American Medical Biographies* (3 vols., Baltimore, 1920), 2:124 ff.; Moncure Daniel Conway, *Omitted Chapters in History Disclosed in the Life and Papers of Edmund Randolph* (New York, 1888), 45, 50, 385 ff., and *passim.*

[10] Farrand, *Records,* 3:589; Kate Mason Rowland, *The Life and Correspondence of George Mason* (2 vols., New York, 1892); Helen D. Hill, *George Mason, Constitutionalist* (Cambridge, 1938); Robert A. Rutland, *The Birth of the Bill of Rights* (Chapel Hill, 1955), 30–40.

the elder Morris had, in turn, planned to manage Washington, who was living in Philadelphia as Morris' house guest. Rutledge did not tell Wilson, but he, too, was doing some other conspiring, and his would be far more effective.)[11] The second South Carolinian was Charles Pinckney, twenty-nine years old, a fiery orator, and a precociously brilliant politician. Pinckney hurt inside, because the Revolution had come when he came of age, thus precluding his being educated in London—a deficiency Carolinians regarded as only slightly less damning than being born out of wedlock or entering trade—and what was worse, his father had become a Loyalist. To quiet the pain, Pinckney aspired to nothing less (and nothing more) than to replace Rutledge as head of the local aristocracy.[12] The aspiration could be creative or destructive, as circumstances necessitated; on the one hand Pinckney could turn his considerable ability to nation-making, and on the other, he could lie, cheat, and defame so as to enhance his reputation as a nation-maker.[13]

---

[11] Richard Barry, *Mr. Rutledge of South Carolina* (New York, 1942), 303–50 and *passim;* Smith, *James Wilson,* 218; Freeman, *Washington,* 6:87.

[12] Perhaps most revealing of Pinckney's character is the story of the spurious Pinckney plan, his effort to assume credit as virtually the sole author of the Constitution; for details see Farrand, ed., *Records,* 3:427, 431, 446, 479, 501–15, 534, and especially 595–609. Likewise revealing, and more pathetic, is Pinckney's lifelong effort to pretend that he was four years younger than he actually was, so as to substantiate his claim that he had been the youngest member of the convention.

[13] There is no full-length biography of Pinckney; sketches may be seen in James B. O'Neall, *Biographical Sketches of the Bench and Bar of South Carolina* (2 vols., Charleston, 1859), 2:141 ff., and in the *Biographical Directory of Congress* and the *Dictionary of American Biography.* The Pinckney Family Papers in the Library of Congress contain much information, but their use is restricted. Barry, *Mr. Rutledge,* has a great deal of data

The next day a fourth state appeared, in the persons of Alexander Hamilton and Robert Yates of New York. Hamilton was a fluke choice: he was sent as the most available minority delegate, but lest he lead New York into mischief he was deliberately outweighed by two fellow delegates who were unswerving Clintonians. Yates was a vain, self-righteous, and pompous second-string aristocrat (Abraham and Christopher Yates had all the talent in the family) who served the Clinton organization because it had made him a justice of the state supreme court. (The third New York delegate showed up two weeks later. Albany's Mayor John Lansing, Jr., was a rich young man who did what Clinton told him to do because Clinton had made him mayor of Albany and a richer young man.)[14]

For a week these nineteen men, representing four states, planned strategy and sat and wondered whether enough delegates would show up so that they would have somebody to practice their strategy upon. The week's returns were discouraging. Seven stragglers straggled into town: Rufus King of Massachusetts had enough native ability and had married enough wealth to ensure his place in the world; but the others—a dirt farmer, a silversmith, a small-town lawyer, a

---

and penetrating analysis, and Brant's *Madison,* 3:27–29, has an excellent capsule description. That it was his father's Loyalism and his not being educated in London that underlay Pinckney's peculiar personal makeup is my own surmise, based on long study of South Carolina and its social values. Another element that might have been important is the fact that Pinckney inherited no wealth—his father's estate having been confiscated —but married a wealthy girl; and under South Carolina's sociolegal system, her property remained her property, and would pass to her daughters.

[14] For an analysis of New York's choice of delegates, see E. Wilder Spaulding, *New York in the Critical Period, 1783–1789* (New York, 1932), 186–88; much information about Yates and Lansing is in the same volume. For a sketch of Yates, see Senate Document 728, 60th Congress, 2d Session.

religious crackpot, a North Carolina planter, and an impetuous and impecunious young bootlicker—were scarcely the stuff of which empires are made. But between them, they formed quorums of two more states, and with one more state represented the convention itself would have a quorum.[15]

On Friday the twenty-fifth—the end of the second week —arrived seven more delegates. Three of them represented New Jersey, and so the convention could now organize itself and get to work. Otherwise, however, in the arrivals no nationalist saw cause for rejoicing. For one thing, the work would be nominal unless a few more states were soon represented. For another, the New Jersey and Delaware delegates were bound, explicitly or implicitly, to oppose any alterations that would change the one state–one vote system of representation in the Confederation Congress. For yet another, the seven newcomers were as lusterless as their seven immediate predecessors. Charles Cotesworth Pinckney, a planter and lawyer, was more stable but less able than his young cousin; Pierce Butler, the fourth South Carolinian, was an Irish-born nobleman who traced his ancestry all the way back to somebody-or-other but who, stripped of

---

[15] Farrand, *Records,* 3:87–98, 587–90; Charles R. King, *Life and Correspondence of Rufus King* (6 vols., New York, 1894–1900). The second-rate characters, in order, were William Few, Jacob Broom, George Read, Richard Bassett, Richard Dobbs Spaight, and William R. Davie, for information on whom see sketches in the *Dictionary of American Biography;* "Autobiography of William Few," in *Magazine of American History,* 7:352 ff.; *Papers of the Delaware Historical Society,* vol. 29 (1900), vol. 51 (1901); William T. Read, *Life and Correspondence of George Read* (Philadelphia, 1870); Sanderson, *Biographies of the Signers* (1831), 3:351 ff.; John H. Wheeler, *Sketch of the Life of Richard Dobbs Spaight* (Baltimore, 1880); John G. de Roulhac Hamilton, *William Richardson Davie* (Chapel Hill, 1907); Blackwell P. Robinson, *William R. Davie* (Chapel Hill, 1957).

his genealogy, would scarcely have been noticed by his next door neighbor. Alexander Martin, a former governor of North Carolina, had lived in luxurious isolation on his back-country plantation for so long that (it was rumored) he (a) had abandoned any nationalist sentiments he had ever held; (b) had taken to writing poetry; and (c) had begun doing things with his slaves that made even rednecks blush. (The first two rumors were warranted; the third was never documented.) Another North Carolinian, Hugh Williamson, was a kind of poor man's Benjamin Franklin who had never had opportunity to move in fast enough company to become a rich man's Franklin. Of the three New Jerseyans, two were soon to die, and it made little difference. They were William C. Houston, a nonentity skilled in acquiring petty but lucrative government jobs, and David Brearley, chief justice of the state supreme court. The third, Attorney General William Paterson, was so short that even Madison could see the top of his head without standing on tiptoe, but what he had inside made him a tall man in any gathering. Indeed, Paterson was the only one of the last fourteen besides King whom anyone would ever have heard of, had not attendance in the convention immortalized them.[16]

---

[16] Farrand, *Records*, 3:90–97, 574–75, 587–90; biographical sketches in *Biographical Directory of Congress* and *Dictionary of American Biography;* James Herring, ed., *National Portrait Gallery of Distinguished Americans* (4 vols., Philadelphia, 1854), vol. 4; O'Neall, *Bench and Bar of South Carolina*, 134 ff.; Samuel A. Ashe and others, *Biographical History of North Carolina* (6 vols., Greensboro, 1907), vols. 3, 5; Roger Powell Marshall, "A Mythical Mayflower Competition: North Carolina Literature in the Half-Century Following the Revolution," in the *North Carolina Historical Review*, 27:188 (1950); McCormick, *Experiment in Independence*, 97–98, 257–59; Julian A. C. Chandler and others, *The South in the Building of a Nation* (13 vols., Richmond, 1909–13), 1:518 ff.; Gertrude S. Wood, *William Paterson of New Jersey, 1745–1806* (Fair Lawn, N.J., 1933).

"Seven states being now represented," George Washington confided to his diary in the expectation that it would someday become revered public property, "the body was organized and I was called to the chair." And, lest others present and taking notes should fail to record it for all posterity, he gratuitously added that the call came "by a unanimous vote."[17]

Never mind that Washington was preoccupied with his image as father of his country. Never mind, either, that twenty-four of the thirty-three unanimous voices were voices that few would have listened to anytime, anywhere. For nine voices (and three more soon to come) were voices of men possessed of an idea of a great nation, and possessed of the ruthlessness and the daring and the skill that make ideas into reality: the two Morrises, Franklin, Wilson, Rutledge, Paterson, Madison, Hamilton, and King, already present, and Roger Sherman, Oliver Ellsworth, and John Dickinson, on their way.

At ten in the morning, Monday the twenty-eighth of May 1787, George Washington called the Philadelphia Convention to order. He stood on the speaker's platform in a chamber of the Pennsylvania State House, the very building where, a decade earlier, a set of grubby little men had considered depriving him of his commandership-in-chief. When he sat down—in a chair on which was painted a rising or sinking sun, no one knew which—he surveyed what might have struck him as an equally grubby group of men. (Madison sat just below the speaker's table, back to the speaker; the others were clustered, by state delegations,

---

[17] Washington's Diary, May 25, 1787, in Farrand, *Records*, 3:27.

in front of him.)[18] They were doubtless somewhat better dressed than their predecessors of the late seventies, for simple republican homespun was no longer so fashionable, now that British fineries were available again. But it was, in the main, a pompous, overfed band of lawyers and planters who faced Washington, the kind of far-from-the-shooting politicians with whom he always felt least at ease.

What took place the first day could have added little to the comfort of the man of action who sat in the chair. First, an hour or so was used up in presenting and reading the credentials of five more delegates attending for the first time: James McHenry of Maryland, once Washington's aide-de-camp; Caleb Strong of Northampton, Massachusetts, a sort of eighteenth-century Calvin Coolidge; Nathaniel Gorham of the same state, a sailor and artisan's son who had made in privateering a fortune that he would soon lose in land speculations; Gunning Bedford, a Delaware lawyer whose main distinction was that he was even fatter than most delegates present; and Oliver Ellsworth of Connecticut, a shrewd, stingy, and extremely able and dedicated nationalist. (Important men from the three last-named states were soon to come: from Massachusetts, Elbridge Gerry, a financier and sometime Marblehead merchant, a disciple of Sam Adams whose stutter and haggling habits alienated most who came into close contact, and whose brittle republicanism and political shrewdness matched that of his mentor; from Delaware, the celebrated John Dickinson, an emaciated figure invariably dressed in black, a man of ponderous and pretentious ways balanced by great good

---

[18] Madison's Preface, in Farrand, *Records,* 3:550; other physical details are scattered throughout the same volume.

sense; and from Connecticut, Roger Sherman, a gnarled old man whose speech was as grotesque as his appearance, but perhaps the shrewdest backroom politician on the continent.)[19]

The rest of the day was consumed in trying to agree on house rules. Delegates from Pennsylvania had spent the weekend vainly seeking support for rules that would give the more populous states a greater voice in the convention, instead of giving all states, even pipsqueak Delaware, one vote. Now, thirty-eight grown men, possessing a combined experience in legislatures and Congress of perhaps three centuries, and thus being well versed in the conventional rules of procedure, wasted roughly four hours in deciding what their rules of procedure would be. The only departure from the norm that was seriously considered was a proposal that the proceedings be completely secret; but though almost everyone agreed that they should be secret, it was not until the next morning that suitable rules were adopted. And on

---

[19] Official Journal (hereafter cited as Journal), Madison's Journal (hereinafter cited as Madison), May 28, and Pierce's Sketches, in Farrand, *Records,* 1:7–13, 3:87–90; Bernard C. Steiner, *The Life and Correspondence of James McHenry* (Cleveland, 1907); Henry Cabot Lodge, "Memoir of Hon. Caleb Strong, LL.D.," in the *Proceedings of the Historical Society of Massachusetts,* 1:290–316 (1874); Sedgwick Papers, Massachusetts Historical Society, *passim;* Timothy T. Sawyer, *Old Charlestown: Historical, Biographical, Reminiscent* (Boston, 1902), 189 ff.; James F. Hunnewell, *A Century of Town Life: A History of Charlestown, Massachusetts, 1775–1887* (Boston, 1888), 117, 157; Sumner, *Financier and Finances of the Revolution,* 2:253 ff.; William G. Brown, *The Life of Oliver Ellsworth* (New York, 1905); Kenneth B. Umbreit, *Our Eleven Chief Justices* (New York, 1938), 79–110; Benjamin Austin, *Life of Elbridge Gerry* (2 vols., Boston, 1829, 1830); Charles J. Stille, *The Life and Times of John Dickinson* (2 vols., Philadelphia, 1891); Forrest McDonald, ed., *Empire and Nation* (Englewood Cliffs, N.J., 1962), ix–xvi; Roger S. Boardman, *Roger Sherman, Signer and Statesman* (Philadelphia, 1938).

that occasion, more time was wasted and the states were divided five to four over the trivial question, whether a standing committee should be appointed to supervise the minutes. At the present rate, the delegates would get around to the exigencies of the Union by about 1800.[20]

But things were moving far faster than they appeared to be. Most men present knew that the delegates from Massachusetts, still quaking from the winter's rebellion and even more anxious about the malaise that underlay it, were ready to concede almost anything to strengthen the national authority. Most also knew that some of the delegates from Pennsylvania, Virginia, and South Carolina had come prepared to scrap the Confederation altogether, in favor of a "high-toned" national government, and had conferred in advance and worked out some kind of plan. The first step in that plan was, in fact, revealed before noon on the second day, the twenty-ninth. What no one knew, however, was how the several equal-voiced states would line up for and against that plan.[21]

The most educated guess was that of Madison, who had too schematic a mind to see the obvious. Madison saw six states as being committed on one side and five on the other. The majority were what he viewed as the "large states" and the "nationalist" bloc, the minority were the "small states" and the "states-rights" bloc.[22]

---

[20] Journal, Madison, May 28, in Farrand, *Records,* 1:7–13.

[21] William Grayson to James Monroe, May 29, 1787, George Mason to George Mason, Jr., May 20, 1787, Madison, May 28, 29, Yates, May 29, all in Farrand, *Records,* 1:10–13, 17–24, 3:22–24, 30; Barry, *Mr. Rutledge,* 315–18.

[22] Madison's view, which is implicit in his journal, almost daily until July 16, is also the conventional historical view.

Madison was wrong on both counts. In the first place, the states in the initial majority were not significantly more populous than their rivals. True, Virginia was the mammoth and Delaware was the midget; but exclusive of these, the average population of the "large" states was roughly 307,-000, and that of the "small" roughly 278,000—a difference of approximately 10 percent. Secondly, the lineup was more nearly sectional than large-versus-small: states south of the Potomac consistently voted with Madison's "large states" bloc, 4 to 0; those north of it (counting New Hampshire, when its delegates arrived) voted as "small states," 6 to 2. Third, the lineup was even more precisely one of the landed states versus the landless. Massachusetts, Pennsylvania, Virginia, North Carolina, South Carolina, and Georgia had access, through colonial charters or some other means, to enormous surpluses of unoccupied lands; all voted as "large" states, which is to say for rearranging the Confederation so as to deprive states of equal votes. New Hampshire, Connecticut, New York, New Jersey, Delaware, and Maryland had no such lands; all voted as "small" states.[23]

If any general alignment of nationalist and antinationalist states existed, it was one of weak or strife-torn states against

---

[23] Population figures from *Census of 1790*. The landed vs. landless states alignment given here is in close accord with that reported by Brant, in *Madison*, 3:55–70 (chapter 5, "The Men and Their Motives"). There is one apparent misfit in each camp, South Carolina and New York. But South Carolina, while nominally not a landed state, had easy access to the abundant lands of Georgia, and South Carolinians acquired Georgia lands on a vast scale; see the manuscript volume, Land Grants, Washington and Franklin Counties, in the Georgia Department of Archives and History (for example, Wade Hampton's acquisition of 1,000 acres in 1784, p. 118). And New York had lost Vermont (about which it was furious), did not have title to the western third of the state, which belonged to Massachusetts, and much of the remainder was inhabited by hostile Indians.

strong or prospering states. But the alignment was not so clean as that, for delegates were individual human beings (some bound by instructions, some not) who had, in the convention, to vote as states. New York was divided, Hamilton favoring and Yates and Lansing opposing a national government; and as a matter of strategy it sided, at the outset, with what appeared to be the states-rights group, the apparently small states. Massachusetts began firmly united, but as time wore on Gerry and Strong developed the kind of nearsightedness that comes from dealing too long and too closely with a problem, and thus forgetting that the world was on fire back home, tended to divide and cancel their state's efforts in the convention. Randolph and Mason of Virginia, becoming similarly affected, began to vote against Washington and Madison, and thus (when two delegates went home) threw the deciding vote of the delegation into the hands of Judge Blair, who wavered from side to side. Finally, Maryland's delegation was a mess. In place of its five delegates who had refused to serve it had elected James McHenry, John Francis Mercer, Luther Martin, Daniel of St. Thomas Jenifer, and Daniel Carroll. McHenry was a devout nationalist (provided that certain local prejudices could be accommodated), but he left after four days because of his brother's fatal illness and did not return until August 5. Mercer was a rich smart aleck in his twenties who appeared late in July, commented that those present were a lot of monarchist clods, and left. Jenifer was a petty local government official who customarily had his hand in the public till or was helping someone else's to reach it; but, being in the habit of supporting authority, he voted in the convention as a nationalist. Luther Martin, a Chase man and (anachronistically) a doctrinaire republican, reputedly showed up sober on but half a dozen occasions in his life, none of them being in the Philadelphia Convention; whenever he spoke, it would be against what was going on, and it might take all day. Carroll was a faint-hearted nationalist who attended only irregularly. That left Maryland divided against itself most of the time.[24]

The first phase of the convention lasted from May 29 until July 27. During it, the delegates spoke and voted as if the question before them were *what kind* of national government would be created, and their debates constituted one of the most brilliant displays of learning in political theory ever shown in a deliberative assembly. But all this was only a parliamentary surface that masked the real issue. The real issue, throughout, was whether there would be a national government—and therefore a nation—at all.[25]

Governor Randolph "opened the main business" with a long speech denouncing the structural defects of the Articles of Confederation and the existing state constitutions. The essential weakness and "our chief danger," he said, "arises from the democratic parts of our constitutions." Voicing a

---

[24] These matters are implicit, when not explicit, in the various records of the convention, the biographical sources previously cited, and the sources cited in chapters two to four herein.

[25] This is just the way the issue was put by Gouverneur Morris, who commonly came closer to the heart of questions than did the other delegates; Madison, September 17, in Farrand, *Records,* 2:645. That my interpretation of the convention differs widely from conventional interpretations, though all historians have the same limited body of sources with which to work, derives in large measure from viewing the convention in this perspective. I believe that if one views the debates in terms of their historical context (the question of whether there would be a government) and if one is familiar with that context (the background in Congress, sketched in chapter one, herein, and the background in the states, chapters two through five), the following interpretation is inevitable. My own interpretation is much closer to Brant's than to that of anyone else; Brant was probably better versed in the state background than any previous writer.

sentiment that all but a handful would soon echo, Randolph added, "It is a maxim which I hold incontrovertible, that the powers of government exercised by the people swallow up the other branches. None of the constitutions have provided sufficient checks against the democracy." He then presented fifteen resolutions—called variously the Large States Plan, the Randolph Plan, and the Virginia Plan— designed to serve as the outlines for debate.[26]

The Virginia Plan would drastically alter the form of the Confederation, but nowise alter its substance: it substituted three branches of government for one (the old Congress), and divided the legislature into two houses, membership and votes in which would be apportioned according to the population of each state, instead of being equal by states; but it endowed the new authority with only the powers of the old Congress, plus a power to legislate in cases where the several states were incompetent.[27] Inasmuch as the states had quite competently levied tariffs upon and regulated international commerce, settled boundary disputes, disposed of treaties, and raised armies and navies, that left little for the national government to do, however it might be organized.[28]

Ignoring a more elaborate set of proposals made by

---

[26] McHenry, May 29, in Farrand, *Records,* 1:26–27; Madison, Yates, and Paterson also record parts of the speech.

[27] On the following day, Randolph made it clear that he did not intend that his resolutions be read so as to interpret them as a blanket grant of power to the national authority; rather, he said, he "only meant to give the national government a power to defend and protect itself. To take therefore from the respective legislatures or states, no more sovereignty than is competent to this end." See James McHenry's notes, May 30, in Farrand, *Records,* 1:42, and also the discussions of May 31, regarding the meaning of the grant of powers.

[28] Madison, May 29, in Farrand, *Records,* 1:20–22; see also *ibid.,* 3:593–94.

Charles Pinckney, the convention resolved itself into a committee of the whole house (in which rules of debate would be less formal) and debated Randolph's resolutions for two weeks. At the end of that time the "small" states presented a counterplan, authored by Paterson and called variously the New Jersey Plan, the Paterson Plan, and the Small States Plan.[29]

The New Jersey Plan likewise proposed a three-branch government, its executive and judicial branches to be chosen by essentially the same methods as in the Virginia Plan, but it would retain a unicameral legislature and retain the system of equal representation by states within it. Given these minor modifications of the form of the Confederation, however, the New Jersey Plan would drastically alter its substance. The plan granted a long list of powers to the central authority, and these, together with others advocated by virtually all its adherents and a clause making acts of Congress paramount to all state laws—and binding upon individuals as well as states—would have made the national government truly sovereign.[30]

The New Jersey Plan was rejected and the Virginia Plan, as somewhat modified by the committee of the whole, was adopted, both by votes of six states to four. The Virginia Plan was then debated in convention for a month. All its aspects but two could have been disposed of in a day. The two disputed parts were the constitution of the executive and legislative branches.

The problem of the executive branch appeared to be wellnigh insoluble, and views of it appeared to be well-nigh

---

[29] Madison, Yates, McHenry, Paterson, Journal, May 30–June 14, *ibid.*, 1:29–240.

[30] Journal, Madison, Yates, King, June 15, *ibid.*, 1:241–47; see also *ibid.*, 3:611–16.

irreconcilable. A few of the more republican delegates (Randolph among them) so distrusted executive power as to insist that it could be safely lodged only in a plural head, preferably three men. The others entertained no such fears, but saw objections to every manner of choosing the executive. Some delegates favored direct popular election, but time and space made it seem unlikely that any candidate after Washington, the obvious choice for first chief executive, could ever draw more than a small fraction of the votes. (If one had asked a back-country Carolinian just to *name* a man from another state, he would have been stumped for an answer.) Final choice would then probably have to be made by the Congress. Most delegates favored having Congress elect the president directly (as both Randolph's and Paterson's plan proposed), but that raised problems of duration of term and eligibility for reelection. If his term were short and he could be reelected, he would be a mere tool of the legislature; to give him sufficient independence, he would have to be made ineligible for reelection and chosen for a dangerously long term. All the objections inherent in this means of election could be obviated by having the state legislatures make the choice, but dependence upon fickle state legislatures had rendered the Congress impotent, and few were anxious to place control of the national executive in their hands. Again, the state governors might be the electors, but many delegates viewed that as an invitation to corruption and cabal—the executive would become an elective monarchy, "the most tyrannical kind." This issue consumed more of the convention's time than any three others combined.[31]

---

[31] For a fairly good summary of this problem, see Madison to Jefferson, October 24, 1787, *ibid.*, 3:132–33.

More heated, in the initial phase, was the question of the structure of the national legislature. Early in the convention John Dickinson arose and wisely pointed out that the delegates could save themselves a good deal of time and save their nerves a good deal of wear by making the legislature bicameral, with representation apportioned by population in one branch and with each state having one vote in the other, for that was the only way their differences could be compromised. But few were yet ready for compromise. The landless states made one concession, agreeing on a bicameral legislature with representation proportional to population in the first branch. But as to the second branch, neither side conceded an inch.[32]

The adamant advocates of proportional representation depicted themselves as being more national-minded, but in fact it was otherwise, at least for the three most populous states. When Virginia, Pennsylvania, and Massachusetts demanded a voice in the national counsels that was commensurate with their population, they were simply taking a position that would enhance the influence of their own states, not the power of the nation. (Nor was their stand more "democratic," as some of them claimed, for most would have left the choice of congressmen to the legislatures.)[33]

---

[32] Madison, June 2, 6, *ibid.*, 1:87, 136.

[33] For examples of opposition to democracy by large-state members, see Randolph in McHenry, May 29; Gerry and Butler, in Madison, May 31; Charles Pinckney in Madison, June 6; Madison in Madison, June 6, 26; Rutledge in Madison, June 21; G. Morris in Madison, July 2; all *ibid.*, 1:26–27, 48, 50, 132, 135, 359, 430, 511–14; and King in Jackson Turner Main, *The Antifederalists: Critics of the Constitution, 1781–1788* (Chapel Hill, 1961), 171. On the comparative nationalism of the "large" and "small" states, see the following footnote.

The attitude of the advocates of equal representation was more complex, having essentially a dual character. On the one hand, they sought for their states a share in the great domain of unoccupied lands. This they proposed to obtain by lodging control of such lands in the second branch of the national legislature, and by giving states equal votes in that branch. (Or, give the small states equal benefit from "the common lands . . . the great states have appropriated to themselves," said Read, "and then if you please, proportion the representation, and we shall not be jealous of one another.")

On the other hand, far from being advocates of state supremacy, all but three of the delegates in the equal-representation bloc (Lansing, Yates, and Luther Martin) were willing, even eager, to abolish the states entirely and place all power in the hands of a national government. They insisted only upon consistency: if the states were to be preserved, they should retain rights to vote as states on matters relating to their existence as states. Given that, or given an equal distribution of claims to unoccupied lands, or given a total abolition of the states as units of government—*any of these*—the "small" and "states-rights" states were willing to grant to the national government every power enjoyed by the king and Parliament of England combined.[34]

Throughout June the debate raged on. The temperature soared—the wettest spring in years now turned into the

---

[34] On this question in general, see Brant, *Madison,* 3:62–69, 101–12; for specific examples of the extreme nationalism of small-state delegates, see Dickinson and Read on June 6, Farrand, *Records* (1:136–37), Brearley on June 9 (*ibid.,* 1:176–77), Paterson on that day and June 16 (*ibid.,* 1:178, 251, and 275), and Ellsworth on June 30 (*ibid.,* 1:487). The quotation

hottest summer—and with it tempers soared also. A little work was accomplished, along the lines of filling in and tightening Randolph's resolutions; but in the main the delegates marked time and argued about representation and grew increasingly bad-tempered. At one point, Franklin proposed that a chaplain be engaged to open each day's session with prayer, a proposal that was irritably dismissed by all but two or three delegates. At another, the obese Mr. Bedford of Delaware, perhaps suffering more in the heat than the others, lost patience with his opponents and blurted out that if the large states did not concede, the small would find some foreign ally to "take them by the hand."[35]

There appeared to be only two dim hopes for a break: that someone would come up with an acceptable compromise, or that someone would change his stand. Franklin, Wilson, and Pinckney suggested various compromises, some

---

from Read is in Yates, June 25 (*ibid.*, 1:412); on the same subject, see Paterson's speech in Yates, June 16 (*ibid.*, 1:259).

The nationalism of the members of the "small-states" bloc is abundantly borne out by their conduct after the compromise on representation, July 16; and it is to be noted that the three delegates who in the end refused to sign the Constitution (including Randolph, who presented the original plan on which it was ostensibly based) were from Virginia and Massachusetts; too, it is to be noted that the small states ratified the Constitution quickly and in some cases unanimously, despite the lack of equal representation, and had been the slowest to ratify the Articles of Confederation, though the Articles had provided equal representation—and the opposite pattern of ratification prevailed in the "large" states. Notice also that the only vote after the compromise of July 16 which saw exactly the same alignment of states as that on the representation question was a vote on the dividing up of the lands of large states; Madison, August 29, *ibid.*, 2:455.

[35] Johnson's Diary, *ibid.*, 3:552 (recording 15 hot days and 6 cool days between June 11 and July 4; the New York *Daily Advertiser* of July 23 reported that the temperature in Philadelphia had reached 91 degrees on July 3); Madison, June 28, 30, and Yates, June 30, in Farrand, *Records*, 1:450–52, 492, 501.

giving the states equal votes on certain issues, others apportioning the second branch on a basis halfway between equal and proportional representation. No one supported them. But toward the end of the month two states in the proportional-representation camp began to waver. Massachusetts began to divide against itself, King and Gorham on one side and Gerry and Strong on the other. Georgia, heretofore voting for proportional representation despite its tiny population, likewise began to split: William Houstoun, a latecomer who stayed only a few weeks, continued to favor proportional representation, but Abraham Baldwin, born in Connecticut and educated there before he moved to Georgia, regressed to his youth and started sitting with and voting the same as the Connecticut delegates.[36]

Until the second of July the convention avoided a showdown vote on the question. That morning Jenifer (who had been canceling Luther Martin's vote) was late in arriving, and Ellsworth of Connecticut seized the moment to bring the issue to a head. The maneuver failed, for the states split five for equality, five against, and Georgia divided. "We are now," said Sherman, "at a full stop"; and he proposed that a committee of one delegate from each state be appointed to work out a settlement. Not many liked the idea, but all states save one voted for it, and business was stopped until the committee should come up with something.[37]

On the fifth, the committee offered a compromise proposed by Franklin: the large states would concede equality in the second branch, the small would concede that all bills

---

[36] Madison, June 30, July 2, and Journal, June 22, 23, July 6, 7, 12, *ibid.,* 1:371, 385, 488–89, 507, 510–11, 549, 591.

[37] Madison, July 2, *ibid.,* 510–16; Martin, "Genuine Information," *ibid.,* 3:187–88. The postponement was also occasioned because the delegates wanted to honor the Fourth of July.

concerning the raising and spending of money should (as was traditional) originate in the popular branch. No one cheered; spokesmen for proportional representation grunted sourly that the provision regarding money bills was no concession at all. Things were still at a full stop. The only hope that remained was that one of the wavering states would change its vote.[38]

Lansing and Yates of New York now moved to dash that last hope. Totally disapproving of the effort to establish a national government, they had heretofore participated largely for the purpose of obstructing. If they should walk out, leaving ten states present, they might be able to obstruct permanently. Should Massachusetts or Georgia cross over, the states would again be deadlocked, 5 to 5. Should both change their votes, the delegates from Pennsylvania, Virginia, or South Carolina (judging by their extreme statements) might well walk out. Should neither change its vote, the delegates from Connecticut, New Jersey, or Delaware (judging by their extreme statements) might well walk out. In any of these eventualities, the convention would be dead, and with it would die the Union of American states.[39] Accordingly, on Tuesday the tenth Lansing and Yates abruptly took their leave.[40]

---

[38] Yates, July 3, Journal, Madison, Yates, July 5, *ibid.*, 1:522–36.

[39] Yates, July 5, *ibid.*, 1:536. For various explanations of the departure of Lansing and Yates, see Martin, "Genuine Information"; Yates' and Lansing's report to George Clinton; Mason's account, September 30, 1792; all *ibid.*, 3:190, 244–47, 367. None of these rings true; and given their known attitudes and the context in the convention, the explanation given here seems to me the most likely one.

[40] The exact date on which Lansing and Yates left is not absolutely certain; Yates' journal ends on July 5, but both the official journal of the Convention and Madison's notes record New York as voting until the 10th, and Hamilton had left on June 29.

For a few days the convention flirted with another suggestion, that representation be based on wealth instead of what had been proposed—until someone raised the explosive issue of whether slaves would count as people for one branch and as property for the other. The week ended with nothing settled and with hope for settlement apparently gone. (One favorable omen—and perhaps it was more than omen—did appear. On Friday the thirteenth a cold front blew in and broke the heat wave. The air was suddenly fresh, and it remained so for three weeks.)[41]

On Monday the sixteenth the vote came on the Franklin committee's "compromise." The roll call began, state by state, north to south. Massachusetts was divided. Connecticut and New Jersey, next in order, voted in favor, then Pennsylvania voted no. Delaware also voted in favor. Then came Maryland, heretofore divided. But as Lansing and Yates had walked out, Daniel Carroll had walked in. He sided with Martin and Maryland voted aye, and the tally stood 4 to 1, with one divided. (With Georgia sure to split and Virginia and the Carolinas sure to vote nay, the convention had but a few minutes to live.)

Virginia did the expected: four states to two. "North Carolina," Washington called. One of its delegates was absent, and the second voted no, but then, unaccountably, the other three voted in favor. That assured passage of the compromise, even though South Carolina followed with a nay and Georgia's delegation, uniting again, also voted no.[42]

There was no general sigh of relief; but neither did the defeated delegates walk out. Their hearts were not in the

[41] Madison, July 5, 6, 9, King, July 5, *ibid.*, 1:533–34, 536–37, 541–42, 559–62.
[42] Journal, July 9, Madison, July 16, *ibid.*, 1:557, 2:15.

proceedings that day or the next, and betweentimes they caucused in a vain effort to agree on some common policy, but in the main they took their defeat and stuck with the convention, albeit grumblingly.[43]

The end of the preliminary stage was not over, for the question of the executive branch had yet to be settled. Settling it took ten more days and the settlement—making the president elective by the Congress for a seven-year term and ineligible for reelection—really satisfied no one. But it was settled, and during those ten days the jubilant "small-states" bloc joined with archnationalists from the other states and pushed through proposals to load the new government with powers.[44]

By July 26 the convention had gone as far as it could go in dealing with general principles; it was now time to pull its resolutions together into the form of a concrete system. On that day it turned over the proceedings to a five-man Committee of Detail and adjourned for ten days. For whatever use they might be, it also referred to the committee the discarded plans of Pinckney and Paterson, along with a few incidental proposals made just before the adjournment. Thus ended the first phase.[45]

The work of the Committee of Detail constituted the second phase. The committee consisted of Wilson, Rutledge, Ellsworth, Gorham, and Randolph. Randolph was unreconciled to the vote of July 16 and uneasy about going too far in giving powers to the national government. His

---

[43] Madison, July 16, 17, *ibid.,* 2:19–20, 25.

[44] Madison, July 17–26, *ibid.,* 2:25–128.

[45] Madison, July 26, *ibid.,* 2:128.

voice in the committee was therefore inaudible, for the other four members were archnationalists. Gorham's was scarcely more audible, for the other three operated largely upon the basis of agreements that had been settled privately, not on the convention floor.[46]

Formally, what the committee did was codify the sense of the convention. Two days before the full group reconvened, the committee drew up and had printed copies of a complete constitution, consisting of a preamble and twenty-three articles. The document bore strikingly little resemblance to Randolph's original plan. It looked a little more like the one Pinckney had proposed. It looked a good deal more like a polished and padded version of the original Paterson Plan —the only obvious variation being the addition of a second branch of Congress, apportioned by population. Overall, the document was well calculated to reflect the expressed views of the delegates, avoid unpalatable flaws of form, and establish a strong national government.

What the committee did also involved considerations that were far more subtle. The document was skillfully enough drawn so that during the convention's third phase (which lasted a month) there was—on the surface—little objection to the idea of creating a national government, and none to the general form it would take. But August was special-

---

[46] Records of the Committee of Detail are extremely limited, consisting almost exclusively of scraps in the Wilson Papers, Historical Society of Pennsylvania; they are all reproduced in Farrand, *Records,* 2:129–74. What happened in the committee has to be inferred from what had gone before, the positions and known private agreements of the committee members, and the committee's draft. Useful information and interesting speculations are contained in Smith, *James Wilson,* 245–49, and Barry, *Mr. Rutledge,* 338–50. For the most important private deal, see the discussion of the dinner meeting between Sherman and Rutledge, below.

interests month: while agreeing on the general form and substance of a constitution, the delegates haggled and traded, like so many fishmongers, over special features to protect their own interests or those of their groups or sections. It was concerning these matters that private agreements had determined the doings of the committee.

In the broadest sense, four sets of interests contended for special favors. One was that of the landless states—Connecticut, New Jersey, Delaware, Maryland, and New Hampshire (whose delegates had finally arrived on July 18). Having won equal representation in the Senate, these states now wanted to ensure that land disputes be settled there.[47] Some wanted to go even further, and now prepared an audacious scheme for what was little else than stealing the lands of other states.[48]

The second general interest was that of the carrying trade, which by delegations meant Massachusetts and, to some extent, Pennsylvania. (Outside the convention the shippers had strong support from another group, the artisans and mechanics of the cities.) These sought to endow Congress —or rather, a bare majority of a quorum of Congress— with power to enact the kind of navigation laws that Massachusetts had been working for, as well as to negotiate such commercial treaties as the one lately discussed between Jay and Gardoqui.[49]

---

[47] Madison, August 29, 30, Martin, "Genuine Information," in Farrand, *Records,* 2:454–56, 461–65, 3:223–27.

[48] The scheme was to endow Congress with power to dismember the landed states by dividing off portions and admitting them as separate states.

[49] This and the two following paragraphs are derived from a multitude of sources, as cited in chapters two through five, herein, together with the speeches and motions of the delegates in the convention.

The third was that of the Southern planters. All these sought to prevent taxes on exports. Those below North Carolina sought protection of the slave trade also, and those from North Carolina to the Mason-Dixon line sought provisions requiring two-thirds majorities for the passage of navigation acts and the ratification of treaties. The logic of the first two demands was obvious. As to the third, Southerners opposed navigation acts for the same reason that Yankees favored them: they could result in a monopoly for American shippers and consequent high freight rates. The provision regarding treaties was designed to protect Southern land speculators against just such pacts as that proposed by Jay and Gardoqui. It too ran against the interest of the carrying states and, for a curious reason, it ran against those of the landless states as well.

Finally, there was the moneyed interest, which meant, in effect, public creditors and stockholders in the Bank of North America. The first were without influence as an articulate group in the convention. Though most of the delegates held securities, mere discussion of the subject aroused tirades against speculators; and advocates of public credit felt it best simply to leave the matter alone and let everyone assume that when the national government had money it would pay its debts in a way that would satisfy all. As to the bank, it had only the Pennsylvania delegates to speak for it. Its interests ran counter to no one's, save the imagined interests of Virginia, but they ran counter to the sentiments of many delegates. For the bank, a completely unobtrusive kind of protection had to be devised.

Almost every delegate participated, at one time or another, in private discussions in behalf of some interest or another. By far the most effective negotiator was John

Rutledge of South Carolina, a man with great instinctive knowledge of who was important (as opposed to those who merely appeared important), and a comparable skill in winning their support for ends he sought. He consulted with many during the course of the convention, but his most important single transaction took place during the evening of June 30. At a private dinner in his quarters (he had left Wilson's house and rented chambers) Rutledge entertained Roger Sherman of Connecticut. Sherman was, on the one hand, a difficult man to deal with, for he combined incorruptible moral rectitude with wily political talent; but on the other, what he sought for his state from the nation was obvious despite his close-mouthed shrewdness, for he had been seeking it since 1776. What he sought was many things, but in essence it was one thing: enough land for his overcrowded state to perpetuate its system of farming and speculating in lands for a long time—say, the lifetime of everyone living.[50]

A year before, through skillful negotiations that were in some respects scarcely distinguishable from blackmail, Sherman had won for Connecticut the huge tract west of Pennsylvania called the Western Reserve. But the winnings, though approved by various other authorities, rested fundamentally on the willingness of the Assembly of Pennsylvania to keep its bargains, a willingness for which that Assembly was not notorious. Now, in the constitutional convention, Connecticut sought the creation of a strong national government—which by its very existence would benefit Connecticut in a general way—but only if that government

---

[50] Barry, *Mr. Rutledge,* 329–32; Boardman, *Roger Sherman,* 82–86, 148–64; Wadsworth to King, June 3, 1787, in Farrand, *Records,* 3:33–34; see also footnote 54 below and chapter four herein.

could be so devised as to protect the state's gains in the Ohio country. The way to do that was to take the issue out of the hands of the fickle Pennsylvania Assembly and lodge it with the Congress. Or, if the convention persisted in insisting on a bicameral Congress, the second house should preserve equal representation and jurisdiction over all land questions should be lodged in it. If this were done Connecticut could, by teaming up with other landless states, expect weighted chances of success.[51]

South Carolina, too, could expect general gains from the creation of a national authority only if certain local interests could be protected. As Rutledge viewed these,[52] they required only that the national government's control over commerce, while broad in the extreme, should not encompass power to interfere with the slave trade or to tax exports.[53]

Rutledge and Sherman struck a deal: that South Carolina (and if Rutledge could deliver it, Georgia) would support Connecticut on the land matter, and Connecticut (and if

---

[51] James Monroe to Richard Henry Lee, May 24, 1786, Charles Pettit to Jeremiah Wadsworth, May 27, 1786, William Grayson to Madison, May 28, 1786, and Monroe to Jefferson, June 16, 1786, all in Burnett, ed., *Letters of Members of Congress,* 8:365–66, 368–69, 373, 391–92; Burnett, *Continental Congress,* 648–49; Brant, *Madison,* 3:65.

[52] Rutledge's views were not universally held in South Carolina; for illustration of his adamant stand on slavery and the opposition of some of his fellow-citizens, see the debates in the state legislature, as published in the *Charleston Evening Gazette,* September 28, 1785. Four times during the convention Rutledge stated that protection of the slave trade (and on some of these occasions, prohibition of export taxes) was the sine qua non of South Carolina's participation in a strong union; interestingly, a delegate from Connecticut supported him on each occasion.

[53] Madison, August 16, 21, 22, September 10, in Farrand, *Records,* 2:306, 364, 374, 559. Interestingly, a delegate from Connecticut supported him on each occasion.

Sherman could deliver them, other Northern states) would support South Carolina on the matter of slave trade and exports. One problem remained. Rutledge could swing South Carolina and Georgia behind a plan to lodge jurisdiction over land disputes in the Senate, but it had not yet been decided that states would have equal votes in the Senate. On this question Georgia was hopelessly divided and Rutledge could not control his own delegation (young Pinckney had bolted Rutledge's authority, and the older Pinckney was adamant against equal representation). Rutledge had, however, an ace up his sleeve. Late in the evening a caller appeared at the door: Hugh Williamson of North Carolina. Until now, Williamson had voted for proportional representation, along with William Blount and Richard Dobbs Spaight and against Alexander Martin and William R. Davie, thus placing North Carolina solidly in the "large-states" camp. But Blount was about to leave for New York to serve a month in Congress. Williamson was prepared to change his vote when the issue came to a showdown. That was enough to seal the bargain between Rutledge and Sherman.[54]

---

[54] The trade and the meeting are narrated in Barry, *Mr. Rutledge,* 329–32; but Barry, following Madison (August 29, note, in Farrand, *Records,* 2:449) and the various appendixes cited by Farrand (2:449n), mistakenly assumed that Connecticut, for its part, wanted protection of the carrying trade. Clearly, as is indicated in the port records of Portsmouth, Beverly, Boston, Providence, Newport, New Haven, Philadelphia, Baltimore, Annapolis, Alexandria, Norfolk and Charleston, Connecticut had no carrying trade; equally clearly, Connecticut was seeking protection of its land claims; and also equally clearly, some trade was made—if there were no evidence, the vigorous defense of slavery by Ellsworth and Sherman (August 22) would lead one to suspect it. The inescapable inference, borne out by the Committee of Detail's draft, is that protection of Connecticut's land claims was Sherman's price.

Thus when the vote on equal representation in the Senate was taken on July 16, eight men knew the outcome in advance: the four delegates from South Carolina, the three from Connecticut, and Williamson of North Carolina. Eleven days later, when Rutledge, Sherman's alter ego Ellsworth, and Rutledge's bosom friend James Wilson were appointed to the five-man Committee of Detail, the same eight men knew how the committee's draft would reconcile the several contending economic groups in the convention. The draft included an absolute prohibition against taxes on exports and against interference by Congress in the slave trade. It also gave the Senate exclusive jurisdiction over disputes between states about titles to lands. For good measure, it took care of another interest by stipulating that acts regarding commerce could be passed only by a two-thirds majority of both houses of Congress, and still another by requiring that treaties could be ratified only by a two-thirds majority of the Senate. Something for everyone.[55]

It did not, however, end up that way. Not that Rutledge and Ellsworth (who took over floor management of Sherman's end of the deal) fumbled; indeed, few assemblies have been so artfully managed, without the knowledge of those being managed, as was this convention during the middle of August. But certain external circumstances changed and certain internal alignments changed also, and

---

The analysis of votes in the North Carolina delegation is arrived at by process of elimination. Williamson was privy to the deal, Blount was absent on July 16, and Spaight voted against equal representation; therefore, to have carried the state in favor of equal representation, both Davie and Martin must have so voted. Furthermore, Davie had indicated on the very day of the Rutledge-Sherman dinner that he was willing to compromise; Madison, June 30, *ibid.*, 1:487–88.

[55] Madison, August 6, *ibid.*, 177–89.

Rutledge and Ellsworth, with the consummate skill of master politicians, adapted their operations in a way that was less than invisible.

The main external change was that on July 23—four days before the Committee of Detail took over—Congress, sitting in New York, concluded the sale of a huge tract of land north of the Ohio River to the Ohio Company. The deal, in fine, was that Congress sold the Company a million acres of land for two-thirds of a million dollars, payable in public securities, in installments and at par. Because the Company was now dominated by Connecticuters instead of the residents of Massachusetts who had originally promoted it, the sale vested Connecticuters with about a third as much vacant land as the entire area of the state. Because the purchase was payable in securities instead of cash, the amount of specie necessary to its completion was roughly eighty to a hundred thousand dollars, or eight to ten cents an acre. Sherman learned of this transaction during the ten-day vacation.[56]

It thus became less advantageous for Connecticut to have land disputes settled in the Senate, where it would have weighted chances of success; and instead made it in the state's interest to lodge them in the Supreme Court, where they would be removed from politics altogether. Accord-

---

[56] *Journals of Congress,* 32:334–43, 33:399–401 (July 13, 23, 1787); Jensen, *New Nation,* 355–59. Sherman's last recorded speech before the adjournment was on July 18. It is certain that he went through New York, for he was in New Haven for a funeral on July 26 (F. P. Dexter, ed., *Literary Diary of Ezra Stiles* [3 vols., New York, 1901], 3:271–72). It is entirely possible that, having seen to the success of the equal representation vote of July 16, he headed for New York to check on the doings of the Ohio Company in Congress. In any event, he was back in Philadelphia when the convention reconvened.

ingly, during the debates on the Committee of Detail's report the elaborate procedure for settling land questions was quietly dropped, and jurisdiction was quietly shifted to the court.[57]

The internal development during the month of August was less easily handled. Luther Martin of Maryland had been unhappy with developments before the adjournment, and while the committee was in session he had returned to Baltimore to confer with his intimate political and personal friend Samuel Chase. They published no record of their discussions, but the gist of them is clear from Martin's tactics after August 6. He gathered about him a group that met nightly in his quarters to drink and discuss the doings of the convention. In such circumstances Martin was at his persuasive best, for at the point when most men began to lose control of their tongues and their wits—say, after the seventh drink—Martin was just beginning to think clearly and sharply and cunningly.[58]

The group consisted of Martin and occasionally Mercer and McHenry of Maryland, Mason and Randolph of Vir-

---

[57] Madison, August 24, in Farrand, *Records,* 2:400–401. Rutledge made the motion for this change; Johnson of Connecticut seconded it, and Sherman spoke for it, as did Dayton, the New Jersey land speculator whose organization (the Miami Company) consummated, in October, a purchase much like that of the Ohio Company.

[58] The evidence of these meetings and of their personnel is in Martin's "Reply to the Landholder" (Ellsworth), March 14, 1788, *ibid.,* 3:282. The meetings began shortly after August 14; Martin was in New York from the seventh until then. What took place in them can only be surmised; but the discontents of each member, about to be summarized, are clear from their remarks in convention throughout August. For information on Martin's operating tactics in such circumstances, as well as general information about him, I am deeply indebted to Mr. Paul S. Clarkson of Baltimore, who for many years has sought out and studied everything written or said by Martin and everything his contemporaries wrote or said about him.

ginia, Gerry of Massachusetts, Charles Pinckney of South
Carolina, and once in a while delegates from Delaware,
New Jersey, and Georgia. In a general sense, the group was
one of watered-down old republicans, but each had some
kind of personal or economic axe to grind.

Martin himself had a number of reasons for objecting to
what was happening. The whole affair was a bit too high-
toned for his taste, and he devoutly and genuinely opposed
the institution of human slavery, which the convention was
proposing to sanction. More tangibly, as a Marylander he
was dissatisfied with the backing off from the clause lodging
jurisdiction over land in the Senate, and he was equally dissatisfied with the clause requiring two-thirds majorities for
navigation acts (because it did not go far enough; he and
the other Maryland delegates thought that acts regarding
commerce should not be passed without the approval of
two-thirds of the Representatives from each state—in substance, that each state should have a veto over such acts).[59]
The occasional delegates from other landless states came
along, as Martin encouraged them to do, because they, too,
were dissatisfied with the shift in jurisdiction over land
questions, despite the general advantages the proposed new
system would afford. Mason and Randolph concurred with
Martin's objections regarding the "tone" of the proceedings
and regarding navigation acts, and also with his objections
to sanctioning the slave trade. Whether both sincerely opposed slavery, as they maintained, or whether they wanted
to stop the importation of slaves so that Virginians and
Marylanders could become slave farmers instead of tobacco

---

[59] On commerce, see McHenry, August 6; on slavery, Madison, August
21; on land, August 30; in Farrand, *Records,* 2:191, 364, 461–70.

and wheat farmers—which would have enriched both men —is beside the point.[60]

Gerry and Pinckney joined the group out of personal pique. Gerry had come into the convention more anxious to accommodate others in the interests of national union than any other delegate. From time to time before the Committee of Detail was appointed, he balked at what was happening; and doubtless more than once he squirmed in discomfort at finding himself in the same camp with such old and dear enemies as Robert and Gouverneur Morris, James Wilson, and Alexander Hamilton. Furthermore, he had an inordinate capacity for becoming irritated with people upon close contact, and was thus particularly susceptible to convention myopia—that is, to forgetting the broad considerations which had brought him into an accommodating spirit, and bickering overmuch about unpleasant details. But each time he started to waver he checked himself. That is, he did so until the middle of August, when Charles Pinckney suddenly furnished an excuse for a 180-degree turn.[61]

Pinckney, as indicated, was a brilliant young man with a neurotic need to be recognized as a person of worth. The convention, up to mid-August, scarcely afforded that recognition. The prestige Pinckney had won by being appointed to the convention was quickly dissipated. Before the South

---

[60] See the debates cited in footnote 59, the debate on slavery, August 22, and Mason's and Randolph's remarks throughout September.

[61] For information on Gerry's personal makeup and his behavior in the convention, beyond that which is implicit or explicit in Farrand's *Records* (including a great deal in the appendixes, vol. 3) and in biographical sources, I am indebted to Professor George Billias of Clark University, who for some years has been engaged in research on a biography of Gerry.

Carolina delegates had left for Philadelphia, John Rutledge had convened them in Charleston, upon which occasion Pinckney had brashly presented a full plan for a national constitution. Rutledge, with the overbearingly condescending manner he could affect, made no comment but also made it clear that he had other plans. Early in the convention—on the very day that Randolph presented the Virginia Plan—Pinckney introduced his own, only to have the convention treat it even more summarily than Rutledge had. Throughout June and July Pinckney arose to make brilliant speeches about something or another, only to be greeted with the same lack of enthusiasm. Doubtless the delegates were too gentlemanly to call him "Sonny," but politely ignoring him accomplished the same effect. Equally doubtless, by mid-August Pinckney must have been beside himself with anxiety to lead or join a group of dissenters that would take control of the convention from its proud leaders.[62] The group gathering around Martin was tailor-made for his aspirations. (Should the Martin group fail, Pinckney could always sign the document approved by the winners, and then go out into the hustings and modestly claim that it was *really* he who had written the document—which is just what he did.)[63]

---

[62] During August, while meeting with the Martin group after hours, Pinckney made on the convention floor a flurry of minor proposals, many of which found their way into the Constitution; significantly, however, most were not directly approved and incorporated, but referred to committees, from which they reemerged later, anonymously. That is the cardinal point: not that Pinckney's ideas on many matters were not accepted, for they decidedly were; but that he was not credited with them when he made proposals.

[63] On the Rutledge episode, see Barry, *Mr. Rutledge,* 312–14; on Pinckney's ineffectiveness in the early phase, see Madison, May 29, June–July, *passim,* and postconvention sources in Farrand's *Records* cited in footnote 13, above. On Pinckney's attendance at the Martin meetings, see Martin's

For the present, which is to say in the middle of August, Pinckney began to attend Martin's evening sessions. Martin was wise enough and skillful enough to humor Pinckney without actually listening to him, but after a few nights that must have rankled the young aristocrat also. It was inevitable, under the circumstances, that he should attempt to attract attention by hinting darkly, in the manner of raw youths, that he was privy to secret information that could blow the convention apart. It was also inevitable that Martin, who could drink any man under the table, should sooner or later get Pinckney so drunk that he would reveal what he knew. What he knew was the details of the "corrupt bargain," the deal between Sherman and Rutledge. However Martin learned the details, he had learned them by the third full week of August. When Martin learned, Gerry and Mason and Randolph and then everybody else in the convention who was aware of anything learned also.[64] Gerry, every puritanical and republican instinct outraged, immediately made the reversal he had been threatening to make for some time. So also threatened to do a number of other delegates.[65]

"Reply to the Landholder," March 14, 1788, *ibid.,* 3:282. Martin says only that "an honorable member from South Carolina" was at the meetings, not naming Pinckney; but given the personalities and commitments of C. C. Pinckney, Rutledge, and Butler, it is inconceivable that Martin could be referrring to anyone but Charles Pinckney. As to Pinckney's immediate postconvention claims, see his "Observations," October 1787, *ibid.,* 3:106 ff.

[64] Madison learned of the deal on August 29 and recorded a note about it, but he clearly misunderstood what had happened, for he thought the trade involved navigation acts and slavery. Historians have generally followed his mistaken lead.

[65] That the deal became generally known is clear; see Madison's note, August 29, *ibid.,* 2:449, and references under August 5, footnote 8; see also footnotes 54, above, and 66, below. From the debates, the freezing of atti-

At this moment—about the twenty-second of August—
Martin stood on the brink of complete victory, which meant
so dividing the convention against itself that it would adjourn without accomplishing anything.[66] Martin now had

tudes in late August is likewise obvious. That Pinckney was the source of the
information is surmise, but in the context the surmise seems inescapable.
Only eight men knew of the deal; it is unthinkable that either Rutledge or
any of the three close-mouthed delegates from Connecticut told. That
leaves the two Pinckneys, Butler, and Williamson. Of these, there is no
evidence that any but Charles Pinckney had any significant or intimate
out-of-doors relationships with any other delegates, and for C. C. Pinckney
and Butler, such relationships would have been entirely out of character;
furthermore, both supported Rutledge and the Connecticut delegates in
the complex maneuvers of late August, and Charles Pinckney opposed
them. In short, only Pinckney had the motive, the occasion, and the inclination. Assuming that it was Pinckney who told Martin, alcohol seems the
most likely agent.

[66] The deal was not common knowledge on August 22, for on that date
G. Morris suggested on the floor that there were ingredients of a deal in
the disagreement over slavery and navigation acts; the defense of slavery
by Connecticut delegates on the same date indicates that their part of the
bargain had long since been sealed. Madison knew about it by August 29,
and it was on August 29 and 30 that the Martin group made its most
determined effort. The revelation therefore must have taken place between
August 22 and 29.

George Mason, in his account of September 30, 1792 (presumably to
Jefferson; Farrand, *Records,* 3:367), set the date as "a fortnight" before
the end of the convention, but he clearly refers to the last week of August.
Mason also got the story wrong—which further attests the skill of the
delegates from South Carolina and Connecticut. Mason thought the South
Carolinians and Georgians feared "that Congress would immediately suppress the imporn of slaves," and "therefore struck up a bargain with the
3 N. England states, if they would join to admit slaves for some years, the
2 Southernmost states wd join in changing the clause which required
2/3 of the legislature in any vote." What Mason was forgetting was that
the Constitution, as it stood before the trade, prohibited Congress from
interfering with the slave trade forever. See article 7, section 4 of the Committee of Detail report, *ibid.,* 2:183, which was unanimously approved on
August 8 (*ibid.,* 2:223). The matter was revived in a different connection
on August 21, and that, in turn, revealed strong antislavery sentiment in
the convention.

not only his own group to work with, but also various other delegates who were opposed to the slave trade, and others who were opposed to the two-thirds clause on navigation acts, and still others who were opposed to the two-thirds clause on treaties, and an indeterminate number who were incensed at the corrupt bargain. The critical moment in the history of the nation as a nation was at hand, and this crisis, unlike the one in mid-July, had not been managed in advance.

But Rutledge and Ellsworth, with all the coolness of a pair of twentieth-century congressmen from Texas, rose to the occasion. To those who objected to the bargain but did not particularly object to its contents, they gave the impression that they had retreated. To those who did not object to the bargain but opposed its fruits, they gave the impression that they had sacrificed its fruits. To all, they gave the impression that the bargain had been something that it had not been. In fact what they did was to take a calculated risk on forever alienating the irreconcilables, but winning, in the process, all others who believed that immense gains of principle or of interest would ensue from the establishment of a national government.[67]

In fine, they came up with a new "compromise" proposal, namely one abolishing the two-thirds clause for navigation

---

[67] Rutledge and Ellsworth were not alone; C. C. Pinckney helped considerably; Ellsworth himself was called away on urgent business on August 27, and Johnson and Sherman picked up his floor tasks. As to what happened, the debates of August 22–30 must be read with great care, noting what changes were being made and who was for and against each. See also the following footnote. The reference to Texas congressmen is, of course, to Sam Rayburn and Lyndon Johnson, who, during the Eisenhower administration, were speaker of the House and Senate majority leader, respectively.

acts and allowing Congress to regulate or even prohibit the slave trade after twenty years.[68] This maneuver alienated, once and for all, Martin, Mason, Randolph, Mercer, and Gerry. It also won, once and for all, all the disgruntled delegates from north of the Mason-Dixon line, and at the same time it preserved the essential features of the private agreement between South Carolina and Connecticut. Thenceforth, the nationalists were in complete control, and the convention could race home to a finish.

One other matter of form remained—the constitution of the presidency—and that afforded occasion for a last-ditch battle by the dissidents. Deals and debates to the contrary notwithstanding, the constitution that the delegates were working with as late as a week before the practical finish of the convention was, in form and in substance, little different from the original Paterson Plan. That is to say, it would establish a government of broad but enumerated powers, to be exercised by a Congress—one that differed from the existing Congress only by being split in half, with one branch popularly apportioned—and by executive and judicial branches of the Congress. As the constitution stood on

---

[68] This proposal, which was made by a committee, was no compromise at all. A compromise involves mutual concessions by contending parties; in this instance, "the South" was yielding on both points, and the pair of proposals constituted a retreat. They were not, however, a retreat from what South Carolina and Connecticut had agreed upon, but a retreat from what most thought they had agreed upon. When the proposal was debated on August 29, Charles Pinckney of South Carolina, Luther Martin of Maryland, and Edmund Randolph and George Mason of Virginia led an assault against it; Rutledge, Sherman, C. C. Pinckney, Butler, Madison, and delegates from the carrying states (Massachusetts and Pennsylvania) defended it.

September 5, the executive and judicial branches were no more than that, arms of the Congress, the president being elected by the Congress and the judges being appointed by the president, subject to approval by the Congress.[69]

Off and on throughout the convention the question of the presidency had been debated. Through August, even as the Martin group was being formed, the dissenters agitated the issue. They did so at first because they were genuinely concerned about it; later, when they perceived that it was the only question that regularly provoked the nationalists to fight one another, they began to employ it for that reason. Each time the problem was settled, Martin or Gerry or Mason or Randolph opened it again, and the matter was debated and settled again, each time in a slightly different way; and each time it went full circle more delegates became dissatisfied with any solution that had been proposed.[70]

The question was finally settled on September 6. A committee, appointed to consider an assortment of miscellany, came up on September 4 with what was the only real governmental innovation devised by the convention: the electoral college system, in which the people (or the legislatures, as the legislatures should determine) should elect as many

---

[69] There is no draft of the document as of September 5, but it is possible to construct one by starting with the Committee of Detail's report, contained in Madison's notes for August 6, and tracing the changes adopted during the next month. What one emerges with is the Paterson Plan, modified by the addition of a second and popularly apportioned branch of Congress, an assortment of minor powers proposed largely by Madison and Pinckney, and the supreme law clause proposed by Martin and subsequently refined, together with the special features arranged by Rutledge and Sherman. Structurally, it still provides for a congressional government.

[70] See Farrand, *Records,* 3:642–46, Index by Clauses of the Constitution.

electors as the number of their representatives and senators. The electors would meet in their respective states but all on the same day, and vote for two persons, one of whom had to be from another state. Whoso got the most votes would become president, and whoever got the second most votes would become vice president. It was an awkward scheme, irrational almost to the point of absurdity, and it was so greeted by most of the delegates; and yet as they argued about it, it became increasingly clear that this was a system that would overcome every objection that had been raised against every other method. After two days, during which numerous minor modifications were proposed and a few were adopted, the plan was approved.[71]

(And thus, almost by accident, was created the magnificent system of checks and balances of the United States Constitution. Until September 6, the constitution agreed upon was one that would have established a congressional government. On that day, the government became a mixed one, for in rendering the presidency independent of Congress, the delegates rendered the judiciary relatively independent also. This one stroke, by crystallizing the whole structure, resulted in a form of government more peculiarly adapted to the nature of the human animal than anything devised before or since.)

Such sublime considerations, however, were related neither to what the delegates were thinking nor to what the committee had sought to do. The committee had devised the electoral college as a half-baked compromise with an immediate issue, and as such it worked. The convention's most vexing problem had been solved, and dissenters had been

---

[71] Madison, McHenry, September 4–6, *ibid.,* 2:496–531.

deprived of their last weapon. Only three more days of debate were required to bring "the main business" to a conclusion.

There was a last important touch. On September 10 the convention appointed a Committee on Style, assigning it the function of "editing" the approved constitution—that is, making sure that its grammar was clear, its language finished, its topics orderly, and so on. The committee consisted of Johnson, Hamilton, Madison, King, and Gouverneur Morris. These, in turn, assigned the function to Morris, who was well known for his skill as a literary craftsman, and so in the end it was he who "wrote" the Constitution.[72]

The document itself attests the excellence of Morris' performance. Less visible are the liberties he took with the text. In rendering the language graceful, he also rendered parts of it ambiguous (and therefore elastic, and therefore viable). Elsewhere, he used words that slanted the meaning of clauses, and in at least one instance he audaciously inserted a clause that had been explicitly rejected by the convention. This would, in the passage of time, prove to be one of the most important details in the Constitution: the clause prohibiting the states from passing laws "impairing the obligation of contracts." In context, all Morris meant by it was to give the Bank of North America the subtle protection it sought, by preventing the legislature of Pennsylvania from again revoking its corporate charter—which was

---

[72] Madison, September 8, 10; Baldwin's résumé to Ezra Stiles, December 21, 1787; Madison to Jared Sparks, April 8, 1831; all *ibid.*, 2:553, 557–64, 3:170, 499.

legally a contract.[73] (Morris tried another and even more audacious insertion: a change in punctuation that would have given Congress virtually unlimited powers. Roger Sherman caught that one, however, and the original punctuation was restored.)[74]

On September 17, 1787, the Constitution was signed by thirty-nine of the forty-two delegates present. Not everyone liked it: Randolph, Mason, and Gerry flatly refused to sign; Lansing and Yates had long since walked out, and Luther Martin and Mercer had gone by early September. Hamilton

---

[73] That Morris could make minor changes was possible largely because the members had no official full draft; the changes are easier for the historian to detect because Farrand (*Records*, 2:565–80) constructed a draft which can be compared with the draft of the Committee on Style. As to the contract clause, King had proposed it on August 28 and Morris had opposed it and Wilson and Madison supported it; it was defeated (*ibid.*, 2:439–40). Whether it was Wilson, King, or Madison who persuaded Morris to insert it cannot be ascertained, but Wilson is the most likely candidate. For one thing, Wilson, as the bank's lawyer, was acutely sensitive on this point; for another, he had a particular awareness of the effect of such a clause on corporate charters; see Journal of the Council of Censors, August 27, 1784, vol. 2, pp. 520–26, in the Public Records Division, Harrisburg, and Wilson's arguments before the Pennsylvania legislature in behalf of the bank's charter, in *Philadelphia Evening Herald*, September 7–8, 1785. See also Baldwin's résumé to Ezra Stiles, December 21, 1787, in Farrand, *Records*, 3:170, wherein Baldwin gives Wilson equal credit with Morris as author of the final draft.

[74] The punctuation change was the insertion of a semicolon after the words "To lay and collect taxes, duties, imposts and excises" in the enumeration of congressional powers, article 1, section 8 (see Farrand, *Records*, 2:594). That would have transformed the subsequent words, "to pay the debts and provide for the common defense and general welfare of the United States," into a positive and broad grant of power. When the semicolon was replaced with a comma, upon Sherman's discovery of the trick (Albert Gallatin in the House of Representatives, June 19, 1798, *ibid.*, 3:379), the "general welfare clause" again became, as Madison laboriously pointed out in *Federalist* Number 41, a restriction on the taxing power rather than a separate grant of power.

said that "no man's ideas were more remote from the plan than his"; Blount signed only after the style of the signatures was changed from one indicating individual approval to one merely attesting that all the state delegations present approved; McHenry was "opposed to many parts of the system"; Franklin said there were many parts he did not approve and would never approve. But most agreed with Franklin that it was the best, under the circumstances, that could be hoped for; and with Hamilton that the alternative to the Constitution was "anarchy and convulsion."[75]

Most also had to agree with Gouverneur Morris. "With all its faults," Morris said, "the moment this plan goes forth all other considerations will be laid aside, and the great question will be, shall there be a national government or not?"

---

[75] Madison, McHenry, September 17, in Farrand, *Records,* 2:641–50. Strictly speaking, only thirty-eight persons signed the Constitution on September 17; George Read signed for himself and, at Dickinson's request, for Dickinson as well, for Dickinson had to be absent.

Chapter Seven

The Constitution

M orris was right: the question, during and before and after the convention, was not what kind of national government would be created, but whether a national government would be created at all. Writing the Constitution had been a great achievement in practical, not theoretical, politics. Getting it ratified would be an even more difficult practical political achievement.[1]

To pull it off, to overcome inertia and a host of centrifugal forces, friends of the Constitution had to manage a thousand variable and sometimes unpredictable factors; which meant, first off, to know what the variables were. Most were prosaic, for in America local habit and prejudice were matched only by the pocketbook in dictating men's votes. But successful politicians knew that even before being moved by these, Americans paid superstitious, almost re-

---

[1] Since this chapter consists of analysis of the Constitution itself and of summary and analysis of data presented and documented in the foregoing chapters, it would be sheer pedantry to document the data and analysis here. Accordingly, footnotes will be offered only as explanation or elaboration of points made in the text, or as documentation of information cited here for the first time.

ligious, homage to certain ideological "givens." Accordingly,
though the establishment of the Constitution was far from a
philosophical matter, the issue had to be argued as if it were.

In point of theory, the Constitution would be America's
organic law—which is to say, the fundamental definition of
the means by which political power was to be exercised.
Inside the Anglo-Saxon scheme of things, the sum total of
governmental power that was regarded as legitimate was
virtually boundless, being subject to only two significant
limitations. One was the contract, public or private. The
other was tradition, largely as embodied in the common
law, which was in essence a set of personal rights in the form
of procedures that governed the exercise of power. Together
these placed life, liberty, and property morally beyond the
caprice of kings, lords, or popular majorities. But these two
theoretically unbreakable limitations were the only restrictions on otherwise unlimited power.[2]

There was, however, one other controlling given: that
power was not only divisible but, in fact, always divided
between the multitudes of agencies that, taken together,
constituted government. The perpetual question was not
"What power is legitimate?" (the answer to which was un-
changing) but "Where are the suitable repositories of power?" (the answer to which was continually changing). The
great disputes during the last days of the empire and all
great political events of the era since 1763—resistance to
the Stamp Act and other measures of Parliament, the Declaration of Independence, the Articles of Confederation, the

---

[2] During the Confederation period both these limitations were sometimes
transgressed by the state legislatures. The Constitution's express prohibition
of such violations is therefore important from a theoretical as well as a
practical point of view.

proposed amendments to the Articles, and the Constitution itself—turned on that point.

The Declaration of Independence, almost everyone agreed, amounted to some kind of reversion to first principles; as a result of it, all power had reverted to its ultimate source, wherever that might be. As to where, in practice many different stances had been taken. Some held that sovereignty, the whole power, devolved upon Congress, others that it devolved upon the states, still others that it devolved upon the whole people, the people of the states, and even the people of the towns.[3] State governments had

---

[3] In Massachusetts and New Hampshire the position taken was that sovereignty reverted to the towns, and these states' constitutions of 1780 and 1784 were legally erected on that principle. In Rhode Island and Connecticut, colonial charters were retained, and thus sovereignty theoretically reverted to the states as such; Rhode Island emphasized this stand with a separate declaration of independence. New York likewise made a separate declaration, but there, as in most states to the south, the dominant position held was that power had reverted to the people of the several states, severally. Very few people anywhere held that sovereignty went to the Congress or to the whole people, though a case was made for this position by the fact that the Treaty of Paris, 1783, by which the United States became independent, dealt with the states as a unit. This matter was muddled, however: in the Declaration of Independence, the plural form was used ("these states are"); the treaty with France, 1778, was between France and the Congress of the United States (thus presumably binding them all, though the Congress did not yet have any legal existence); the peace treaty itself was ratified by some states separately, and in New Hampshire it was ratified by the individual towns. James Wilson was the ablest spokesman for the theory that sovereignty devolved upon Congress or the whole people; his arguments were made in a political context, and few took them seriously.

When the framers of the Constitution referred the proposed supreme law to the people of the states, in their capacities as people of states—rather than having it ratified in any of several ways—they were in fact asserting that that was where sovereignty lay. The Congress, the state governors, the state legislatures, and the voters in every state, each in their turns, had opportunity to reject this assertion; when they unanimously confirmed the procedure, they necessarily confirmed the assertion.

been created on a motley collection of these theories, and
the question, until 1787, was not specifically answered. By
direct implication, the promulgation of the Constitution
gave a firm answer to this question.

In an ultimate sense, the Constitution confirmed the
proposition that original power resided in the people—not,
however, in the people as a whole, but in them in their
capacity as people of the several states. In 1787 the people
were so divided because, having created or acquiesced in
the creation of state governments, they were bound by prior
contracts. They could create more local or more general
governments, but only by agreeing, in their capacity as
people of the several states, to relocate power previously
lodged with the state governments. All powers not thus
relocated, and not reserved by the people in explicit state
constitutional limitations, remained in the state governments. In short, national or local governments, being the
creatures of the states, could exercise only those powers
explicitly or implicitly given them by the states; each state
government could exercise all powers unless it was for-
bidden from doing so by the people of the state. But in the
Constitution, the states went a step further, and expressly
denied to themselves the exercise of certain powers, such as
those of interfering with the obligations of private contracts,
passing ex post facto laws, and refusing to honor the laws
of other states. This is the essence of the American federal
system: the division of power along a vertical axis by re-
moving some of it from the central originating point, the
states, and shifting some of it up and some of it down the
axis.

At the same time that the Constitution was providing for
the creation of a national government by shifting powers

upward on the vertical axis, it provided that the powers so shifted should be further divided on a horizontal axis. That is, the national government's powers would be distributed in accordance with the three traditional aspects of government, legislation, execution, and adjudication.

So far, nothing new. Such a division was but a formalization of the theory and practice of government in England and its adaptation in British North America. And though such practice had been "discovered," as Dickinson put it, through experience and not through reason, it had, by the late eighteenth century, a thorough-going rationalization. That rationalization was that the definition of tyranny was the unchecked expression of the will of the sovereign; the only way to prevent such tyranny was through a mixed government. A mixed government meant one in which power was so distributed that no particular person, faction, class, group, or segment of the population, no matter what its numbers, could ever gain control of all the parts of the multifaceted government. "Give all power to the many," said Hamilton, and "they will oppress the few. Give all power to the few, they will oppress the many."[4]

There was, however, one cardinal difference between Britain and America which made a mere copying of the British system unfeasible. England had a hereditary monarchy and a hereditary nobility, each of which, along with the people, prevented the other from an unchecked expression of its will; and the two combined checked the people. In America, which lacked these hereditary institutions, it was necessary to devise some kind of structural substitute.

---

[4] The quotations are from Madison's Journal, June 18, August 13, 1787, in Farrand, *Records,* 1:288, 2:278.

This did not mean creating an artificial monarch and an aristocracy of wealth or education, as some of the delegates, notably Hamilton and Gouverneur Morris, proposed; but dividing the people into various aspects or capacities of themselves.

In other words, "the people" were not, in any part of the multilevel government, allowed to act as the whole people. Instead, for purposes of expressing their will they were separated from themselves both in space and in time. This was accomplished by separating the people, both in space and in time, from those they elected.

The national government would have four parts: House of Representatives, Senate, Presidency, and Court. The House was the "democratic" branch, all its members being elected directly by the people every two years—not, however, by the people as a whole, but by the people as citizens of subdivisions of states. The Senate was elected by the legislatures of the several states, and was therefore chosen by the people indirectly through their directly elected representatives, and represented the people not as residents of districts, but of states. Senators were removed further from the people by a time barrier, one-third of them being elected every two years for six-year terms. The chief executive was chosen by electors who were chosen by one of three means, as the state legislatures should direct: by the people in districts, by the people in the state as a whole, or by the state legislatures themselves; his term was four years, intermediate between that of the two houses of Congress. The fourth part of the national government, the Court, was chosen by the president (who was chosen by electors chosen by the legislatures chosen by the people), with the approval of the Senate (chosen by legislatures chosen by the people), and for life. And in state and local governments comparably cumbersome arrangements would continue to prevail.

The result of this jerry-built structure was that government in the United States would be of (that is, from) the people; hopefully, it would be for the people; but by no means would it be by the people. The people had no instrumentality through which to exercise "the general will" immediately, and they could express it directly only by achieving a fantastic unanimity and sustaining that unanimity for fifteen or twenty years.

The division of every voter into many artificial parts of himself was one of three aspects of the genius of the American constitutional system. The second stemmed from the fact that the division and definition of power, on both axes, were neither static nor precise. The executive and legislative branches, though separate, each had a foot in the door of the other; many powers were ambiguously stated; the court structure was only outlined, leaving it to Congress to fill in the details and even permitting Congress to incorporate state courts as part of the national court system. This very fact—that power was ill-defined and free to shift from one place to another, as time and circumstance should dictate—made the system viable. It could live through wars and revolutions and the most profound economic, social, and technological changes the world had ever seen, and be amended more than twenty times, and still its essence would remain the same.

The third aspect concerned the actuating principle of the governmental system. Montesquieu had taught that the proper actuating principle of a republic was virtue. The Founding Fathers, being skeptical of man's virtue, designed a republic whose actuating principle would be the opposite. The untidiness of the system necessitated that the operation

of American government would ever recapitulate its process
of birth. That is, the system was born of compromises—
some arrived at openly and some under the table, some
arrived at through "respectable" means and others through
"corrupt" deals—and it could be made to work only through
similar methods. So cumbersome and so inefficient was the
system that the people, however virtuous or wicked, could
not activate it. It could be activated through deals and de-
ceit, through bargains and bribery, through logrolling and
lobbying and trickery and trading, the tactics that go with
man's baser attributes, most notably his greed and his love
of power. And yet, in the broad range and on the average,
these private tactics and motivations could operate effectively only when they were compatible with the public good,
for they were braked by the massive inertia of society as a
whole.

Such a system was scarcely calculated to appeal to fundamentalist republicans. Its lack of symmetry, its blurring of
powers that should theoretically be separated and well de-
fined, its irrationality ran directly counter to their deification
of rationalism. Its thwarting of the general will ran directly
counter to their faith in the goodness of the people in the
aggregate. Its implicit endorsement of evil as the proper
moving force of government ran directly counter to their
every fiber.

From the point of view of republican ideologues, the Constitution had another fatal defect: it had no bill of rights. To
have had a bill of rights, as a matter of fact, would have
been inconsistent with the overall theory on which the Constitution was based, and the nationalists in the convention
as well as Federalists in the ratifying conventions were
quick to point this out. That is, if the national government
was a creature of the states or of the people of the states,

then it could have only such powers as were expressly granted it, together with certain powers implied in the general power to "make all laws which shall be necessary and proper for carrying into execution" the specified powers. After it enumerated all the powers the national government could exercise, it made no sense for the Constitution then to enumerate certain powers that it could not exercise. As Hamilton said, "Why declare that things shall not be done which there is no power to do? Why, for instance, should it be said that the liberty of the press shall not be restrained, when no power is given by which restrictions may be imposed. . . . This may serve as a specimen of the numerous handles which would be given to the doctrine of constructive power, by the indulgence of an injudicious zeal for bills of rights." But whatever the logic of the position of the creators of the Constitution, the absence of a bill of rights was likely to win enemies among doctrinaire republicans. In addition, it provided an excellent popular ground on which certain other opponents of the Constitution, themselves motivated by personal interest, could attack the document.[5]

In short, to those republicans who viewed the "grand question" as what kind of national government should be created, rather than whether one should be created at all, the Constitution would likely be unpalatable.

On the more practical level: More than anything else, accessibility to transportation—and through it to communication—predisposed Americans to be narrow or broad in their loyalties, to oppose or favor the establishment of a national government. Simply by virtue of living in one place

---

[5] Farrand, *Records,* 2:587–88; James Wilson, in *Pennsylvania Packet,* October 10, 1787; Hamilton, in *Federalist* Number 84.

instead of another, Americans were less or more prone to think nationally, to be aware of the existence of national problems, and to think of themselves as Americans before thinking of themselves as citizens of their particular states or towns.

Given existing technology, it was far more natural for most Americans to think in local terms than in national terms and, when they thought about it at all, to prefer local authority to national authority. Even the most enlightened inhabitants of the interior of New Hampshire—and of the Berkshire Hills and Worcester County, Massachusetts, and of Pennsylvania west of Harrisburg, and of the piedmont of lower Virginia and all of North Carolina and the South Carolina up-country—normally did not have contact with national authority from one year to the next, felt the existence of their state governments only through the militia muster and the annual visit of the taxgatherers, and encountered information, ideas, or people from the outside world only two or three times a year. To them it was as unreasonable to suppose that the thirteen states could be well governed by a single national government as it had been to suppose that the thirteen colonies could be well governed from London. Accordingly, for most people all the force of inertia was opposed to the Constitution, and it took something special to bring them to think otherwise.

But in the contest over the Constitution it was not necessary that they should all be brought to think otherwise. People who lived in the "busy haunts of men" already thought otherwise; for even the lowliest inhabitants of Philadelphia—and of New York and Boston and Norfolk and Charleston—came into regular contact with persons and news from the other states and, indeed, from Europe as well. And though such people constituted only a small fraction of the population, they had a political advantage over their country cousins. To a large percentage of Americans who lived outside towns, an arduous trip of a day or even two or three days was necessary to appear at a polling place. Accordingly, the difficulty of movement dictated that many of the most removed (and most local-minded) citizens, even when not indifferent to the outcome of the contest over ratification, would not bother to take part in it. In the several elections held for delegates to state ratifying conventions, some 480,000 of the roughly 640,000 adult males in the country would not participate—some of them because of being disfranchised by law, the vast majority because it was simply too much trouble.[6]

Recent experience had changed some of these habitual attitudes. For one thing, the war had converted many to the

[6] On voting in general, see Chilton Williamson, *American Suffrage from Property to Democracy, 1776–1865* (Princeton, 1962); on voting in Massachusetts, see Robert E. Brown's *Middle-class Democracy and the Revolution in Massachusetts* (Ithaca, 1955), and on Virginia, see Robert E. and Katherine B. Brown's *Virginia, 1705–1786: Democracy or Aristocracy?* (East Lansing, 1964); on voting in New Jersey, see Richard P. McCormick, *History of Voting in New Jersey* (New Brunswick, 1953). My estimate of the vote on the Constitution is based upon these works and upon tabulations of votes recorded in the town meeting records in the Microfilm Collection in the New Hampshire State Library; Papers Relating to the Adoption of the Constitution, 17–36, and Acts and Proceedings of the General Assembly, 13:465, in the Rhode Island Archives; Jedediah Huntington to Andrew Huntington, May 1787, in Connecticut Historical Society *Collections*, 20:471 (1923); *New York Journal,* April 24, May 1, June 5, 1788; New York *Daily Advertiser,* June 3, 7, 14, 1788; Poughkeepsie *Country Journal,* June 3, 1788; Philadelphia *Independent Gazetteer,* November 18, 1787 (see also Brunhouse, *Counter-Revolution,* 328–44); Annapolis *Maryland Gazette,* January 22, 1789; *Maryland Journal and Baltimore Advertiser,* October 5, 1787, October 14, 1788 (see also Crowl, *Maryland During and After the Revolution,* appendix); Charleston *Columbian Herald,* April 17, 1788; Savannah *Gazette of the State of Georgia,* December 6, 1787.

national view. Among those so converted, three groups were most important: First, those who had learned firsthand the idiocy of attempting to wage a war or defend a country without a government, which would include particularly those persons who had been in Congress or in important administrative positions when the republican-dominated Congress collapsed in 1779–80. Second, those who fought in the war, particularly those in the continental line and most particularly those who had served in close proximity to Washington. Third, those who inhabited areas which had suffered great devastation or long occupation at the hands of the British during the war—which would include especially the cities of Newport, New London, New York, Norfolk, Charleston, Savannah, most of the tidewater of South Carolina and Virginia, and all of New Jersey.

The peacetime experience had likewise convinced many of the necessity of a national government, but its effect was largely on whole populations of whole states—that is, those states whose experiments in independence convinced the inhabitants that their states could not make a go of it alone. Making a go of it appeared impossible for a variety of reasons: in Connecticut because of a popular fixation on an obsolete way of earning a livelihood, and also because of a fiscal system that prevented the successful operation of either government or economy; in New Jersey because of an overwhelming burden of public debt; in Maryland because of a political movement that portended revolutionary social upheaval; and in Delaware for no particular reason and a host of general reasons.

But postwar experience also saw the development, in some quarters, of vested interests in the continuation of the primacy of the state governments. Normally this had to do with the pocketbook, but it also involved lust for prestige and power, the driving force of most of the state political leaders and of some of their followers. Either way, when successful policies designed for the good of the state as a whole were combined with policies that worked to the particular advantage of particular individuals, as was the case in New York and Virginia, vested interests in state primacy grew broad and deep. In Rhode Island the habit of mixing public policy and private gain was long standing and thoroughly manifest in postwar politics, and there almost everyone but the operators in Continental Loan Office certificates had a stake in continuing the existing system. In Massachusetts and Pennsylvania dynamic state programs worked to private advantage but contrary to public interest, and there vested interests in state supremacy were not so deeply rooted. And in three other states—Connecticut, Maryland, and North Carolina—such interests had developed but were narrow and generally lacking in appeal to the electorate.

So far predispositions; and philosophical bent, habitual narrowness or breadth of view, and recent experience weighed heavily in the contest. But the issue turned upon expectations as well, and among these the most vital were two: that adoption of the Constitution would alter existing relations between debtors and creditors, and that it would change the probabilities of success for special interest groups seeking favors from government.

Debtors and creditors, public and private, had been and would continue to be the most dynamic elements in American politics. In the system prevailing under the Articles of Confederation, their fates were in the hands of the state

legislatures; the legislatures were free to interfere with relations between private debtors and creditors, and to dis-
tribute the burden of public debt, which is to say taxes, at
will. Most states had, in practice, passed at least some
temporary legislation designed in behalf of private debtors,
most commonly laws postponing the collection of debts.
And most had levied the major portion of the tax load
as direct taxes on real property, and only secondarily as
duties on imported goods.

Adoption of the Constitution would drastically alter this
system. On the one hand, the Constitution expressly prohibited the states from continuing to enact laws for the relief
of private debtors. On the other, it was generally viewed as
likely that the United States would take on most or all of the
burden of the public debts, and that the burden of taxation
would be shifted from direct taxes to import duties, from
land to commerce.

Who would favor and who would oppose these changes
depended upon who owed whom, how much and under
what conditions. As to private debts, in the simplest and
most general terms the structure was as follows: There was
a considerable but undeterminable amount of conventional,
short-term consumer and mortgage debt, largest in the
busiest places and smallest or nonexistent in the most isolated places. In general, as far as can be ascertained, this
kind of debt was not particularly potent politically, except
when acute shortages of currency made all debtors hyper-
sensitive.[7] But there were three major forms of private in-

---

[7] It is worth repeating that the strong paper-money movements in New
England were designed to wipe out public debts, not private debts; and
that the opponents of these measures in New England, the large public
creditors, were the very persons who were most embarrassed by their

debtedness which were peculiar to the postwar decade and which were extremely potent politically. The first of these was the postwar debt of the plantation aristocrats of South Carolina. The second was the debts that American importers accumulated after the war, some of which were passed on through the sale of goods to retailers and consumers, some of which, especially that in Boston and Providence, were not. The third was the debt of Virginia and Maryland planters to British and Scottish merchants, accumulated before the war and at least temporarily wiped out through governmental intervention during and just after the war. Debtors of the first description, the South Carolinians, had benefited from special legislation which ratification of the Constitution would close to them; but as it happened, most of them could expect compensating gains from ratification. Debtors of the second description, those in Boston and Providence, had not so benefited and had, in fact, to some extent been victims of such legislation; and as it happened, they could expect vast gains from ratification. Debtors of the third description, those in Virginia and Maryland, had benefited much; and most of them could expect little in the way of tangible gains from ratification.

As to public debts, every adult male in the United States was a public debtor—that is, he was responsible for paying a share of the taxes necessary to carry the burden of interest and principal on state and congressional obligations. Since

---

private indebtedness. Paper money in New Jersey was designed to support public debts; in New York and Pennsylvania it was designed to service both public and private debts, but not to wipe them out through depreciation. In South Carolina the paper money was clearly designed for the relief of private debtors, the planters. Elsewhere the aims of paper-money advocates were mixed.

most of the people in the country were farmers, most of the farmers were proprietors, and most taxes were being levied directly on real property, ratification of the Constitution offered the direct prospect of immediate and great tax relief for a large portion of the population, by shifting the burden of taxes from land to trade.

The Constitution should therefore have had, and to some extent did have, a broad appeal to those on whom the existing tax burden fell most heavily—the small farmers north of the Mason-Dixon line, and most particularly, those who had recently been involved in rebellions in New England. But there was a countervailing psychological force that largely overcame this appeal: the very idea of a strong, vigorous, and high-toned central government suggested repressing the poor, an idea implanted and nourished by two decades of anti-British propaganda. Those who had been most vocal and most violent in protesting the burden of direct taxes, the Shaysites, were particularly obsessed with this notion—that central authority meant oppression. Too, there was another countervailing influence that worked on tax-ridden farmers. Many, many of the places where there were concentrations of such farmers were places where communication was slowest and poorest. Accordingly, the inhabitants were not only ill-informed, they were beyond the reach of the normal means of quick political persuasion, and so champions of the Constitution had little opportunity to appeal to them on the basis of prospective relief from taxes. But in those areas of small farmers in which communication was reasonably good—particularly New Jersey, Delaware, southern New York, eastern Pennsylvania, the back country of Maryland, and the Shenandoah Valley of

Virginia—farmers to whom tax relief was important could
be counted on to welcome the Constitution.

Finally, there were the special interest groups seeking
governmental action in their behalf. Among the more vocal
of these were the artisans and mechanics in the cities. Because they were concentrated in small areas, these persons
were more important as voting blocs than their relative
numbers would indicate; but even so, they had not usually
been influential enough to get what they wanted from government, and when they got legislation it was ineffectual.
Such had been the history of the agitation for legislation by
artisans in Boston and some other Massachusetts cities, and
in Philadelphia, New York, Portsmouth, and Baltimore.
Primarily, what they sought was protection from or outright
prohibition of competition from foreign manufacturers. On
general inspection it appeared likely that effective legislation
to this end could be obtained if the Constitution were
adopted, and the assertion of its likelihood, repeatedly made
by writers of propaganda in favor of the Constitution, reinforced that expectation.

To a considerable extent, the interests of shippers and
shipowning merchants closely paralleled those of artisans
and mechanics, and in general shippers were more direly in
need of positive help from government than any other group
in America. But not all shippers shared equally the same
needs: certain needs were felt by all, others only by special
groups.

The needs shared by all shippers were the direct result of
American independence. Without the powerful protection
of the British flag, American vessels began to fall prey to

the piratical raids of Algerian corsairs immediately after the establishment of peace. For a decade after 1784, except for a brief time in 1787–88 when an epidemic of black plague slowed down the Algerians, no American vessel could sail into southern European or north African waters without danger of plunder and capture by pirates. Related to this problem were the discriminatory insurance rates charged on American shipping in London: five percent on American vessels and only two percent on British or French vessels on identical voyages. Adoption of the Constitution would make possible the building of a strong navy to protect American shipping and obviate the need, if real need existed, for such high insurance rates. Too, by permitting the creation of a surplus of liquid capital through the funding of war debts, adoption of the Constitution would make it possible to establish American insurance companies which could free American shippers from this dependence on London. Another matter of vital concern to all American shippers was free interstate commerce—a condition they enjoyed, but were not assured, under the existing system—and this was guaranteed by the Constitution.

On the other hand, restrictions placed against American shipping by foreign governments, while worded so as to operate generally, bore hardest on particular shippers. The two groups hit hardest were concentrated in New England: those in trade with the British West Indies and the operators of fishing vessels.

The closing of the British West Indies to American shipping at the end of 1783 did not merely deprive Americans of a share in a lucrative freight business; it almost paralyzed the New England carrying trade. To be operated economically, the larger vessels owned by New Englanders had to make one annual European voyage with an American staple and two or three supplementary trips to the West Indies, either for direct trade in provisions or for freight from the islands to the mainland. Furthermore, the West Indies were the only adequate source of specie for making international payments. It is true that the French West Indies were opened to American bottoms even as the British islands were being closed, but the French islands offered markets principally for livestock and lumber, which were best carried in specially built small craft. For this reason, the new markets could not take the place of the old; and besides, the French markets did not yield specie on anything like the magnitude of the British islands.

The shipowners who were in the fishing business had fared somewhat better in 1783, for John Adams had negotiated into the peace treaty a clause that guaranteed free access to the best fishing banks. But the act that closed the British West Indies to American bottoms in 1783 was followed two years later by a French *arrêt* that substantially excluded American fish from the French West Indies. As a result American fishermen found themselves with an abundance of fish and no place to sell them. For similar reasons, compounded by the wartime migration of whales, the whaling industry suffered even more. Exactly what the proposed new government could or would do about these maladjustments was open to question. But New Englanders, especially the new-rich merchants in Boston, thought that the only solution was to fight Britain with tariffs and navigation acts. Massachusetts' all-out effort to fight Britain with state legislation had proved ineffectual, but adoption of the Constitution would make it possible to conduct such a war on the national level, where success seemed more likely. Most shippers in other states, though not suffering the dislocations that plagued Massachusetts, stood to benefit from such action.

But if legislation designed against foreign shippers were forthcoming, it would work directly counter to the interests of other important groups. For one thing, the mercantile system laboriously developed by the Virginia planters had been designed to promote an excess of competition between American and foreign shippers. For another, all international importing merchants who were not shippers—the proportion of whom in the mercantile population increased as one moved south—had a vital interest in free trade. At best, legislation designed to promote American shipping at the expense of foreign shipping would do the merchants no good, and it could be clearly inimical. Navigation acts and protective tariffs would definitely work contrary to their interests. Within limits, duties for revenue could be passed on to consumers, but protective duties, being by design taxes that force prices of imports above a competitive level, would deprive importers of commodities and markets.

But in two important ways merchants themselves could foresee tangible benefits arising from the adoption of the Constitution. One was that public credit could be expected to be placed on a more substantial footing, and more tangibly, the prices of the various forms of public securities would doubtless rise. Because the flow of everything that passed as money was toward and through merchants, and because public securities were one of the things passing as money, merchants had accumulated large quantities of securities at sizable discounts; appreciation of their values would yield windfall profits. Again, the general expectation was that treaties with foreign powers would be easier to negotiate if the national government were established under the Constitution—despite the clause requiring a two-thirds majority of the Senate for adoption of treaties—and favorable trade treaties could be expected. Particularly, a treaty with Spain, along the lines proposed in the Jay-Gardoqui negotiations, seemed likely, and with it would come the opening of Spanish America to wheat grown in the United States. The benefits of that development were incalculable.

But the advantages that the merchants could foresee brought them, in turn, into direct conflicts of interests with other groups. To increase the likelihood of a Spanish treaty was to increase the likelihood that the interests of Western settlers and their more powerful allies, speculators in Western lands, would be sacrificed. Again, the interests of land speculators, while affected both favorably and unfavorably by what could be expected from ratification of the Constitution, were likely to conflict with the interests of merchants as public security holders.

The ways in which adoption of the Constitution would favorably affect land speculators were two: by strengthening claims to certain titles, and by providing for the establishment of a national government which could create armies to remove the threat of Indians in newly settling territories. The foreseeable unfavorable effects were also two: one general, applying to large and disparate groups of buyers of public property, and one specific, applying only to buyers of confiscated Loyalist estates.

The general effect depended upon the terms under which public property was purchased. Since most land-sales programs were geared to the retirement of war debts, the most common form of contract for large purchases involved payment in public securities as well as cash. Buyers contracted to pay specific sums, usually making a small down payment in specie and agreeing to pay the remainder in public securities at their par value within a specified period of months or years. In modern parlance, they were selling securities "short"—that is, they were promising to deliver, in exchange for land, securities that they did not at the time possess. Like short sellers of a later day, they expected to be able to buy the securities on the open market at a price less than that at which they had contracted to deliver them—actually, from an eighth to a fourth of face value.

If the Constitution were ratified and the national government under it should take decisive steps to fund the public debt, the market prices of securities would double and then treble. A buyer of public lands priced at $100,000 would, prior to 1787, have expected to be able to pay for them for something like $20,000. Should the Constitution be adopted, the hard-money cost of retiring his debt would run to more than $60,000 and perhaps as high as $100,000. The restoration of public credit would mean his ruin.

Buyers of confiscated property were doubly jeopardized. Not only were most of them "short sellers" of public securities; they stood, as well, to have their titles entirely invalidated should the Constitution be adopted. The Constitution provided that treaties "made or which shall be made" should become a part of the "supreme law of the land," and the peace treaty of 1783 had provided for the restoration of property confiscated by both sides.

These were the underlying facts and attitudes which, along with the accidental and the coincidental, would condition the contest over ratification. They would operate whether politicians knew about them or not, and no politician knew them all. But they were only the stuff of the contest, not the contest itself.

The nationalists—or Federalists, as they shrewdly and misleadingly began calling themselves—were in a much better position than were their opponents to know and manage these ingredients. Almost by definition, they were a ready-made national political organization. They shared a common goal and, to a considerable extent, a common general attitude toward government. They knew one another and, despite the fighting over money that had separated them, they did business with one another. Many of them had worked together in Congress and in state politics, and others had fought in the war together and joined the Society of the Cincinnati together. Between them, those of their leaders who had served in the Philadelphia Convention were personally acquainted with perhaps half the influential nationalists in the thirteen states. Those leaders participated in the initial planning and subsequent execution of the campaign for ratification and, indeed, built into the Constitution itself part of the strategy of the campaign.

The opponents of the Constitution—or anti-Federalists, as the nationalists christened them—had the numerical strength to carry the issue, but they could carry it only if they could organize and coordinate their efforts. And almost by definition, they were difficult if not impossible to unite. They had no common positive program: as advocates of state primacy, they shared only a negative attitude. In the main, they did not know one another, and previously had known little and cared little about what went on outside the limits of their own states. The old interstate coalition of republicans—the Massachusetts-Virginia alliance—had broken down when postwar events had driven Massachusetts republicans at least temporarily into the nationalist ranks. Ripe for formation was a new coalition between the old republicans in Virginia and the newly converted states-righters who made up New York's dominant political group. Whether anti-Federalists could defeat the Constitution depended, in the last analysis, upon whether Federalists could carry the contest before this Virginia–New York republican coalition could be put together.

Chapter Eight

From the Many, One

The Philadelphia Convention flowed, without perceptible interruption, into the contest over ratification. The rules of the game were built into the Constitution. The amending procedure prescribed by the Articles of Confederation—requiring approval by all thirteen legislatures—was entirely ignored. Instead, the Constitution was sent to Congress, with a request that Congress pass it along to the state legislatures, who would in turn be asked to submit it to popularly elected special conventions in each state, "for their Assent and Ratification." If the conventions of nine states should ratify, the Constitution would become binding on those nine states, and they could proceed to organize a government. Whether any other states subsequently joined the reconstituted union was up to them, individually.[1]

The Constitution and an accompanying resolution and letter of transmittal reached Congress in New York on September 20, 1787. Discussion was set for a week later, and when the day arrived, Congress for once had a quorum,

---

[1] Constitution, Article VII; Resolution of the Convention, September 17, 1787, and Washington to the Congress, September 17, 1787, in Farrand, *Records,* 2:665–67.

and it was nationalist dominated: eighteen of the thirty-three members present were men who had come up from the Philadelphia Convention.[2]

Old republicans Richard Henry Lee and William Grayson of Virginia, supported by Hancock man Nathan Dane of Massachusetts and Clintonian Melancton Smith of New York, tried to effect an abortion. Lee proposed that Congress should add a number of amendments before sending the Constitution to the states; the states could then ratify the original document or an amended one, and their combined recommendations could be the subject of a second convention. (Such a procedure would have been disastrous, for the Constitution's friends and enemies alike recognized that it was now or never for the Union.)[3]

Federalist congressmen would have preferred sending the document out with a full endorsement, and they probably had the numbers to carry the point. But they chose not to do battle, for they could not afford a noisy and time-consuming fight. In the first place, for the psychological effect on

---

[2] *Journals of Congress,* September 20, 28, 1787; Madison to Washington, September 30, 1787, in Gaillard Hunt, ed., *The Writings of James Madison* (9 vols., New York, 1900–1910), 5:4–8; William Bingham to Thomas Fitzsimons, September 21, 1787, and Lee to Adams, October 27, 1787, in Burnett, ed., *Letters of Members of Congress,* 8:646, 669; Edward P. Smith, "The Movement Toward a Second Constitutional Convention in 1788," in J. Franklin Jameson, ed., *Essays in the Constitutional History of the United States* (Cambridge, 1889), 54.

[3] *Journals of Congress,* September 28, 1787; Edward Carrington to Madison, September 23, 1787, in Farrand, *Records,* 3:98–99; Madison to Washington, September 30, 1787, in Jonathan Elliot, *Debates on the Adoption of the Federal Constitution* (main title varied; 5 vols., Philadelphia, 1896), 5:566; Madison to Jefferson, October 24, 1787, *ibid.,* 5:568; Lee to Mason, October 1, and Lee to Samuel Adams, October 5, 1787, in James C. Ballagh, ed., *The Letters of Richard Henry Lee* (2 vols., New York, 1911, 1914), 2:438–39, 445.

voters it was important to create an illusion of unanimity in Congress. Equally important, carrying one difficult and key state possibly depended upon swift action. Accordingly, the Federalists chose to compromise. On September 28, Congress resolved to send the "Report of the convention" to the states without congressional recommendations, pro or con. Then the resolution was leaked to newspapers in such a way as to suggest that a unanimous vote on this compromise had meant unanimous approval of the Constitution.[4]

The difficult and key state was Pennsylvania. Its nationalist-dominated legislature was sitting in a session that was legally required to end on Saturday, September 29.[5] If that legislature could act on the Constitution, it could call elections for a ratifying convention so soon that the opposition could not organize; indeed, the elections could be held so soon that there would scarcely be time to publish the Constitution in the back country, where much of the anti-nationalist strength lay. Such was the delicacy of the balance of party power in Pennsylvania, however, that should the issue be postponed until after a new legislature were elected in October and convened in November, a dangerous delay of many months was likely and total defeat of the Constitution was possible.[6]

Instantly upon the passage of the congressional resolu-

---

[4] Madison to Washington, September 30, 1787; *Journals of Congress,* September 28, 1787; Lee to Randolph, October 16, 1787, in Elliot's *Debates,* 1:503–5.

[5] The legislature had already seen a copy of the Constitution, forwarded by Franklin, but it could not act upon it until it received the document officially from Congress.

[6] Robert L. Brunhouse, *Counter-Revolution in Pennsylvania* (Harrisburg, 1942), 200–201; Charles Page Smith, *James Wilson, Founding Father, 1742–1798* (Chapel Hill, 1956), 262–63.

tion, a special courier sped on horseback for Philadelphia. He arrived Friday night; the legislature was scheduled to adjourn in a matter of hours. The nineteen members of the antinationalist party in the Assembly resorted to a desperate stratagem: they simply disappeared, thus preventing a quorum. A large band of men was dispatched to search the city, and barely in time they found two of the absent members, seized them, and forcibly dragged them into the House. The quorum thus achieved voted that an election be held in early November for delegates to a convention that would begin on November 21.[7]

The timing of the special election was brilliant. It was early enough to prevent effective organization of the opposition. It was late enough so that the antis could not employ their most effective electioneering device, for to call out the militias for the special election meant to lose them for the regular election. And while antis cursed the maneuver and raced home to try to group their forces, the Federalists launched a massive propaganda campaign.[8] They concentrated their attack in the critical area, the City and County of Philadelphia; for in the decade since the Declaration of Independence, the party that controlled the ten seats of the city and county had dominated the state, party

---

[7] Tench Coxe to Madison, September 28, 29, 1787, in Andrew H. Allen, ed., *Documentary History of the Constitution* (5 vols., Washington, 1905), 4:304–6; Brunhouse, *Counter-Revolution,* 200–202; *Journal of the Pennsylvania Assembly,* September 28, 29, 1787; John B. McMaster and Frederick D. Stone, eds., *Pennsylvania and the Federal Constitution, 1787– 1788* (Philadelphia, 1888), 1–5.

[8] The antis had attempted to prevent being outmaneuvered for time by having prepared a series of articles against the Constitution long before it was finished. These were signed "Centinel" and are believed to have been written either by George Bryan or by his son Samuel; they were circulated both as pamphlets and in newspapers in the back country; see the *Carlisle Gazette,* October 24, 1787.

strength elsewhere being relatively stable and split almost equally.[9]

The merchants and speculators in the city were divided, as they had been for years, but the question was not in their hands. The decision lay with the artisans and mechanics and tradesmen in the city and the farmers around it. These folk had once unquestioningly supported the anti-Morris radicals, but just now things were different. Tangible gains were in store for them if the Constitution were adopted, but that was not it; they were in a mood to vote their pride, not their pocketbooks. In 1786 the anti-Morris faction had sought to do them the favor of exempting them from taxes, a favor that had the incidental effect (if not the primary aim) of depriving them of the vote. The nationalists saw to the repeal of this measure, and though repeal cost the artisans and mechanics money it restored their right to vote and won their loyalty. In the election on the Constitution they showed that loyalty: the Federalists won by the overwhelming margin of 1,198 votes to 160.[10] In the county they elected all five delegates, and they picked up five more in normally

---

[9] *Freeman's Journal, Pennsylvania Packet, Evening Herald, Pennsylvania Gazette, Pennsylvania Mercury,* October–November 1787; *Carlisle Gazette,* October 24, 31, 1787; Tench Coxe to Madison, September 27, October 21, 1787, in Allen, ed., *Documentary History of the Constitution,* 4:296–97, 338–39; McMaster and Stone, eds., *Pennsylvania and the Federal Constitution,* 73–203. For George Bryan's appraisal of the contest, see the undated paper in George Bryan Manuscripts, 1785–87, in Historical Society of Pennsylvania; for Gouverneur Morris', see Morris to Washington, October 30, 1787, in Elliot's *Debates,* 1:505–6. My appraisal of party strength, 1776–89, is based on tabulating votes as recorded in the *Journal of the Assembly;* for a summary of shifting party alignments during the period, see Brunhouse, *Counter-Revolution,* 321–25.

[10] The antis headed their ticket in Philadelphia with Franklin, purely as a stratagem. Three of the other four anti candidates, Charles Pettit, John Steinmetz, and William Irvine, were merchants and speculators in securities, holding several thousand pounds among them.

antinationalist (and militia-dominated) Northampton and Northumberland counties. Elsewhere the voting followed usual patterns; the Federalist victory in three counties won the election.[11]

While this was happening, Federalists were building momentum elsewhere. In the forty days between the debates in Congress and the special elections in Pennsylvania, six more legislatures called elections for ratifying conventions. In the next forty days another three did so, four more states held elections, and one state ratified by a unanimous vote in convention. Before 1788 was two weeks old, five states had ratified: Delaware on December 7, by a convention vote of 30 to 0; Pennsylvania on December 12 by 46 to 23; New Jersey on December 18 by 38 to 0; Georgia (shocked out of its particularism by an Indian uprising) on January 2 by 26 to 0; and Connecticut on January 9 by 128 to 40. And by the end of that month all states save Rhode Island had called conventions.[12]

But these were only battles, not the war; and in winning them Federalists had met reversals that only chance had

---

[11] Brunhouse, *Counter-Revolution*, 192; *Journal of the Assembly,* September 7, 1786; *Evening Herald,* September 16, 20, 1786; *Independent Gazetteer,* November 18, 1787; New Loan Certificates, Book A, 2169–77, 2914–15, 2253–63, 5381–83, Book C, p. 37, in Public Records Division, Harrisburg. For a more detailed analysis of the contest and the contestants in Pennsylvania, see McDonald, *We the People,* 163–82.

[12] State actions are summarized in Elliot's *Debates,* 1:319–37. For more detailed accounts and analyses of action in these states, see Munroe, *Federalist Delaware;* McCormick, *Experiment in Independence,* 261–79; Coleman, *Revolution in Georgia;* Bernard C. Steiner, "Connecticut's Ratification of the Federal Constitution," in the *Proceedings of the American Antiquarian Society,* 25:70–127 (1915); McDonald, *We the People,* 116–48.

prevented from becoming fatal. In the very act of calling a ratifying convention, the Virginia legislature, dominated by anti-Federalists and led by staunch anti-Federalist Patrick Henry, followed the plan of opposition that Richard Henry Lee had laid down. The legislature instructed Governor Randolph to circularize the other governors in an effort to gain support for a second general convention, and provided for defraying the expenses of Virginia's delegates to it.[13]

Lee himself was in New York City, grinding out anti-Federalist propaganda, conferring with Clintonians, and counting on Henry and Mason and Randolph to carry the counterattack in Virginia. But Virginia Federalist politicians were shrewder: they went to work on, and won, Edmund Randolph.[14] Exactly who converted Randolph to Federalism —or how or when—no one knows. That Washington, Madison, and John Marshall tried to convert him is known. So also are some facts that suggest the means of conversion: that Randolph's objections were doctrinaire, and thus subject to persuasive reasoning; that he was financially embarrassed in 1788 and emerged in 1790 on solid footing and as the holder of more than $10,000 in public securities;

---

[13] Hening, ed., *Statutes of Virginia,* 12:462; *Journal of the House of Virginia,* October 25, November 30, 1787; Randolph to Madison, September 30, 1787, in Moncure D. Conway, *Omitted Chapters of History Disclosed in the Life and Papers of Edmund Randolph* (New York, 1888), 95; Lee to Randolph, October 16, 1787, in Ballagh, ed., *Letters to Lee,* 2:450–55; John Pierce to Knox, October 27, 1787, in Knox Papers, Massachusetts Historical Society.

[14] Lee did not neglect Randolph; see his letter urging Randolph to support a second convention, October 16, 1787, in Lee, *Life of R. H. Lee,* 2:76. Madison was not sure of Randolph as late as April; see Madison to Jefferson, April 22, 1788, in Hunt, ed., *Writings of Madison,* 5:121.

that he was politically ambitious and emerged in 1789 as the first attorney general of the United States.[15]

For whatever reason, Randolph did not send out the legislature's circular letter until December 27. And for whatever reason, George Clinton did not receive his copy of the letter until March 7. Accordingly, when the New York legislature took up the question of ratification late in January, the Clintonians had no definite plans. Though controlling the legislature, they failed by two votes in each house to carry a resolution censuring the Philadelphia Convention for exceeding its powers, and in the end they effected only a fumbling and futile delaying action, by setting the ratifying convention for the following June. Had Clinton received Randolph's letter in normal time, New York could have joined Virginia in the movement for a second convention. He did not, and New York did not. The first effort to forge the Virginia–New York alliance had miscarried.[16]

Even so, the Federalists' momentum had been broken by the time the New York legislature acted. Pennsylvania's defeated anti-Federalists, finally united and focused, began

---

[15] John Pierce to Knox, October 27, 1787, in Knox Papers, Massachusetts Historical Society; Madison to Randolph, October 21, November 18, 1787, January 10, 1788, in Elliot's *Debates,* 5:567, 568, 570 ff.; Randolph to Madison, October 23, 1787, cited in Freeman, *Washington,* 6:122n; Randolph to Madison, February 29, 1788, July 19, 1789, in Conway, *Randolph,* 100–101, 126–28; Randolph to Washington, October 8, 1789, *ibid.,* 129–30, and also pp. 45, 50, 385 ff.; Smith, "Second Constitutional Convention," 63; Virginia Loan Office, Register of Assumed Debt, vol. 1113, folio 86, in Old Loan Records, National Archives.

[16] Conway, *Randolph,* 109–10; *Votes and Proceedings,* New York Assembly, January 31, 1788, New York Senate, January 31, 1788; *New York Journal,* September 27, 1787, and throughout the next four months; *Albany Journal,* February 23, 1788.

a noisy campaign for amendments to the Constitution, particularly in the form of a bill of rights. South Carolina antis, led by aristocrat and former Tory Rawlins Lowndes, failed by only one vote in an effort to prevent the calling of a ratifying convention, and that was close enough to create fear (ill-founded, as it turned out) that the aristocracy would not support the Constitution. The Rhode Island legislature flatly refused to call a convention and called a popular referendum instead. More dangerous yet, the lethargic citizenry of New Hampshire elected delegates who, it was widely expected, were decidedly opposed to ratification. Only if Massachusetts met before New Hampshire and acted swiftly and strongly in favor of the Constitution, said local observers, could New Hampshire be induced to ratify.[17]

Such action in Massachusetts was not forthcoming. When its convention met on January 9, no one knew exactly how the delegates lined up, for at the special town meetings which had chosen them a month earlier, only two dozen towns had bound their representatives with instructions. But it was clear that a majority were skeptical of the virtues

---

[17] Arthur Campbell to Adam Orth, March 9, 1788, and to Francis Bailey (publisher of the *Freeman's Journal*), March 8, 1788, in George Bryan Manuscripts, Historical Society of Pennsylvania; McMaster and Stone, *Pennsylvania and the Federal Constitution, passim; Pennsylvania Packet,* December 18, 1787; Elliot's *Debates,* 4:253–317; Papers Relating to the Adoption of the Federal Constitution, 17–36, and Acts and Proceedings of the General Assembly, 13:465, both in Rhode Island Archives; Joseph B. Walker, *A History of the New Hampshire Convention for the Investigation, Discussion, and Decision of the Federal Constitution* (Boston, 1888), *passim;* Portsmouth *New Hampshire Spy,* January 1788; Nicholas Gilman to John Sullivan, October 31, 1787, and Sullivan to Jeremy Belknap, February 26, 1788, in Hammond, ed., *Sullivan Papers,* 3:543, 566.

of the Constitution. One member predicted that there would be 192 votes against the Constitution and only 144 for it.[18]

Superficially, at least, the Massachusetts convention seemed to pit riches and education and talent against poverty and semiliteracy and wary, ignorant suspicion. A host of splendidly clad Federalist lawyers and merchants and clergymen defended and expounded the Constitution. On the opposite side, sullen and silent, clothed in bumpkin's homespun, sat nearly a score of men who a year earlier had been marching, armed, against the state; and fourscore more who had sympathized with the insurgents. ("It takes the best men in the state to gloss this Constitution," one of them grumbled. "If these great men would speak half as much against it, we could complete our business and go home in forty-eight hours.")[19]

But the power—and the contest—lay not with these extremes. It lay with a great uncommitted middle, comprising more than a hundred men from all walks of life, and with two old revolutionary heroes who had not exchanged a friendly word in eight years. If so persuaded, Samuel Adams could deliver upwards of twenty of these delegates for ratification. If so persuaded, John Hancock could deliver up-

---

[18] Orin G. Libby, *Geographical Distribution of the Vote of the Thirteen States on the Ratification of the Federal Constitution, 1787–1788* (Madison, 1894), 75–78; Sedgwick to Van Schaack, January 18, 1787, in Sedgwick Papers, Massachusetts Historical Society; Samuel B. Harding, *The Contest over the Ratification of the Federal Constitution in the State of Massachusetts* (New York, 1896), 67 n.

[19] For an analysis of the personnel in the convention, see *ibid.* and McDonald, *We the People,* 191–202; see also Madison to Washington, February 3, 1788, in Hunt, ed., *Writings of Madison,* 5:95 ff.

wards of fifty. Neither liked the Constitution, but each was amenable to conversion.

The Federalist tactic was as obvious as it was delicate and time-consuming. The Constitution must be discussed, explained, "glossed," clause by clause, line by line, word by word. This might convert a few of its enemies; but more important, it would forestall a test of strength for weeks, until the balance of strength could be shifted. Meanwhile, out of doors, Federalists could privately seduce their opponents, man to man and one by one (salesmanship, expense-account style, was not invented in the twentieth century; dozens of penurious back-countrymen, having to pay their own bills in expensive Boston and hope that their towns would later reimburse them, might have welcomed a generous invitation to a sumptuous dinner with a well-heeled Federalist; and more than one might thereby come to realize that the "great men" who advocated the Constitution were not such bad fellows, after all).[20]

And meantime, too, in due season Adams and Hancock could be worked on. There was no doubt that Adams needed working on, for he clearly disliked the Constitution. He had been startled that it proposed "a national government instead of a federal union of sovereign states"; his

---

[20] "I must tell you I was never treated with so must politeness in my life as I was afterward by the tradesmen of Boston merchants and every other gentleman," one backwoods member wrote: quoted in Morison, *Maritime History of Massachusetts,* 39. On Federalist tactics, see Smith, "Second Constitutional Convention," 71 ff.; Harding, *Contest over Ratification,* 82–106. The debates are published in part in Elliot's *Debates,* vol. 2; fuller accounts are in three separate editions, published in Boston in 1788, 1808, and 1856, the last being a publication of the state and the most thorough coverage.

protégé, Elbridge Gerry, had refused to sign the document; and Adams confided to his old friend and ally, anti-Federalist leader Richard Henry Lee, that he had "a poor opinion" of the Constitution.[21]

To win Adams' support, the Federalists resorted to a tactic that he might have devised himself. Adams' political strength had always lain with the artisans and mechanics of Boston and the other seaport towns. Secretly, Federalists engaged Paul Revere and others to stage a "mass meeting" at the Green Dragon Inn, one-time headquarters of Adams' Sons of Liberty. The meeting adopted strong resolutions in favor of ratification and appointed Revere head of a committee to present the resolutions to Adams. The Sam Adams of 1775 would have seen through the maneuver in a moment; but this was not the Adams of old. Embittered by a total defeat by Hancock in 1780–81, after a vicious struggle for power; disillusioned by Shays' Rebellion in 1786–87; confused and heartbroken by the death of his son just as the convention opened—this was the Sam Adams of 1788. When "his people," the common folk of Boston, spoke, he did not ask whether political ventriloquists were at work. On the floor of the convention, he announced his conversion to the cause of ratification.[22]

With Adams won, Federalists had enough votes to approach Hancock and negotiate from strength. The governor

---

[21] Lee to Adams, October 5, 27, 1787, in Ballagh, ed., *Letters of Lee,* 2:444–47, 456–58; Adams to Lee, December 3, 1787, in Cushing, ed., *Writings of Adams,* 4:325; Gerry to the Massachusetts legislature, October 18, 1787, in Farrand, *Records,* 3:128–29.

[22] *Massachusetts Centinel,* January 9, 1788; Harding, *Contest over Ratification,* 95–97; King to Madison, January 27, 1788, in King, ed., *Life and Correspondence of Rufus King,* 5:95 n; Smith, "Second Constitutional Convention," 75–76.

was, on the one hand, a shallow and vain man, and on the other, an almost incredibly astute politician. These qualities, in combination, proved his undoing. Federalist leaders invited him to a secret meeting: it was attended by Hancock, his confidential advisor James Sullivan, the newly converted Adams, and Federalist strategists Nathaniel Gorham, Theophilus Parsons, ex-governor James Bowdoin, and Rufus King. The amenities are readily imagined: Federalists might have asked after the governor's gout, which would have been a polite way of asking how he thought the contest would go. They might also have expressed the hope that in future his gout should not become unbearable, which would have been a way of suggesting that they might be able to win without him, an idea "dreadful to one whose love of popularity was so great."[23]

The actual business transacted is more nearly a matter of record. At the outset and throughout, the Federalists assured Hancock that only his popularity could swing the contest, that only he could be the savior of his country. Then came a request designed both to flatter and to mask a power play: Parsons, the Federalists said, was about to move that the question be taken. They wanted also to propose a bill of rights, in the form of nine recommendatory amendments. Would the governor, as one of the nation's most celebrated patriots and friends of liberty, be so kind as to introduce the amendments himself? Next, outright political bribery: Washington, the father of his country, would doubtless be the first president, but someone, doubtless a New Englander,

---

[23] This account is derived from Amory, *James Sullivan,* 1:223 ff.; Theophilus Parsons, *Memoir of Theophilus Parsons* (Boston, 1859), 71–80; Harding, *Contest over Ratification,* 85–87; King to Knox, February 1, 1788, in King, ed., *King,* 1:319.

would become the first vice president and logical successor; and who was better qualified for the support of Massachusetts Federalists, and of their influential Federalist friends elsewhere, than the governor himself? It was not unthinkable, indeed, that Virginia might withhold ratification so long as to render Washington ineligible, and in that event, who could say? ("Loaves and fishes," Gouverneur Morris had predicted, "must bribe the demagogues. They must be made to expect higher offices under the general than the state governments.")[24]

Hancock went for the "noble bait." When Parsons moved the adoption of the Constitution, Hancock left the president's chair and introduced the nine amendments. They had been composed by Parsons and were in Sullivan's handwriting, but "with a confidence astonishing to all who were in the secret," Hancock "called them his own, and said they were the result of his own reflection." Adams seconded the proposals and gave a brief speech endorsing them. Then, just before putting the question, Hancock said baldly that "I give my assent to the Constitution in full confidence that the amendments proposed will soon become a part of the system." The vote was taken: it was 187 for, 168 against. Ten country rubes, unswayed by these histrionics, could have stopped the campaign for ratification dead in its tracks.[25]

This was February 8. Six states had ratified. Three to go.

Two of the three came easily. Late in April, to no one's surprise, Maryland ratified by an overwhelming majority. There was some resistance: Samuel Chase and Luther

---

[24] The quotation is from Madison's Journal, July 2, in Farrand, *Records,* 2:513–14.

[25] Parsons, *Life of Parsons,* 71; Elliot's *Debates,* 2:122–23, 130, 174–81.

Martin led a frenetic opposition campaign, as clever in its demagoguery as any Chase had previously conducted. But Chase and his friends were too much in disrepute because of the recent scandals to be of great influence; and the Maryland aristocracy was too unnerved by Chase's political doings to reject the sanctuary promised by the creation of a strong national government; and the Constitution afforded the state opportunity for a share of the national domain, lands too badly needed and too long sought to forgo at this late date. The popular vote for delegates favorable to ratification was about 6,500 to 3,500. The convention vote was 63 to 11.[26]

Late in May, South Carolina followed. By virtue of apportionment of representation that was designed for the purpose, the decision was in the hands of the planters; the handfuls of merchants and small farmers on each side could not alter the outcome. Some wealthy planters opposed, out of various motives. But to most, all the conditions were conducive to acceptance of the new system. For one thing, times were troubled, and had been for years, and widespread was the craving for what a later politician would call normalcy. For another, the tangible gains for the planters were obvious and the tangible losses, if any, were invisible. For still another, the Constitution pleased Carolina planters' vanity, for in a broad sense it was, in considerable measure, their own handiwork; nearly half the 149 men who voted for ratification were related, directly or indirectly, through blood or marriage, to the Rutledges and the Pinckneys who had sat in the Philadelphia Convention. For yet another, it appealed to their pride—their wellspring motive—for they

---

[26] Philip A. Crowl, "Anti-Federalism in Maryland," in the *William and Mary Quarterly,* 3d series, 4:446–69 (1947); Crowl, *Maryland During and After the Revolution, passim;* McDonald, *We the People,* 148–60.

thought of themselves as the broadest minded and best educated and most cosmopolitan of all Americans. And so they
debated the Constitution with the pomposity and solemnity
it deserved, and then voted for it by more than two to one.[27]

But the ninth state would not be easy to find. The dilatory
tactics that won the contest in Massachusetts lost it in New
Hampshire. Federalists there had Langdon and Sullivan, on
the same side for once, but they had no Bowdoin, no Parsons, no King, no Gorham, to "gloss" the Constitution.
Moreover, the hoped-for momentum in the wake of Massachusetts' favorable action failed to materialize. Massachusetts' ratification had taken too long, and had involved too
much machination, and had in the end been too close.
Finally, in New Hampshire some of the "great men" did
speak out against the Constitution, giving the anti-Federalists courage to end the business, not quite within forty-eight
hours, but within 240.[28]

The chief anti-Federalist spokesman was a lawyer and
former Tory from Amherst named Joshua Atherton.[29] Ather-

---

[27] *Ibid.*, 202–35; William Schaper, "Sectionalism and Representation in
South Carolina," in the *Annual Report of the American Historical Association,* 1900, pp. 5 ff.; *Charleston Morning Post, Charleston Evening Gazette,
State Gazette,* October 1787 to May 1788; Elliot's *Debates,* 2:253–317.
The kinship ties of the delegates were worked out from genealogical
sources by Ellen S. McDonald, as an appendix to "An Ethnographic Study
of South Carolina About 1790" (unpublished paper, Brown University,
1964).

[28] Sullivan to Belknap, February 26, 1788, Gilman to Sullivan, March 22,
1788, Knox to Sullivan, April 9, 1788, in Hammond, ed., *Sullivan Papers,*
3:566, 576, 580; Walker, *New Hampshire Convention, passim.*

[29] Nicholas Gilman, apparently reflecting a general feeling among Federal-
ists, thought that Atherton was only the spokesman, and that Nathaniel
Peabody and Jonathan Moulton were behind the opposition. See Gilman to
Sullivan, March 22, 1788, in Hammond, ed., *Papers,* 3:576.

ton knew his state well enough to realize that argument based on political theory or even on political expedience would weigh little there. Instead, he denounced the Constitution as sinful, on the ground that it sanctioned slavery. To those to whom such an equation mattered—and they were numerous—such logic was irrefutable. In combination with the conservatism that characterized even the not so religious in the New Hampshire convention, it was sufficient to prevent a favorable vote on ratification.[30]

It was not quite, however, enough to elicit an unfavorable vote. In a way, the question of ratification was like an examination question at the Last Judgment: no clear procedure was prescribed if the answer were negative. It hardly seemed proper to go to all the trouble of holding special town meetings to elect delegates to a convention—and the representation at it was the most nearly complete that the state had ever seen—only to say no. No, and then what? This was a question that taxed the imaginations of politicians far more subtle than the simple New Hampshire country folk; and it was this that stretched the forty-eight hours beyond 200.

At about the two hundredth hour Federalist Samuel Livermore, a Princeton-educated lawyer and judge who before the war had moved to New Hampshire's northern frontier, where he enjoyed immense respect among his neighbors, privately persuaded several of them to favor ratification. At Livermore's suggestion, they approached John Langdon, leader of the Federalists in the convention, and told him they were bound by instructions to oppose ratification, but would seek new instructions if the convention should tem-

---

[30] *New Hampshire Convention;* Elliot's *Debates,* 2:203–4; *New Hampshire Spy,* February 23, 1788.

porarily adjourn. Langdon seized the opportunity to bridge the impasse, and through his influence the convention agreed not to vote yes or no. Instead, it adjourned until June 18.[31]

And now, in the spring of 1788, the contest came rushing to a climax. The Federalists, only one state short of their immediate goal, dispatched riders to village after village and farm after farm in efforts to convert the back country of New Hampshire to the cause. They sought to persuade not through reason but through ignorance, through influence and rumor and fear: to some they bore messages and propaganda-filled newspapers from relatives in arch-Federalist Connecticut, to others they brought talk of invasion from Canada and even suggestions that the Indians and Papists had joined forces once again—a rumor three decades out of date. In New York, over the signature Publius, Hamilton and Jay and Madison ground out their monumental propaganda pieces in behalf of the Constitution, the *Federalist* essays; and in Virginia these arguments were reinforced by others and by hard-nosed politicking, including hauling out all the old war heroes Federalists could find to run as their candidates for the convention.[32]

But the spring belonged to the antis. In March North Carolinians held their elections and returned delegates opposed to ratification by more than two to one. In April

[31] Sullivan to Belknap, February 26, 1788, in Hammond, ed., *Sullivan Papers,* 3:566; Jeremiah Libbey to Belknap, February 19, 22, 1788, in *Belknap Papers,* 3:388–90; Walker, *New Hampshire Convention,* 22–30, and Langdon to Rufus King, February 23, 1788, quoted therein, 29 n.

[32] *New Hampshire Spy,* April 15, 1788; *Connecticut Courant,* March 3, 10, 1788; *Keene Recorder,* April 1788; Grigsby, *Virginia Convention of 1788,* vol. 1, p. 32; and newspapers of Portsmouth, New York, Richmond, and Alexandria, February–May 1788.

Rhode Islanders held their referendum and voted ten to one against ratification. New Yorkers went to the polls about the same time; and despite the plausible Publius, roughly 14,000 of the 20,000 votes cast were for delegates opposing ratification. Federalists carried only four counties and nineteen delegates against nine counties and forty-six delegates for their opponents. Only in Virginia were the elections not decisively against the Constitution: there the returns were ambiguous, Federalists winning just over eighty delegates, antis winning about sixty-five, and almost twenty being uncommitted.[33]

Even more ominously, the antis at last not only got organized but came up, as well, with an appealing positive program. Its aim was the same as Lee's had been back in September, the calling of a second convention, ostensibly to amend but actually to destroy the work of the first. But now it had an attractive rationale, well calculated to gull the gullible: the increasing agitation for a bill of rights. There was some base to build on. True, only the conventions of Massachusetts and South Carolina among the first eight

---

[33] Louise I. Trenholme, *The Ratification of the Federal Constitution in North Carolina* (New York, 1932), 107–32; Masterson, *William Blount,* 142–44; Archibald Maclaine to Iredell, January 15, 1788, in Griffith J. McKee, *Life and Correspondence of James Iredell* (2 vols., New York, 1847), 2:216; *New York Journal,* April 24, June 5, 1788; Papers Relating to the Adoption of the Federal Constitution, 17–36, in Rhode Island Archives; New York *Daily Advertiser,* June 3, 7, 14, 1788; Poughkeepsie *Country Journal,* June 3, 1788; David Henley to Samuel Henley, April 18, 1788, in Personal Miscellaneous File, Library of Congress (containing a county-by-county breakdown of the returns in Virginia); Randolph to Madison, April 17, 1788, in Conway, *Randolph,* 101; *George Nicholas to* Madison, April 5, 1788, in Hunt, ed., *Writings of Madison,* 5:114; William Grayson to John Lamb, June 9, 1788, in John Lamb Papers, New York Historical Society.

ratifying had recommended the adoption of a bill of rights, but the defeated minorities in Pennsylvania and Maryland had joined in the demand; and anti-Federalist propagandists were hammering away daily at the theme. If, on top of this, each of the five states remaining outside should ratify only conditionally, the condition being that the Constitution be amended so as to guarantee certain liberties, that would do the job. It would turn out to be impossible to reconcile the various amendments with one another and with the unqualified ratifications of the first eight states—impossible, that is, without calling another general convention for the purpose.[34]

The plan was likely to fail only if something was badly fumbled in the execution; and the interstate coordination of efforts was not left to chance. For practical purposes, since North Carolina and Rhode Island were likely to refuse to ratify for a time whether amendments were made or not, coordination actually involved only three states: New Hampshire, Virginia, and New York. The crucial function was entrusted to a small group operating out of the New York customs house under the direction of General John Lamb, a seasoned professional whose political career had begun in the 1760s as one of New York's original Sons of Liberty. This Federal Republican Club, as Clinton and Lamb styled the organization, had served for months as an informal nationwide clearing house for anti-Federalist propaganda. Now, in May, it set up a secret courier and mail system and established contact with proven anti-Federalist

---

[34] Gilman to Sullivan, March 22, 1788, in Hammond, ed., *Sullivan Papers,* 3:576; Smith, "Second Constitutional Convention," *passim;* Elliot's *Debates,* 2:176–77, 547 ff.; Edward Rutledge to Jay, in Johnston, ed., *Correspondence of Jay,* 3:252; Robert A. Rutland, *The Birth of the Bill of Rights, 1776–1791* (Chapel Hill, 1955), 126–58; Washington to Charles Carter, published in *Massachusetts Centinel,* January 23, 1788.

leaders in several key states—Atherton in New Hampshire, Chase in Maryland, Mason and Henry in Virginia, Timothy Bloodworth and Willie Jones in North Carolina, Rawlins Lowndes in South Carolina.[35]

The conventions of all three critical states were assembled in June: Virginia on the second, New York on the seventeenth, New Hampshire on the eighteenth. The last to start was the first to finish. In New Hampshire, all delegates whom extraconvention techniques could win had been won. Now, the state's Federalist leaders indulged in debates only long enough to give them time to count heads. (As they did so, a delegate here and a delegate there might have drifted into their camp, for the like of Langdon, Sullivan, and Livermore were no longer dependent upon their own wits for coining persuasive arguments; thanks to Hamilton, Jay, Madison, Wilson, Tench Coxe, and others the Federalist explanation for every punctuation mark in the Constitution was well established.) After three days, the alignments were as close as they could be brought by every weapon the Federalists had at their command.[36]

John Sullivan, a politician so methodical that he would soon be able to survey and classify and count every eligible voter in every town in New Hampshire, now surveyed the convention. At worst, the Federalists might fall two or three short. Taking no chances, they scheduled a final vote for the afternoon of June 21; and in the forenoon a pecunious citizen of Concord (where the convention was meeting) in-

---

[35] Isaac Q. Leake, *Memoir of the Life and Times of General John Lamb* (Albany, 1850), 305–16; Lamb Papers, New York Historical Society, *passim;* Spaulding, *New York in the Critical Period,* 174, 221–22.

[36] Walker, *New Hampshire Convention,* 31–43; "Journal of the Convention," in *New Hampshire State Papers,* 10:2–18; Whittemore, *John Sullivan,* 216–17.

vited six impecunious anti-Federalists to lunch. The lunch was liquid and alcoholic, and a half dozen anti-Federalists failed to show up at the convention until late afternoon. By that time, the vote had been taken and the Federalists had won.[37] The requisite nine states had ratified, and Federalists could begin to organize a government under the Constitution.[38]

But the union was far from complete. The states that had ratified formed three unconnected geographical areas, and since these areas did not include Virginia, George Washington was now an alien. Unless Virginia could be brought into the Union, the plan for a second convention could still succeed. For, on the one hand, few would trust the awesome powers of the president to anyone but Washington; and on the other, "popular demand" for a bill of rights—managed from the New York customs house—had reached such proportions that Federalists could no longer ignore it. In all likelihood, if both New York and Virginia should ratify, but only on condition that certain amendments for the protection of the rights of the people should first be adopted— and North Carolina and Rhode Island should remain outside—the other states would have no choice but to convene again and seek to secure those rights.

What the anti-Federalists in New York and Virginia had to do was do the same thing: ratify with conditions. But the wheel of history turns upon petty pivots, and the pivot now

---

[37] In all likelihood, it should be added, the Federalists would have won by two or three votes without this maneuver.

[38] Sullivan to Knox, Sullivan to Hancock, June 21, 1788, Knox to Sullivan, June 29, 1788, in Hammond, ed., *Sullivan Papers,* 3:588–90; "Journal of the Convention," 2–7; Walker, *New Hampshire Convention,* 43n (which tells the story of the liquid lunch as a "well-authenticated tradition").

was personal vanity. Until this moment, the Federal Republicans in New York had corresponded with their counterparts in Virginia through the mails and through a secret address in Richmond; all messages from New York to Richmond had been sent care of "George Fleming, Merchant, Richmond." Communications so addressed had reached their destination. But for this final and all-important strategic operation George Clinton felt it proper to address only his equal. Accordingly, Clinton's letter explaining New York's operational tactic in detail was sent not to a fictitious George Fleming but to a very real Edmund Randolph. Whether two or five or twenty people in the world knew that Randolph had already sold out to the Federalists is of no consequence. No one in New York knew, and when Randolph received the message he, in effect, tucked it away in his files.[39]

But for an improbable coincidence, even this miscarriage of intelligence need not have proved fatal. Richard Henry Lee, who knew of and had originally suggested the plan of working for a second convention, suddenly fell ill in the late winter of 1788. Trusting the fate of the nation to his brilliant cohorts, Henry, Mason, Grayson, and the others, he decided that it was not necessary to be in the convention himself.[40] As a result, anti-Federalism in Virginia was left

---

[39] Henry to Lamb, June 9, 1788, and Clinton to Lamb, June 21, 1788, in Leake, *Lamb,* 307–8, 315–16; Smith, "Second Convention," 88–90; Clinton to Randolph, May 8, 1788, and Randolph to the Assembly, June 23, 1788, in Conway, *Randolph,* 110–12, and the text of same, 112–13. Randolph did not precisely file away the letter: he sent it to the legislature at a time when the members were all attending the debates in the convention, which amounted to the same thing.

[40] Perhaps Lee himself would not have helped, for by the time the convention opened he had formulated still another plan, namely that Virginia

in the hands of men marvelously able to execute but totally incapable of planning.[41]

Virginia Federalists had other advantages besides the breakdown of communications between antis. Not the least of these was that a clear, albeit small, majority of the delegates in the convention were on their side from the outset. Another was the formidable array of talent leading the Federalists: Randolph, Edmund Pendleton, George Wythe, George Nicholas, James Madison, John Marshall. For forensic ability, for legal and constitutional knowledge, for understanding of the principles of government, few bodies ever assembled could match the Virginia Federalists in this convention.[42]

But they were matched by one man: Patrick Henry, who rose to the occasion with the most dazzling performance of his life. Henry was abetted by men of no mean talent— George Mason, William Grayson, Theodorick Bland, James Monroe, Benjamin Temple—but he did not need them. Like a legendary swordsman of the people, single-handedly fending off an entire royal guard, Henry held the field for twenty-three days against future presidents, chief justices, cabinet officers, senators, diplomats. On all but five days he

---

should ratify but reserve power to withdraw from the Union if amendments and satisfaction were not obtained within five years. Some New Yorkers were groping in the same direction. See the account of the New York convention, below.

[41] Arthur Lee to Richard Henry Lee, February 19, 1788, *ibid.,* 99–100; R. H. Lee to Lamb, June 27, 1788, in Ballagh, ed., *Letters of Lee,* 2:475; R. H. Lee to Mason, May 7, 1788, in Lee, *Life of Lee,* 2:88–90.

[42] Grigsby, *Virginia Federal Convention, passim;* Brant, *Madison,* 195–228; Elliot's *Debates,* vol. 3; Charles Lee to Washington, April 11, 1788, in Washington Papers, Library of Congress; Washington to Jay, June 8, 1788; *Writings of Washington,* 9:374; see also the Virginia sources cited in footnote 33, above.

took the floor at least once. On many days he did so thrice, and one day five times and another day eight. With one speech he held the floor alone for seven hours.[43]

Every day the hall was packed with spectators, come to hear the most eloquent performance in the annals of forensic virtuosity. Spectators and delegates alike sat frozen, hypnotized, as Henry ranged on and on, now thundering, now whispering, now threatening, now pleading. With masterful skill, he found everyone's most vulnerable spot—his fears, principles, passions, prejudices—and pierced him there. To the poor who feared the wealthy, to Baptists who feared an established church, to Kentuckians who feared loss of the Mississippi, to slaveholders, to those who owed British creditors, to all who loved the Republic, he appealed in turn. He portrayed the coming destruction of liberties so vividly that one spectator "involuntarily felt his wrists to assure himself that the fetters were not already pressing his flesh." Even so worldly a pair of observers as Robert and Gouverneur Morris, in Richmond for the event, sat awed by this man, as if by one demonically inspired. Glumly, Madison wrote Hamilton that though the Federalists had a majority of three or four delegates, he feared that Henry would carry the day.[44]

Madison's apprehension was based on a miscalculation. He perceived, accurately, that the anti-Federalists were stall-

---

[43] Descriptions of Henry's preformance in the convention are numerous: Grigsby's *Virginia Federal Convention,* 1:76 ff.; the biographies of Henry by Wirt and Tyler; Smith, "Second Constitutional Convention," 84–88; Brant, *Madison,* 195–222, 227; and others.

[44] Madison to Hamilton, June 16, 1788, in *Hamilton Papers,* 5:9; see also G. Morris to Hamilton, June 13, 1788, *ibid.,* 5:7; Madison to Washington, June 13, 1788, in Hunt, ed., *Writings of Madison,* 5:179n; Theodorick Bland to Arthur Lee, June 13, 1788.

ing for time, awaiting news daily expected from New York. But he mistakenly assumed from the lurking presence of Colonel Eleazer Oswald, a known secret liaison man between Northern and Southern anti-Federalists, that the Virginia antis knew or would soon know what the New Yorkers were going to do, and would act in concert with them. Accordingly, Madison and the other Federalist captains unwittingly did exactly the right thing: they fought a holding action while awaiting a final surprise attack that never came. Thereby, they let Henry's siege run its course, past the moment at which it could have brought him victory.[45]

Had Henry and Mason been able to announce, at the instant of climax, that New York was definitely going to ratify conditionally, the Virginia convention could have been induced to do likewise. The Federalist majority was slim, and a handful of the Federalists were so favorably disposed toward a bill of rights as to go along with New York in adding amendments before ratifying. But no such announcement was forthcoming, and the wavering Federalists were not willing to have Virginia take such a step alone. At last, Henry had spent his best efforts, and a restless, anticlimactic mood invaded the convention hall, discharging the electric tension that had long dominated it.[46]

---

[45] Madison to Hamilton, June 9, 16, 1788, and Henry Lee to Hamilton, June 16, in *Hamilton Papers*, 5:4, 9–10; William Grayson to Nathan Dane, June 18, 1788, in Dane Papers, Library of Congress; Madison to King, June 18, 1788, in King Papers, New York Historical Society; Madison to Washington, June 13, 18, 1788, in Hunt, ed., *Writings of Madison*, 5:179n, 211n–12n; Henry to Lamb, Grayson to Lamb, June 9, 1788, in Leake, *Lamb*, 307, 311; Elliot's *Debates*, 3:410–531 (the week of June 14–20).

[46] The change in mood took place over the weekend of June 21–22; when they resumed on Monday, June 23, the delegates were no longer engaged

And now rose the specter that haunts every political manipulator: the man of good will who upsets everything by an ingenuous and sincere proposal. George Wythe, a doddering old man, devout and respected as a Federalist but even more devout and respected as a republican, offered a proposal that brought gasps from Machiavels on both sides. On June 24 he called for amendments, to be tacked on after a resolution of ratification, which would remedy the defects of the Constitution; and he turned to Henry with an appeal to accept the amendments in a spirit of compromise. Caught off guard—for he could not reject Wythe's plea without raising the suspicion that his talk of a bill of rights masked other designs—Henry demurred. "Subsequent amendments," he grumbled, would not do; only previous amendments would establish "union, firm and solid." He offered an alternate proposal: to refer a declaration of rights and other proposed amendments "to the other states in the confederacy, previous to ratification."[47]

This sudden impasse gave Madison an opening for offering his own solution as a compromise. Two days earlier, he had secretly determined that the Federalists' best strategy was to offer "to preface the ratification with some plain and general truths that can not affect the validity of the act; and subjoin a recommendation which may hold up amendments as objects to be pursued." Such a maneuver had a hidden advantage: the prefatory "plain and general truths" could be, both in form and in substance, scarcely distinguishable from the renowned bill of rights that prefaced the Virginia

in titanic debate, they were merely quibbling; Elliot's *Debates,* 3:577 ff.; see also Madison to Washington, June 23, 1788, in Hunt, ed., *Writings of Madison,* 5:225 n–226 n.

[47] Elliot's *Debates,* 3:586–96.

constitution. But as a preface such articles would have no legal authority, whatever their emotional appeal; and if the last few days of debates had made anything clear, it was that the delegates were muddled in their ideas of the legal standing of the Virginia bill of rights. Madison's motion was thus a masterpiece of ambiguity.[48]

The delegates slept on it, and the next day they voted on it. Henry's proposal for previous amendments was rejected, 88 votes to 80. Quickly, the Federalists pressed for a final vote, as phrased by Madison. The motion carried by 89 to 79. The tenth and most important state was under the new roof.[49]

In the wake of the actions in New Hampshire and Virginia, the New York convention degenerated almost comically. As the convention assembled in Poughkeepsie on June 17, anti-Federalists outnumbered their opponents by 46 to 19. They were led by a band of men who counted themselves among the shrewdest politicians in America, men bold enough and clever enough to design a plan for totally undoing the work of the great Philadelphia Convention. Within six weeks they were themselves totally undone.[50]

The convention began with a clause-by-clause debate through the Constitution. John Jay, Robert R. Livingston,

---

[48] Madison to Hamilton, June 22, 1788, in *Hamilton Papers*, 5:61; Elliot's *Debates*, 3:516–22; see also Randolph's earlier speech, *ibid.*, 3:70; and Rutland, *Bill of Rights*, 163–74.

[49] Elliot's *Debates*, 3:653–55.

[50] The proceedings of the Poughkeepsie convention are reported in part in Elliot's *Debates*, 2:205–414, and in Francis Childs, ed., *Debates and Proceedings of the Convention* (New York, 1788); Childs' coverage grows thin as the convention proceeds. A narrative of the entire contest in New York is Clarence E. Miner's *The Ratification of the Federal Constitution by the State of New York* (New York, 1921).

and Hamilton defended it brilliantly but futilely. The Clintonians occasionally answered through their ablest spokesmen, Melancton Smith, Samuel Jones, John Lansing, Thomas Tredwell, and Clinton himself; but in the main they followed their customary practice of sitting silent, arrogantly confident of their voting strength. For a week this mock debate droned on, and then came the news that New Hampshire had ratified unconditionally.[51]

Disturbed but not daunted, the anti-Federalists continued as before, secure in the belief that they would soon receive news that Virginia, under the leadership of Governor Edmund Randolph, had ratified only on condition that a second convention be held to add amendments to protect American liberties. Almost playfully, as they waited for the news the Clintonians introduced a host of amendments and wallowed in the fun of watching their favorite enemy, the proud Hamilton, reduced to the humiliating task of debating the phraseology of a proposed bill of rights.[52]

Then came the news from Virginia, as deafening as a great clock that fails to strike. The anti-Federalists reacted in confusion; they caucused to determine what to do next, but they caucused in vain. Kaleidoscopically, they changed their plans even on the convention floor. At one point, Smith made a proposal, then withdrew it under attack from Hamilton; Lansing made it anew, but then Jones offered an amendment which rendered it ineffectual.[53]

---

[51] Elliot's *Debates*, 2:205–309; John Langdon to Hamilton, June 21, 1788, in *Hamilton Papers*, 5:34; *New York Journal*, July 4, 1788.

[52] Elliot's *Debates*, 3:309 ff.; see also Hamilton's speeches in *Hamilton Papers*, vol. 5, *passim;* New York *Daily Advertiser*, June–July 1788.

[53] Elliot's *Debates*, 2:386–412; Jay to Washington, July 4, 8, 1788, in *Documentary History of the Constitution*, 4:766–67; *Hamilton Papers*, 5:193n–94n, and Hamilton to Madison, July 8, in the same, 3:147; Jay to Mrs. Jay, July 5, in Johnston, ed., *Jay Correspondence*, 3:347.

In their befuddled state, the anti-Federalists had two vital weaknesses. One was that only half their men were disciplined party stalwarts; the other half were men of sound heart and feeble intellect who sincerely believed that all would be well if only certain liberties were guaranteed on paper. These latter found it difficult—once the Federalists raised the question—to understand why New York anti-Federalists should be waxing so vocal in demanding a national bill of rights, when New York did not have one for its own constitution, and no Clintonians had ever regarded that as a particularly important oversight. When Robert Yates offered an explanation—"Oh, that's different"—they had accepted it, but with misgivings. Now, these simple souls proved uncontrollable.[54]

The other anti-Federalist weakness was that their opponent was Alexander Hamilton. Once the battle became possible, he rose to it and became almost a Henry on the other side. More telling, he perceived the most vulnerable spot in the whole Clintonian scheme of things: New York City. Clinton had carried the city through the elections of 1786, but that was before he learned to dedicate himself to state sovereignty; and in the only major election since then, the elections to the Poughkeepsie convention, he had lost it so decisively that he had had to run his better Southern District men as candidates from upstate districts to get them into the convention at all. Now, in the convention, Hamilton played upon this weakness: casually, in a speech about

---

[54] Jay to Washington, May 29, June 30, 1788, *ibid.,* 3:334–35, 345–46; Spaulding, *New York in the Critical Period,* 250; Yates' argument in Ford, ed., *Essays on the Constitution,* 299–300; see also the notes to the debates in *Hamilton Papers,* vol. 5, debates of July 9–24. Since these papers include much data from the manuscript minutes of the convention, taken by Gilbert Livingston and never published, they are more valuable for the later stages of the convention than any of the published sources.

a dozen subjects delivered on July 17, he set a trap. "Of course you realize," he said to the Clintonians without quite saying it, "that if you refuse to ratify then New York City will secede from the state and ratify by itself, and where will the Empire State be without its crown jewel?"[55]

Upon that suggestion—which had been made privately before Hamilton offered it publicly, and which was repeated again and again off the floor—even the Clintonian leaders paused. In desperation, they offered to ratify on condition that if life under the Constitution should remain intolerable for six years, New York would have the right to secede. No, said Hamilton coolly, that will not do; and he presented the considered opinion of a learned member of Congress (actually it was only Madison's guess, hastily scribbled on a Sunday evening) that ratifying with any conditions whatsoever would be as unacceptable as ratifying only certain clauses of the Constitution. For the umpteenth time, the Clintonians caucused again; and now they agreed to ratify "in full confidence"—not on condition—that desired amendments would still be forthcoming. The next day, July 26, twelve Clintonians abandoned the instructions of their constituents, and seven abstained, and ratification was carried by a vote of 30 to 27.[56]

Even in defeat the Clintonians had a clear majority, and

---

[55] Leake, *Lamb*, 314; *New York Journal*, June 5, 1788; Hamilton's second speech of July 17, in *Hamilton Papers*, 5:175.

[56] Hamilton to Madison, June 8, July 19, Madison to Hamilton, July 20, speech of July 24, *ibid.*, 5:3, 177, 184, 193; New York *Daily Advertiser*, June 14, *New York Packet*, May 13, 1788; Jay to Washington, May 29, 1788, in Johnston, ed., *Jay Correspondence*, 2:334–35; Spaulding, *New York in the Critical Period*, 254–55; William Dunlap, *History of the New Netherlands, Province of New York, and State of New York, to the Adoption of the Federal Constitution* (2 vols., New York, 1840), 2:281 n; Elliot's *Debates*, 2:412–13.

they had the hollow satisfaction of requiring their enemies to agree to a "unanimous" letter, requesting a second convention, before consenting to give their votes for ratification. But they consented, and the Union now had eleven members.[57]

(Five days before the New York convention adjourned the North Carolina convention assembled. Lacking the sophistication of their northern brethren, they also lacked the temerity; and on August 4 they voted by an overwhelming majority—184 to 84—to reject the Constitution outright, and summarily adjourned. But to anti-Federalists this was a Battle of New Orleans: a victory won after the war was lost.)[58]

In the main, that fall's elections for officers of the new government were uneventful; indeed, a mood of unity, rivaling that of the Spirit of Seventy-six, blanketed most of the nation late in 1788.[59] As to amendments, most people who desired them vaguely felt that they were forthcoming, and most people who opposed them vaguely feared the same thing. In this frame of mind, voters everywhere but in Virginia and New York (and of course North Carolina and Rhode Island, which were outside the Union) chose friends of the Constitution as their representatives in national office.

---

[57] The circular letter, signed by Clinton and dated July 28, 1788, is published, *ibid.,* 413–14. Apparently it was Jay who actually drafted the letter; Johnston, ed., *Jay Correspondence,* 3:353–55.

[58] Elliot's *Debates,* 4:1–252.

[59] These generalizations should be qualified by reference to the continuing campaign for a second convention and the to-do that attended the New Jersey elections; on the latter, see McCormick, *Experiment in Independence,* 287–303.

The first Congress, not counting members from the two malcontent states, consisted of thirty-odd Federalists and less than a dozen anti-Federalists. Such presidential electors as were chosen voted unanimously for Washington as their first choice and, following the lead of Massachusetts Federalists (who abandoned their promise to Hancock as soon as he had paid the price of it), a majority of them voted for John Adams for vice president.[60]

The elections in New York were marked by rancor and indecisiveness. The Schuyler-Hamilton faction gained control of the state Senate and the Clintonians retained their overwhelming predominance in the lower house. One house insisted on one method of choosing electors, the other on another, and as a result no electors were chosen. After that, the houses disagreed again on the manner of choosing congressmen; and thus, though New York City served as the first capital under the Constitution, the state temporarily had the humiliation of not being represented in the first Congress. Perhaps it was not really a humiliation; it could have been that the Clintonians were seeking to prevent a quorum in the first Congress, and their racalcitrance was but a stratagem. In any event, the meeting of the first Congress was delayed many days, but it finally achieved a quorum and settled down to business.[61]

In Virginia, anti-Federalist leader Patrick Henry held unchallenged sway in the legislature. He took the "unusual

[60] Frank F. Stevens, *Transitional Period, 1788–1789, in the Government of the United States* (Columbia, Mo., 1909); I have traced these events in the newspapers of the several states, through the fall of 1788.

[61] *Votes and Proceedings,* New York Senate, December 13, 17, 18, 19, 24, 31, 1788, January 3, 5, 14, 27, February 2, 3, 4, 9, 1789, and corresponding dates in Assembly Proceedings.

liberty" of nominating both candidates for the United States Senate, and in doing so he slighted not only the Federalists' chief pretender to the office, James Madison, but all other Federalists as well: the first two senators from Virginia were Richard Henry Lee and William Grayson. And then, to add injury to the insult of Madison, he arranged for what would soon be known as a gerrymander (after another celebrated anti-Federalist) so as to prevent Madison from attaining even a seat in the nation's lower house: he induced the legislature to place Madison's home county, Orange, in a congressional district with six anti-Federalist counties. (Madison, a persistent campaigner if ever one existed, won a seat anyway by conducting what was in effect America's first house-to-house campaign. His campaign platform: James Madison, Jr., was the true friend of a bill of rights. That turned out to be the only plank of 1788 that had any meaning.)[62]

For all his great capacity for waiting, Madison must have virtually exploded with impatience in the early spring of 1789. First the Congress failed to meet on the scheduled day, March 4; when both houses finally had quorums five weeks later, they concerned themselves not with the fate of the Republic but with the proper form of address for the president. Then they settled down to consider the most pressing general matter, the raising of a revenue by levying import duties; but when Madison, who perhaps more than anyone else appreciated the momentum the anti-Federalists had accumulated in their agitation for a bill of rights, served

---

[62] Brant, *Madison*, 3:235–45, 264 ff.; Madison to Jefferson, October 17, December 8, to Randolph, November 2, 23, to Henry Lee, November 30, 1788, to Washington, January 14, March 4, 8, 19, and to Randolph, March 1, 1789, all in Hunt, ed., *Writings of Madison*, 5:269–331.

notice on May 4 that he would propose certain amendments to the Constitution on May 25, the announcement fell upon the House with a dull thud.[63]

First, some of the staunchest Federalists persisted (stupidly, Madison must have thought) in their original position that a bill of rights was unnecessary. Roger Sherman brushed off the idea of amendments, and arch-Federalist Fisher Ames of Massachusetts vehemently attacked it. And while high Federalists foolishly followed this course, anti-Federalists, heretofore vocal champions of amendments, joined them in attempting to frustrate Madison's efforts: anti-Federalists Aedanus Burke and Thomas Sumter of South Carolina, James Jackson of Georgia, and Elbridge Gerry of Massachusetts, who only weeks earlier had led choruses of voices crying out for amendments, now opposed their introduction. Their motive was simple: if there was any chance left for a second convention, it would be destroyed once and for all by the introduction in Congress of a bill of rights. For precisely that reason, Madison championed a bill of rights. As it happened, the majority of the Federalists in Congress understood what he was about, and they went along with him.[64]

For once, Madison's overtrained, oversystematized way of thinking served the nation well. Methodically, patiently, he sifted the proposals that had been made in the several states. Not counting the two states that still refused to ratify

---

[63] Madison to Jefferson, September 21, October 17, 1788, *ibid.,* 5:264, 269–75; Smith, "Second Constitutional Convention," 94–112; Leake, *Lamb,* 320; *Pennsylvania Gazette,* December 3, 10, 1788; Brant, *Madison,* 3:245–63; Rutland, *Bill of Rights,* 158–89.

[64] The following account, unless otherwise documented, is based on the more detailed versions given in Brant, *Madison,* 3:264–75, and Rutland, *Bill of Rights,* 190–218.

(neither of which had a bill of rights of its own), formal requests for a bill of rights had come in from five states (two of which had no bills of rights). In one way and another proposals for amendments had drifted in from nine states. In all, the various proposals encompassed 186 amendments, or 210 if the twenty-four preamble-type amendments offered by the New York convention are included.[65]

Eliminating duplicates, Madison found eighty substantive proposals. All nine states asked for a prohibition against interference by Congress with the time and place of holding elections, restrictions on the taxing power, and a declaration that all powers not delegated to the general government should be reserved to the states. Seven states spoke for jury trials; six called for an increase in the number of members of Congress, protection of religious freedom, and a prohibition of standing armies in times of peace. Five wanted prohibitions against quartering troops and against unreasonable searches and seizures, and protection of the right of the states to control the militias, the right of the people to bear arms, and the rights of freedom of speech and of the press. Four states requested guarantees of due process of law, speedy and public trials, the rights of assembly and petition, limits on the federal judicial power, and a ban on monopolies, excessive bail, unconstitutional treaties, and the holding of other federal office by members of Congress.

Madison dismissed the least popular and most impractical of these suggestions and reduced the remainder to nineteen substantive amendments. (He introduced one impractical proposal of his own: that the amendments be woven into the

---

[65] The tabulation is from Edward Dumbauld, *The Bill of Rights and What It Means Today* (Norman, Okla., 1957), 32–38.

text of the Constitution, rather than tacked on at the end.) On June 8, the House resolved itself into a committee of the whole house to debate the proposals and by August 24, after intermittent debates, had approved the amendments. They differed little from Madison's original proposals, save for being consolidated into seventeen amendments and being worded so as to be added onto the end of the Constitution. As they emerged from the House, the amendments were designed to apply to state governments as well as the national government. (Hence, for example, states as well as the national government would have been required to have trials by jury and prohibited from restricting freedom of speech.)

On September 2, the Senate took up the proposals. Right away, that body removed the applicability of the bill of rights to the states (hence, for example, states remained free to tax all citizens for the support of established churches, as Connecticut did until 1818 and Massachusetts did until 1833). Otherwise, however, the Senate largely concurred, though it and a joint committee that met on September 25 further consolidated the amendments so that only twelve were left. The first two, concerning the number and salaries of congressmen, were never ratified; the ten others, known as the Bill of Rights, became part of the Constitution on December 15, 1791.

The rest of the story was anticlimax, or rather, the beginning of another story. Once Madison's amendments passed through Congress the movement for a second convention collapsed. On November 21, 1789, after a vigorous educational campaign, North Carolina finally ratified by an even greater margin than that of its initial rejection. (The delay cost the North Carolinians roughly a million dollars, for in the interim between its two conventions Northern speculators, many of them anti-Federalists from New York and Pennsylvania, plundered the state by buying up huge quantities of unfunded public securities.) Five months later Rhode Island, which had been the first to make the break with England, became the last state to ratify the Constitution, and the Union was complete. (The delay cost the nation, not the state, roughly a quarter of a million dollars, for the Rhode Islanders were able to saddle the national government with that much public debt which the state had already paid.)[66]

Sometimes in the course of human events, as the Declaration of Independence had proclaimed, it becomes necessary for people to dissolve political bands. Prudence had dictated that governments long established should not be abolished for light and transient causes; and all experience had shown that mankind is more disposed to suffer, while evils are sufferable, than to right itself by parting with accustomed forms. The experience of the American Revolution itself showed something more: that when a people parts with accustomed forms, its soul is awakened and a nation is born.

The power unleashed in the parting is magnificent to behold; but its greatest power, as the American experience had hinted and Europe's would soon demonstrate, is the power to destroy, for man's accustomed forms are also his sense of self-restraint. The American Revolution was only a beginning in teaching men the process, but once it was done—once the vulgar overstepped the bounds of propriety and got away with it—there was no logical stopping place.

---

[66] McDonald, *We the People,* 312–15, 323, 345–46.

Common Sense led unerringly to Valmy, and Valmy to Napoleon, and Napoleon to the Revolution of 1830, and that to the Revolutions of 1848, and those to the Paris Commune of 1871, and that to the Bolshevik Revolution, and that to the African and Asian Revolutions in Expectations, and those to eternity.

That the American Revolution and the American people —of all the world's peoples the most materialistic and most vulgar and least disciplined—should have produced a governmental system adequate to check the very forces they unleashed; this was the miracle of the age, and of the succeeding age, and of all ages to come. The French, the Russians, the Italians, the Germans, all the planet's peoples in their turn, would become so unrestrained as to lose contact with sanity. The Americans might have suffered a similar history, had they followed the lead of those who, in 1787 and 1788, spoke in the name of the people and of popular "rights." But there were giants in the earth in those days, and they spoke in the name of the nation, and the people followed them. As a result, the Americans were, despite themselves, doomed forever to be free.

Index

This book was linotype set in the Times Roman series of type. The face was designed to be used in the news columns of the *London Times*. The *Times* was seeking a type face that would be condensed enough to accommodate a substantial number of words per column without sacrificing readability and still have an attractive, contemporary appearance. This design was an immediate success. It is used in many periodicals throughout the world and is one of the most popular text faces presently in use for book work.

Book design by Design Center, Inc., Indianapolis
Typography by Weimer Typesetting Co., Inc., Indianapolis
Printed by Hilltop Press, Inc., Indianapolis